Exam Ref 70-695 Deploying Windows Devices and Enterprise Apps

Brian Svidergol

PUBLISHED BY
Microsoft Press
A Division of Microsoft Corporation
One Microsoft Way
Redmond, Washington 98052-6399

Library of Congress Control Number: 2014952206
ISBN: 978-0-7356-9809-3

Printed and bound in the United States of America.

First Printing

Microsoft Press books are available through booksellers and distributors worldwide. If you need support related to this book, email Microsoft Press Support at mspinput@microsoft.com. Please tell us what you think of this book at http://aka.ms/tellpress.

Acquisitions Editor: Alison Hirsch
Developmental Editor: Alison Hirsch
Project Editors: Alison Hirsch and Carol Dillingham
Technical Reviewer: Rhonda Layfield; Technical Review services provided by Content Master, a member of CM Group, Ltd.
Copyeditor: Kerin Forsyth
Indexer: Lucie Haskins
Cover: Twist Creative • Seattle

Contents at a glance

Contents

What do you think of this book? We want to hear from you!

Microsoft is interested in hearing your feedback so we can continually improve our
books and learning resources for you. To participate in a brief online survey, please visit:

www.microsoft.com/learning/booksurvey/

What do you think of this book? We want to hear from you!

Microsoft is interested in hearing your feedback so we can continually improve our books and learning resources for you. To participate in a brief online survey, please visit:

www.microsoft.com/learning/booksurvey/

Introduction

This book helps prepare you for the Microsoft 70-695 exam titled *Deploying Windows Devices and Enterprise Apps*. The exam covers a wide range of technologies, and many readers might not have hands-on experience with all of them. The book uses a combination of fact-based content, step-by-step procedures for key exam topics, real-world experiences, and comprehensive review scenarios and questions to help you prepare for the exam. It's recommended that you use a lab environment to walk through the procedures covered in the book until you have hands-on experience with all the technologies covered on the exam.

The audience for this book includes IT pros with relevant job experience who are interested in passing Exam 70-695 or expanding their knowledge and skills related to deploying Windows and applications.

To maximize your chances of success in learning the material in this book and passing the 70-695 exam, you should have the following prerequisite knowledge:

- Basic working knowledge of Windows Server, especially related to adding and removing roles and features, basic system management, and core networking concepts.

- Windows client operating system management and support, including installation and troubleshooting.

- Operating system deployment knowledge, including automated system deployment concepts. Even if you don't have experience with WDS, MDT, or Configuration Manager, some background in operating system deployments will go a long way when you are preparing for the exam.

- Configuration Manager. Some exposure to Configuration Manager is helpful, even if it is not related to operating system deployment.

- Windows PowerShell. Many Microsoft exams are including more questions and answers with Windows PowerShell commands. Knowing the basic noun–verb pairing and how to construct Windows PowerShell commands in a pipeline will go a long way for the exam.

This book covers every exam objective, but it does not cover every exam question. Only the Microsoft exam team has access to the exam questions themselves, and Microsoft regularly adds new questions to the exam, making it impossible to cover specific questions. You should consider this book a supplement to your relevant real-world experience and other study materials. If you encounter a topic in this book that you do not feel completely comfortable with, use the links you'll see in the text to find more information and take the time to research and study the topic. Great information is available on MSDN and TechNet and in blogs and forums.

Microsoft certifications

Microsoft certifications distinguish you by proving your command of a broad set of skills and experience with current Microsoft products and technologies. The exams and corresponding certifications are developed to validate your mastery of critical competencies as you design and develop, or implement and support, solutions with Microsoft products and technologies both on-premises and in the cloud. Certification brings a variety of benefits to the individual and to employers and organizations.

> **MORE INFO** **ALL MICROSOFT CERTIFICATIONS**
>
> For information about Microsoft certifications, including a full list of available certifications, go to *http://www.microsoft.com/learning/en/us/certification/cert-default.aspx*.

Acknowledgments

I would like to thank Alison Hirsch for her overall guidance on this project as well as her attention to detail. Working with her on the team made things much easier for me. I'd also like to thank Stan Reimer who has put his trust in me on several projects. I always appreciate the opportunities and have enjoyed working with him and his team. Thanks also goes out to Charles Pluta, a friend of mine with extensive technical depth that always makes time to help out. I can count on him at all hours of the night and that goes a long way! Bob Clements, my go-to guy on many deployment projects, came through with an excellent real-world perspective that helped me bring clarity to many topics. Elias Mereb, I've really enjoyed hanging out with you over the past several years. Your love for life and technology is contagious. I appreciate your willingness to take my calls, offer up your words of wisdom, and engage with me on projects.

Finally, I'd like to thank my beautiful wife Lindsay, my son Jack, and my daughter Leah. Although I try never to take away family time for work, I might have rushed around a bit more when we put the kids to bed, knowing that I had a boatload of work ahead of me every night. Lindsay might have gotten less sleep than me on this project, dealing with baby Leah, Jack, and all of the household stuff. I couldn't do these projects without her support, and I am grateful for that.

Free ebooks from Microsoft Press

From technical overviews to in-depth information on special topics, the free ebooks from Microsoft Press cover a wide range of topics. These ebooks are available in PDF, EPUB, and Mobi for Kindle formats, ready for you to download at:

http://aka.ms/mspressfree

Check back often to see what is new!

Microsoft Virtual Academy

Build your knowledge of Microsoft technologies with free expert-led online training from Microsoft Virtual Academy (MVA). MVA offers a comprehensive library of videos, live events, and more to help you learn the latest technologies and prepare for certification exams. You'll find what you need here:

http://www.microsoftvirtualacademy.com

Errata, updates, & book support

We've made every effort to ensure the accuracy of this book. If you discover an error, please submit it to us at:

http://aka.ms/er695/errata

If you need additional support, email Microsoft Press Book Support at:

mspinput@microsoft.com.

Please note that product support for Microsoft software and hardware is not offered through the previous addresses. For help with Microsoft software or hardware, go to *http://support.microsoft.com.*

We want to hear from you

At Microsoft Press, your satisfaction is our top priority, and your feedback our most valuable asset. Please tell us what you think of this book at:

http://aka.ms/tellpress

The survey is short, and we read every one of your comments and ideas. Thanks in advance for your input!

Stay in touch

Let's keep the conversation going! We're on Twitter: *http://twitter.com/MicrosoftPress*.

Preparing for the exam

Microsoft certification exams are a great way to build your resume and let the world know about your level of expertise. Certification exams validate your on-the-job experience and product knowledge. While there is no substitution for on-the-job experience, preparation through study and hands-on practice can help you prepare for the exam. We recommend that you round out your exam preparation plan by using a combination of available study materials and courses. For example, you might use this Exam Ref and another study guide for your "at home" preparation and take a Microsoft Official Curriculum course for the classroom experience. Choose the combination that you think works best for you.

Note that this Exam Ref is based on publicly available information about the exam and the author's experience. To safeguard the integrity of the exam, authors do not have access to the live exam.

CHAPTER 1

Implement an operating system deployment infrastructure

Deploying a client operating system is a routine task that you will perform numerous times in your career as a systems administrator. It's easy to deploy the operating system to a single computer, but the task becomes more daunting and complex in enterprise environments in which you need to deploy the operating system to hundreds, and sometimes even thousands, of devices. To scale operating system deployment to more than a few devices, you need to rely on automation. The more automation you use, the less time you need to spend per device when performing operating system deployments. In this chapter, you learn about implementing the necessary infrastructure to deploy an operating system over the network to thousands of devices.

Objectives in this chapter:

- Objective 1.1: Assess the computing environment
- Objective 1.2: Plan and implement user state migration
- Objective 1.3: Configure the deployment infrastructure
- Objective 1.4: Configure and manage activation

Objective 1.1: Assess the computing environment

Before you can deploy a new operating system, it's important to assess your existing environment to discover which, if any, of the existing devices support the new operating system. By assessing your environment, you can also determine whether hardware upgrades are necessary for any of the devices.

> **This objective covers how to:**
> - Use the Microsoft Assessment and Planning Toolkit (MAP)
> - Assess Configuration Manager reports
> - Integrate MAP with Configuration Manager
> - Determine network load capacity

Using the Microsoft Assessment and Planning Toolkit

Microsoft Assessment and Planning (MAP) is an agentless inventory, assessment, and reporting tool that can securely assess IT environments for various platform migrations, including but not limited to Windows 8.1, Windows 8, Microsoft Office 2013 and Microsoft Office 365, Windows Server 2012 and Windows Server 2012 R2, SQL Server 2012, Microsoft Hyper-V, Microsoft Private Cloud Fast Track, and Microsoft Azure.

MAP is a solution accelerator available as a free download from the Microsoft Download Center. You install the toolkit according to the options that best fit your environment and goals. The MAP page on the Microsoft Download Center has additional information and documentation to help you install MAP correctly.

You can use MAP to scan and assess your organization's readiness for Windows 8.1. MAP uses several agentless methods to connect to your network's computers, assess the hardware and device compatibility with Windows 8.1, and then create comprehensive Microsoft Word and Microsoft Excel reports.

You should tie your use of MAP to a phased approach as part of your overall deployment strategy. There are six distinct phases for you to consider, and the key to a successful MAP experience is to complete each of six phases sequentially. The following sections describe the six phases.

Phase 1: Choose your goals

To use this phase correctly, know what MAP can do. It contains a number of inventory, assessment, capacity planning, and software usage tracking scenarios that fit various situations. MAP uses wizards to perform data collection from which you can make better decisions. The overall purpose of this phase is to understand what you are attempting to do with respect to deploying Windows and to have an overall idea of what the outcome will be. By knowing what you want to accomplish, you can use MAP better to gather information, which is covered in the next phase.

As an example, your goal could be to deploy Windows 8.1 on 300 devices in the Miami office successfully by a specific date.

Phase 2: Gather your data collection requirements

MAP communicates with machines in a network to collect information to use in the assessments, but before you can start collecting data, some prep work is necessary. In this phase, you work on the following data collection requirements:

- **Credentials for target computers** To connect to target computers, you must specify credentials, and they must be able to collect data from Windows-based computers by using Windows Management Instrumentation (WMI). For Linux or UNIX computers, the credentials must be able to connect by using Secure Socket Shell (SSH) and collect data. It is a good practice to use a dedicated service account for MAP communication so you can use local administrative access and avoid using domain admin-level or root-level credentials.

- **Credentials for Active Directory discovery**   To connect to Active Directory to perform queries for discovery, supply Active Directory credentials. These can be the same credentials used for collecting data from target computers.

Phase 3: Prepare your environment

In this phase, you prepare your environment to ensure that MAP can connect and gather information from the target machines successfully. The following list highlights the preparation tasks:

- **Configure target devices to allow MAP communication**   The configuration will vary by platform. If a firewall is in place between the MAP computer and the target device, open ports. If a host-based firewall is in use on devices, you must configure it to allow the MAP communication. For Windows-based devices, you can automate the configuration of the Windows firewall by using Group Policy Objects.
- **Configure logging on target devices**   Logging can be used for troubleshooting purposes and security auditing purposes.

> **MORE INFO   DETAILED FIREWALL AND LOGGING INFORMATION**
>
> At a minimum, familiarize yourself with the general Windows firewall considerations shown at *http://social.technet.microsoft.com/wiki/contents/articles/17809.preparing-your-map -environment.aspx*. If time allows, scan through the remaining details for firewall and logging considerations too.

Phase 4: Install the MAP Toolkit

Before installing MAP, decide how MAP will store the data it collects in your environment. MAP stores collected information in SQL Server databases. You can use the Microsoft SQL Server 2012 Express LocalDB, which is free; it comes with MAP, and you can install it with MAP. Alternatively, you can use a SQL Server database hosted on Microsoft SQL Server 2008, SQL Server 2008 R2, or SQL Server 2012 database server. If you use a full SQL Server installation, you must create a named instance called MAPS before you run the MAP installer.

> **MORE INFO   MAP**
>
> This book uses MAP version 9.1. You can download it from the Microsoft Download Center at *http://www.microsoft.com/en-us/download/details.aspx?id=7826*. You can find the installation steps for MAP on the download page, under "Install Instructions."

To install MAP, perform the following steps:

1. Run MapSetup.exe.
2. In the Microsoft Assessment And Planning Toolkit dialog box, click Next.

3. On the License Agreement page, select I Accept The Terms In The License Agreement and then click Next.

4. On the Installation Folder page, specify the folder where MAP should be installed and then click Next.

5. On the Customer Experience Improvement Program page, specify whether to join the customer experience improvement program and then click Next.

6. On the Begin The Installation page, click Install and, after the install is complete, click Finish.

Phase 5: Collect data

Now you can begin using MAP for the data-collection process. Two wizards collect the data that most scenarios require:

- Inventory and Assessment Wizard
- Performance Metrics Wizard

INVENTORY AND ASSESSMENT WIZARD

The Inventory and Assessment Wizard is the starting point for all MAP scenarios. When you use the information gathered in phases 1 through 3, the wizard prompts you to:

- **Select your inventory scenario**   Your scenario will depend on your goals. For instance, if you want to deploy Windows 8.1, you should select the Windows Computers scenario. This maps back to phase 1: Choose your goals. Although many of the available scenarios won't be covered in this book, it is valuable to know about MAP's capabilities for inventorying an environment. The complete list of available scenarios is:
  - Windows Computers
  - Linux/UNIX Computers
  - Vmware Computers
  - Active Devices And Users
  - Exchange Server
  - Endpoint Protection Server
  - Lync Server
  - Software ID (SWID) Tags
  - SQL Server
  - SQL Server With Database Details
  - Windows Azure Platform Migration
  - Oracle
  - Windows Volume Licensing
  - Client Access Tracking For Windows Server 2012 Or Later

- Client Access Tracking For SQL Server 2012 Or Later
- Client Access Tracking For Configuration Manager
- Client Access Tracking For Sharepoint Server 2013
- Client Access Tracking For Remote Desktop Services

- **Select your discovery method**   You can use any of the following discovery methods:
  - **Active Directory Domain Services (AD DS)**   Use AD DS discovery to retrieve a list of computer accounts from Active Directory during the discovery process.
  - **Windows networking protocols**   Use Windows networking protocols to retrieve a list of computers from the Computer Browser service. This method is used for computers that are part of a workgroup or computers that are part of legacy domains such as those running on Windows NT 4.0.
  - **System Center Configuration Manager**   Use System Center 2012 R2 Configuration Manager to discover computers based on data discovery records (DDRs) that Configuration Manager maintains.
  - **IP address range**   Use the IP address range option to scan IP addresses in a range that you specify. A maximum of 100,000 IP addresses are allowed in a single scan.
  - **Manual entry**   Use manual entries to specify the names of individual computers you want to connect to during the discovery process. When you select this option, you can specify the credentials used for each manually entered computer. This is useful if you have several computers, each of which will have a unique credential, which can be common in a highly secure environment.
  - **Import computer names from a file**   Use this option to import computers from a file based on host names, fully qualified domain names, NetBIOS names, or IP addresses. In addition, you can specify the credentials for each import file.

- **Provide the credentials to connect and inventory the target machines**   You need to specify two sets of credentials to retrieve data successfully during the discovery and inventory process of MAP:
  - **Discovery credentials**   Use discovery credentials to generate a list of computers from which you want to collect inventory data. The credentials used depend on the discovery methods you decide to use. For example, if you use AD DS for discovery, you must specify an account that has Read permission on the containers that store computer accounts in the Active Directory database. By default, all users have Read permissions on containers and organizational units (OUs) that contain computer objects. If you use Configuration Manager, specify credentials that have read rights in the Configuration Manager database.
  - **Inventory credentials**   Inventory credentials are called All Computers Credentials in the wizard. These credentials are used to connect, by WMI, to the discovered computers and must have local administrative rights on the computers from which you want to gather inventory data.

- **Retrieve hardware inventory**   Depending on the scenarios chosen, MAP uses different technologies to retrieve hardware inventory. The technologies used for the most used scenarios are
  - **WMI**   Gathers inventory data from Windows-based computers and from Configuration Manager.
  - **SSH**   Gathers inventory data from Linux and UNIX computers.
  - **VMWare**   Gathers inventory data from VMWare virtualization host servers.

PERFORMANCE METRICS WIZARD

The Performance Metrics Wizard collects specific performance-related information such as CPU, memory, network, and disk usage for Windows-based servers and clients as well as for LINUX-based servers. The information that this collection mechanism gathers supports the capacity-planning features for server consolidation, desktop virtualization, Microsoft Private Cloud Fast Track, and Azure application migration.

USING MAP TO DISCOVER AND INVENTORY COMPUTERS

To discover and inventory computers, do the following:

1. On the computer on which you installed MAP, on the Start screen, type Assessment.
2. In the search results, click the Microsoft Assessment And Planning Toolkit tile. Wait for MAP to start.

   It might take approximately 30 to 60 seconds. The dialog box shown in Figure 1-1 appears.

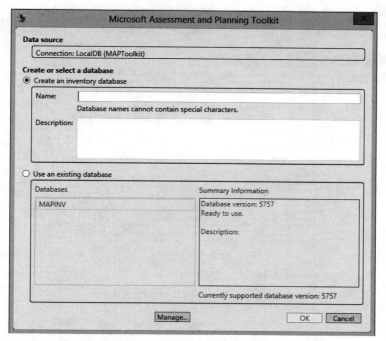

FIGURE 1-1 Microsoft Assessment And Planning Toolkit

3. In the Microsoft Assessment And Planning Toolkit dialog box, in the Create Or Select A Database section, click Create An Inventory Database. In the Name field, type **Client Assessment** and, in the Description section, type **Initial client assessment**. Click OK.

4. In the console tree, select Overview and, in the Where To Start section, click Perform An Inventory to start the Inventory And Assessment Wizard. On the Inventory Scenarios page shown in Figure 1-2, select Windows Computers and click Next.

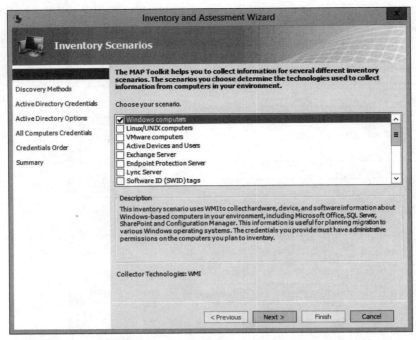

FIGURE 1-2 Inventory And Assessment Wizard, Inventory Scenarios page

5. On the Discovery Methods page shown in Figure 1-3, ensure that Use Active Directory Domain Services (AD DS) is selected and click Next.

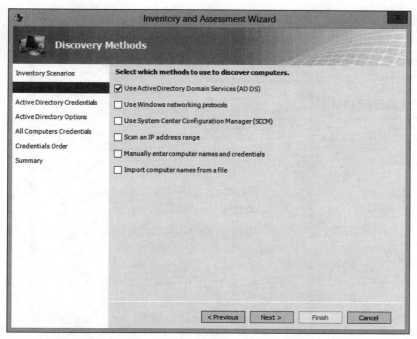

FIGURE 1-3 Inventory And Assessment Wizard, Discovery Methods page

6. On the Active Directory Credentials page displayed in Figure 1-4, enter the following information in the text boxes and then click Next.

   - **Domain**   The name of the domain in which you want to discover computers.
   - **Domain Account**   An account with read rights in Active Directory, for example, CONTOSO\MAP-SVC.
   - **Password**   The password for the account entered.

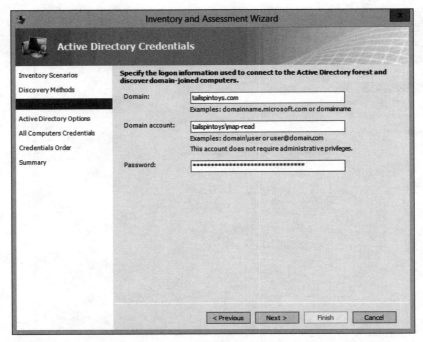

FIGURE 1-4 Inventory And Assessment Wizard, Active Directory Credentials page

7. On the Active Directory Options page, ensure that Find All Computers In All Domains, Containers, And Organizational Units is selected and then click Next. On the All Computers Credentials page displayed in Figure 1-5, click Create to specify an account to be used to gather inventory data from discovered computers and then click Save after entering the account details.

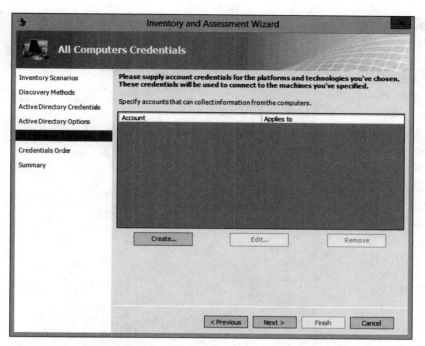

FIGURE 1-5 Inventory And Assessment Wizard, All Computers Credentials page

8. Repeat step 7 if more than one account is required for your environment and then click Next. On the Credentials Order page displayed in Figure 1-6, click Move Up and Move Down to specify the order in which MAP will try to use accounts when gathering inventory data.

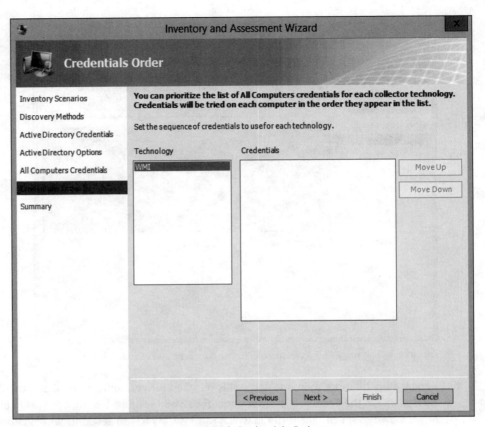

FIGURE 1-6 Inventory And Assessment Wizard, Credentials Order page

9. Click Next and then click Finish.

   Data will appear in the Inventory And Assessment dialog box, as displayed in
   Figure 1-7. You can review the data and then click Close when you are finished.

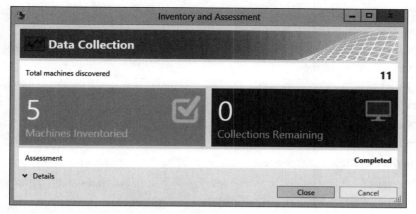

FIGURE 1-7 Inventory And Assessment dialog box

10. To collect inventory data, look at the Environment Summary in the Overview section.

11. Expand Desktop in the console tree and then click the Windows 8.1 Readiness tile.

12. In the Options section, click Generate Windows 8.1 Readiness Report and observe the Report Generation Status dialog box displayed in Figure 1-8. Click Close.

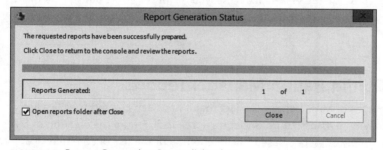

FIGURE 1-8 Report Generation Status dialog box

Phase 6: Review the reports

When you run the data collection wizards, MAP has the information necessary to generate custom reports and proposals that are specific to the environment that MAP inventoried.

To preview Windows 8.1 readiness reports, do the following:

1. In the View menu, click Saved Reports.

2. Open the Excel worksheet report named Windows81Assessment with the date of the process. Look at the following worksheets:

   - **Summary** Displays the number of computers that are ready for Windows 8.1 with, and without, hardware upgrades as well as the number of computers not ready for Windows 8.1 and the number of computers that could not be inventoried.

- **Assessment Values**   Displays the minimum requirements for Windows 8.1. You can change the requirements used for the reports or use the provided ones.
- **ClientAssessment**   Displays a row for each computer and what requirements it meets or does not meet.
- **AfterUpgrades**   Displays a row for each computer that requires an upgrade and its settings after the upgrade.
- **DeviceSummary**   Displays a row for each type of device found, such as USB hubs and processors, and the number of computers that have each specified device.
- **DeviceDetails**   Displays a row per device for each computer inventoried.
- DiscoveredApplications   Displays a row for each application discovered and the number of computers on which the application was found.

EXAM TIP

If you scan a Hyper-V host computer, MAP will automatically attempt to scan the virtual machines (VMs) hosted on the Hyper-V host computer. Watch for exam scenarios in which your MAP reports have data for computers that were not part of your original scope. Those computers might be VMs from a Hyper-V host. In some cases, your user account might not have access rights to scan the VMs. In that case, you might see errors but still see the full set of inventory data you were expecting. Again, this could be due to scanning a Hyper-V host computer.

Assessing Configuration Manager reports

One of the advantages of MAP, besides the fact that it has been created specifically for upgrade and deployment assessments, is that it's a free tool. Before the creation of MAP, IT professionals had to rely on paper-based documentation or the use of commercial applications that gathered hardware and software inventory data.

One such application is System Center 2012 R2 Configuration Manager. Medium to large enterprises use Configuration Manager to collect hardware and software inventory, manage configuration and compliance settings, deploy apps, and deploy operating systems to devices.

Companies that have a Configuration Manager infrastructure can take advantage of the hardware inventory, software inventory, and Asset Intelligence features to collect data that MAP usually collects and view reports from within Configuration Manager itself. Configuration Manager has a much broader range of features and, as such, offers a broader range of flexibility when it comes to gathering data. If you are comfortable with writing your own SQL queries, or have a database admin that can assist, you will find hundreds of attributes that Configuration Manager is gathering automatically. When the necessary inventory data isn't available, you can use custom inventory classes to extend your reporting capabilities further.

The reports in Configuration Manager can also provide a great source of comparison with the inventory you receive from MAP. Taking the reports side by side can help you eliminate questionable clients that did not respond to your MAP assessment.

REAL WORLD **ASSET INTELLIGENCE REPORTS**

I worked on a project to reduce licensing costs. The management team had expressed concerns about licensing costs going up even though the company had not hired additional employees or purchased new software. Using the built-in reports in Configuration Manager, along with software metering to see when or if applications were launched, I was able to deduce that some licensed applications that were needed by only a subset of employees were unexpectedly part of the standard corporate computer image. Thus, every time the desktop team reimaged a computer or deployed a new computer, the licensed applications were installed. We removed those licensed applications from the image and automatically uninstalled the applications that had not been used.

Integrating MAP with Configuration Manager

You can use both MAP and Configuration Manager to determine whether devices in a network can be upgraded to Windows 8.1. Configuration Manager relies on data collected by its client agent, which you can later use to generate compliance reports. MAP uses WMI to collect the same data.

Some people say that you should use Configuration Manager if you have it and MAP if you don't. Configuration Manager is a much broader tool, not just specific to upgrading an environment. MAP has built-in reports that are specific to a migration or upgrade. Should you go through the trouble of discovering and inventorying your environment with MAP when you already have Configuration Manager?

The good news is that you don't have to. You can use discovery data that Configuration Manager inventoried to feed MAP. Configuration Manager can be integrated with MAP to do so. To integrate MAP and Configuration Manager, perform the following steps:

1. From the Start screen, type **Assessment**.

2. In the search results, click the Microsoft Assessment And Planning Toolkit tile. Wait for MAP to start. It might take approximately 30 to 60 seconds.

3. In the console tree, click Overview and, in the Where To Start section, click Perform An Inventory. In the Inventory And Assessment Wizard dialog box, select Windows Computers and click Next.

4. On the Inventory Scenarios page, under Choose Your Scenario, select Windows Computers and click Next.

5. On the Discovery Methods page, select Use System Center Configuration Manager and click Next.

6. On the SCCM Server And Credentials page shown in Figure 1-9, enter the Configuration Manager site server name and account to be used to retrieve data from the site server. The account must have local administrative rights on the site server. Click Next.

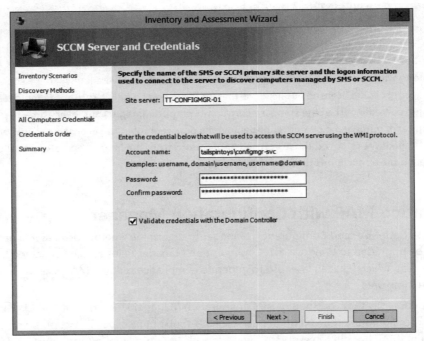

FIGURE 1-9 Inventory And Assessment Wizard dialog box, SCCM Server And Credentials page

7. In the All Computers Credentials section, click Create to specify an account to be used to gather inventory data from discovered computers and then click Save after entering the account details.

8. Repeat step 7 if more than one account is required for your environment. After you have entered all accounts you want to use, click Next.

9. On the Credentials Order page, change the order in which accounts should be tried on individual computers and then click Next.

10. On the Summary page, click Finish.

Determining network load capacity

One of the most common mistakes in the field when using MAP for assessments is to ignore the load it can generate on a network when assessing data from hundreds of computers. Before running MAP to inventory all computers on a network, monitor the network and run inventory on a single computer to measure the network load the inventory process generates.

Vendors offer several tools you can use for network monitoring. You should ask the network team members at your organization which tools they use for bandwidth monitoring in general and check what the average available bandwidth is during different hours of the day to choose the right time to run an inventory scan.

To capture network load for an inventory scan, follow these steps:

1. Install a network capture application such as Wireshark.

   Wireshark is an open-source network capture application available at *www.wireshark.org*.

2. Determine which computer to scan as a test for measuring network load and write down its IP address.

3. Run the network capture application.

4. Filter the capture by changing the IP address to the IP address you wrote down in step 2.

5. Start the network capture.

6. On the Start screen, type **Assessment**.

7. In the search results, click the Microsoft Assessment And Planning Toolkit tile. Wait for MAP to start. It might take 30 to 60 seconds.

8. On the console tree, click Overview and, in the Where To Start section, click Perform An Inventory. In the Inventory And Assessment Wizard dialog box, select Windows Computers and click Next.

9. On the Inventory Scenarios page, under Choose Your Scenario, select Windows Computers and click Next.

10. On the Discovery Methods page, select Scan An IP Address Range and click Next. On the Scan An IP Address Range page, set the Starting Address and Ending Address to the IP address you wrote down in step 2, as displayed in Figure 1-10. Click Next.

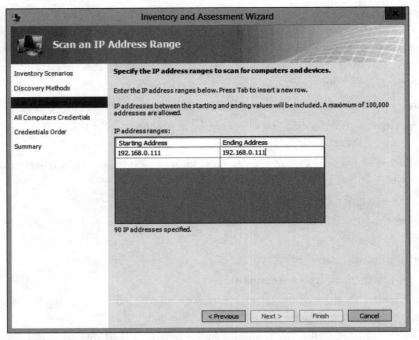

FIGURE 1-10 Inventory And Assessment Wizard, Scan An IP Address Range

11. In the All Computers Credentials page displayed, click Create to specify an account to be used to gather inventory data from discovered computers. Click Save after entering the account details for an account with local administrative rights on the computers to be inventoried.

12. On the Credentials Order page, click Next.

13. On the Summary page, click Finish.

 Data starts to appear in the Inventory And Assessment dialog box. You can click Close after you see that the computer has been inventoried.

14. Switch to your network capture program and stop the capture.

15. Determine with the network team at your organization whether the traffic required is within the limits of the physical network. You must decide whether you need to segment the data collection and when to run it.

Besides using a network capture program, you can also use Performance Monitor to retrieve similar data. However, Performance Monitor will not filter the network traffic data by IP address or process.

> ### *Thought experiment*
> ### Windows 8.1 deployment at Tailspin Toys
>
> Tailspin Toys has a single office in Miami, Florida, with approximately 200 comput-
> ers. Computers run mostly Windows XP, but several run Linux. Tailspin Toys has
> decided to upgrade all computers to Windows 8.1, including the computers cur-
> rently running Linux. All Windows-based computers are part of an Active Directory
> Domain Services domain, tailspintoys.com.
>
> During a customer meeting, you were informed that Tailspin Toys does not use any
> of the System Center products. It also doesn't have any documentation on the hard-
> ware specifications of its computers.
>
> You decide to use MAP to assess the environment. To help you plan better for the
> assessment, answer the following questions:
>
> 1. Which MAP scenarios should you choose to assess?
>
> 2. Which MAP discovery methods should you choose for the assessment?
>
> 3. Which technologies will MAP use to inventory the computers?

Objective summary

- You can inventory your network environment and generate upgrade reports by using MAP or Configuration Manager.
- You can use Asset Intelligence reports in Configuration Manager to determine which computers need hardware upgrades to make them compliant with a new operating system.
- MAP does not require an agent for inventory purposes. It uses WMI for Windows devices.
- Configuration Manager uses an agent to inventory your environment.
- MAP can use discovery data from Configuration Manager, which can save administra-tive time because you might not have to perform an inventory with MAP.

Objective review

Answer the following questions to test your knowledge of the information in this objective. You can find the answers to these questions and explanations of why each answer choice is correct or incorrect in the "Answers" section at the end of this chapter.

1. You use Configuration Manager to manage 500 client computers. You need to discover which computers can be upgraded to Windows 8.1. Which Configuration Manager features should you use? (Choose all that apply.)

    A. Hardware inventory

    B. Software inventory

C. Asset Intelligence

D. Compliance settings

2. Twenty-five client computers need to be upgraded to Windows 8.1. You need to determine whether they can be upgraded without using an agent on them. Which tool should you use?

A. Configuration Manager

B. ACT

C. MAP

D. WDS

3. Which discovery methods can MAP use? (Choose all that apply.)

A. WMI

B. Network protocol

C. AD DS

D. SNMP

4. You have an environment that includes the entire System Center suite of products. You plan to install MAP to assess your environment. You don't want MAP to perform a discovery and instead want to rely on existing data. What should you do?

A. Integrate MAP with Operations Manager.

B. Integrate MAP with Configuration Manager.

C. Integrate MAP with App Controller.

D. Integrate MAP with Service Manager.

5. You need to collect inventory data on 250 client computers. Which environmental prerequisites are required before you can successfully connect to these computers by using MAP? (Choose all that apply.)

A. Remote access to the computers using RDP

B. Firewall access for MAP

C. Configuration Manager client installed

D. A known service account

Objective 1.2: Plan and implement user state migration

At most companies, users have a mapped network drive that is used as their home folder. It's where they are supposed to store all their data. Some of those companies also use folder redirection to map common local storage locations to home folders. However, as you probably know, only some data ends up in the home folder. Quite a bit of the data ends up spread out in multiple locations on the client computers. This poses a challenge for computer upgrades and migrations because the data needs to be available to the users after the upgrade or migration. As part of planning computer upgrades and migrations, you need to account for the data.

Now that you know that there is local data, you need to figure out how to handle it before you begin an upgrade or migration project.

This objective discusses how to handle user state migration by using the User State Migration Tool (USMT) for wipe-and-load and side-by-side migration scenarios.

This objective covers how to:

- Design a user migration strategy
- Estimate migration store size
- Secure migrated data
- Create a User State Migration Tool (USMT) package

Designing a user migration strategy

The User State Migration Tool (USMT) is a free tool from Microsoft to migrate user profiles and data from a source operating system to a destination operating system. It's included as part of the Windows Automated Installation Kit (AIK) and consists of three client tools and some XML files that you can use to configure the specific data that migrates. The following list describes the USMT components:

- **ScanState**   This tool (ScanState.exe) scans a source computer, collects the files and settings, and then creates a migration store that holds the data in a compressed format. ScanState does not modify the source computer. It uses .xml files that dictate which data is part of the migration. The migration store can be stored on a network share, on a folder in a removable drive, locally on the source computer if hard links are used, or on a computer running the Configuration Manager State Migration Point System role.

> **MORE INFO**   **SCANSTATE**
>
> For more information about ScanState, see *http://technet.microsoft.com/en-us/library /dd560781(v=WS.10).aspx.*

- **LoadState**   This tool (LoadState.exe) migrates files and settings, one at a time, from the migration store to a temporary location on the destination computer. During this process, files are decompressed and decrypted if necessary. LoadState then transfers files to their correct locations, deletes the temporary copies, and begins migrating more files. Compression improves performance by reducing network bandwidth usage and the space that the migration store requires. You can turn off compression by using /nocompress.

MORE INFO **LOADSTATE**

For more information about LoadState, see *http://technet.microsoft.com/en-us/library /dd560804(v=ws.10).aspx.*

- **Usmtutils** This tool (Usmtutils.exe) can perform several functions relating to compression, encryption, and validation of a migration store. Usmtutils also can extract files manually if your data store becomes corrupt or your hard-link store becomes locked.
- **Migration XML files** These are the XML files that you use with ScanState and LoadState to control the data migration. They include the MigApp.xml, MigUser.xml, and MigDocs.xml files and any custom .xml files that you create.
- **MigApp.xml** This is one of the .xml files included with USMT. It contains rules for migrating application settings.
- **MigDocs.xml** This is one of the .xml files included with USMT. This file contains rules for the MigXmlHelper.GenerateDocPatterns helper function, which can find user documents on a computer automatically without creating extensive custom migration .xml files.
- **MigUser.xml** This is one of the .xml files included with USMT. This file contains rules for migrating user profiles and data.
- **Config.xml** To exclude data from the migration, you can create and modify the Config.xml file by using /genconfig with the ScanState tool. This optional file has a different format from the migration .xml files because it does not contain migration rules.
- **Config.xml** This file lists the elements that you can migrate. Specify migrate="no" for the elements that you want to exclude from the migration. You also can use this file to control some migration options for USMT. Note that specifying migrate="no" is not the same as removing a line from the file. Removing a line from the file results in that element not being processed.

MORE INFO **USMT .XML MIGRATION FILES**

For more information about the USMT .xml migration files, see *http://technet.microsoft .com/en-us/library/cc766203(v=ws.10).aspx.*

Before you can use USMT to perform user state migration, understand the different scenarios in which you can use USMT, how to determine which data is migrated, and how to store the data during migration.

There are two scenarios to consider when migrating user state data: refresh (one example would be wipe and load) and replace (also known as side by side). In wipe-and-load migration scenarios, the ScanState tool collects the user state in one of two ways:

- **Online** An online migration involves running ScanState while the source instance of the Windows operating system is running.
- **Offline** In an offline migration, ScanState is run against a copy of the Windows operating system that is not running. Do this by performing either of the following tasks:
  - Run ScanState from the Windows PE environment and collect data from an existing version of the Windows operating system.
  - Run ScanState against the Windows.old directory that contains data from the previous Windows installation.

Sample wipe-and-load scenarios

In wipe-and-load scenarios, the source and destination computers are the same computer. Windows 8.1 replaces the old operating system, and you preserve and migrate the user state to Windows 8.1 by using USMT.

There are four scenarios in which you can use a wipe-and-load migration:

- Offline migration by using Windows PE and hard-link migration. A hard-link migration is an in-place migration that enables you to maintain data files on the source computer while the original installation of Windows is removed and a new version of Windows is installed. A hard-link migration greatly reduces the amount of time required to complete an in-place migration.
- Offline migration by using the Windows.old folder and hard-link migration.
- Online migration by using a compressed migration store.
- Online migration by using hard-link migration.

An offline migration by using Windows PE and hard-link migration is normally used when you need to upgrade an existing computer without starting the existing operating system or accessing the network. You can perform this migration by performing the following steps on each computer to be migrated:

1. Boot the computer to Windows PE and then run the ScanState command-line tool, specifying /hardlink and /nocompress. ScanState saves the user state to a hard-link migration store on each computer, which improves performance by minimizing network traffic.

2. Install your company's standard image that includes Windows 8.1 and standard applications.

3. Run the LoadState command-line tool. LoadState restores each user state back to each computer.

An offline migration using the Windows.old folder and hard-link migration takes advantage of the Windows.old folder created by the Windows setup program when upgrading an existing version of Windows to maintain state data. To perform this type of migration, perform the following steps on each computer to be migrated:

1. Install Windows 8.1 without reformatting or repartitioning the operating system drive and then install all required applications.

2. Run ScanState and then run LoadState on each computer with /hardlink and /nocompress.

An online migration using a compressed migration store copies the user state data to a file server or a removable drive and then copies the data back to the computer after the new operating system is installed. To move forward with this type of migration, perform the following steps on each computer to be migrated:

1. Run ScanState and then specify a file share or removable drive as the location for the migration store.

2. Install the company's standard image that includes Windows 8.1 and standard applications.

3. Run LoadState to load data from the migration store created in step 1.

An online migration by using hard-link migration is commonly used when you can start the computer with its current operating system to scan the user state data; then load the same data after installing the new operating system. Using a hard-link migration store will reduce the user-state migration time because it maintains the data in its current location. For this scenario, perform the following steps on each computer to be migrated:

1. Run ScanState with /hardlink and /nocompress. This will save the user state to a local hard-link migration store on the computer. The ScanState process completes faster because the files don't have to transfer across the network or write to an external disk. The files don't even move on the disk but instead are left in their original location.

2. On each computer, install the company's standard image that includes Windows 8.1 and standard applications.

3. Run LoadState, which will restore the user state from the previous version of the Windows operating system.

EXAM TIP

Exam item writers sometimes target easy-to-test areas of a technology. For Objective 1.2, a few areas stand out as easily testable: knowing the difference between MigApp.xml, MigDocs.xml, and MigUser.xml; knowing the order in which you run ScanState (first) and LoadState (second); and understanding how to work with EFS-encrypted files. (ScanState fails if you don't account for them, and you need to use /efs:copyraw with ScanState to bring over the files and keep them encrypted.) It is also worth noting that drives encrypted with BitLocker must have BitLocker suspended before ScanState can read the file system.

Sample side-by-side scenarios

In the side-by-side scenario, the source and destination computers are not the same. Computer-replace scenarios involve migrating user states from one computer to another. Thus, such scenarios don't have to follow the computer-refresh process of scan, install, and load.

You would use a side-by-side migration in three migration scenarios:

- Offline migration by using Windows PE and an external migration store
- Manual network migration
- Managed network migration

Use an offline migration using Windows PE and an external migration store when you have access to the source computers locally but can't start them by using their current operating system, and you don't have access to a network. You then must perform the entire user state migration offline by using an external hard disk as the location for the migration store. For this scenario, perform the following steps:

1. On each of the source computers, start in Windows PE and then run ScanState to collect the user state data and store it on the external hard disk.

2. On each of the destination computers, deploy Windows 8.1 by using the company's standard Windows deployment process.

3. On each of the destination computers, run LoadState, which restores the user state from the external hard disk.

Use a manual network migration when you can start the source computers by using their current operating system and the computers can access the network. In this scenario, you use a file server to host the migration store. Perform the following steps:

1. On each of the source computers, run ScanState to export the user state to the migration store on the file server.

2. On each of the destination computers, deploy Windows 8.1 by using the company's standard Windows deployment process.

3. On each of the destination computers, run LoadState to retrieve user state data from the file server used to store the migration store.

You can use a managed network migration when the source computers are running the System Center Configuration Manager client agent and have access to a network. Use a site role in Configuration Manager named the state migration point. To perform this migration, follow these steps:

1. On each of the source computers, configure System Center Configuration Manager, Microsoft Deployment Toolkit (MDT) 2013, or a logon script to run ScanState. Store the user state data in the migration store on the file server.

2. On each of the destination computers, deploy Windows 8.1 by using the company's standard Windows deployment process. This involves using System Center Configuration Manager or Windows Deployment Services (WDS).

3. On each of the destination computers, configure System Center Configuration Manager, MDT, or a logon script to run LoadState. Restore the user state data from the migration store on the file server.

Determining which settings to preserve

USMT migrates user accounts, application settings, operating-system settings, files, and folders. These default settings frequently are enough for a basic migration. However, you should consider which settings you want users to be able to configure and which settings you want to standardize when determining which settings to migrate.

USMT controls the data that you can migrate by using migration .xml files, including MigApp.xml, MigDocs.xml, and MigUser.xml as well as any custom .xml files that you create.

USER DATA

ScanState uses rules in the MigUser.xml file to collect everything in a user's profile. ScanState then performs a file extension–based search on most of the system for other user data.

By default, USMT migrates the following user data and access control lists (ACLs) by using the MigUser.xml, MigDocs.xml, and MigApps.xml files:

- **Folders from each user profile** USMT migrates everything in a user's profile, including My Documents, My Video, My Music, My Pictures, Desktop files, Start menu, Quick Launch settings, and Favorites.

- **Folders from the All Users and Public profiles** USMT also migrates the following from the All Users profile in Windows XP or the Public profile in Windows Vista, Windows 7, or Windows 8.1: Shared Documents, Shared Video, Shared Music, Shared Desktop files, Shared Pictures, Shared Start menu, and Shared Favorites.

- **Specific file types** The ScanState tool searches the fixed drives and collects and migrates files that have any of the following file name extensions: .accdb, .ch3, .csv, .dif, .doc*, .dot*, .dqy, .iqy, .mcw, .mdb*, .mpp, .one*, .oqy, .or6, .pot*, .ppa, .pps*, .ppt*, .pre, .pst, .pub, .qdf, .qel, .qph, .qsd, .rqy, .rtf, .scd, .sh3, .slk, .txt, .vl*, .vsd, .wk*, .wpd, .wps, .wq1, .wri, .xl*, .xla, .xlb, or .xls*.

- **ACL** USMT migrates the ACL for the files and folders that you specify, from computers that are running Windows XP and Windows Vista.

The MigUser.xml file does not migrate the following data:

- Files outside of a user profile that don't match one of the file-name extensions in the MigUser.xml file

- ACLs for folders that are outside of a user profile

- Operating system components

By default, USMT migrates most standard operating-system features to destination computers that are running Windows 8.1 from computers that are running Windows XP, Windows Vista, Windows 7, or Windows 8. Some settings, such as fonts, are not available for an offline migration until after the destination computer is restarted. For this reason, it's a good idea to restart the destination computer after LoadState has run. There are USMT version limitations, depending on the source and destination computer's operating system version. For example, if the source computer is running Windows XP, you can't use ScanState 6.3 or later. In such scenarios, you can use multiple versions of ScanState and/or LoadState to perform the migration tasks.

The following list includes some of the operating-system components that migrate with USMT:

- Mapped network drives
- Network printers
- Folder options
- Users personal certificates
- Internet Explorer settings
- Supported applications

It's considered a best practice to install all applications on the destination computer before restoring the user state. This ensures that you preserve migrated settings. If you install the application after the user state has been migrated, the installation might overwrite the users' settings.

The versions of installed applications must match on the source and destination computers. USMT does not support migrating the settings of an earlier version of an application to a later version, except for Microsoft Office. USMT only migrates settings that users have changed. Default application settings will not be migrated if the user has not changed the settings from the default values.

Settings USMT does not migrate

USMT does not migrate the following settings:

- **Application settings**   USMT does not migrate settings from earlier versions of an application. In addition, it does not migrate application settings, and some operating-system settings, when you create a local account to use as the user account on the destination computer.
- **Existing applications**   You have to reinstall all applications on the destination computer before restoring the application settings.
- **Operating system settings**   USMT does not migrate these operating system items: local printers, hardware-related settings, drivers, and passwords.
- **Some operating system settings**   Depending on the version of Windows that is installed, USMT will not migrate some settings.
- **Shared folder permissions**   You must share these folders again after the migration completes.
- Files and settings migrating between operating systems with different languages.

- Customized icons for shortcuts.
- Taskbar settings when the source computer is running Windows XP.

USMT requires administrative credentials. If you run the USMT as a standard user, the tool will not run; it only migrate some settings or only the current user. Many factors play into this, including the version of the source operating system on which you are running ScanState and whether User Account Control (UAC) is enabled.

Determining which settings to migrate

As you now know, USMT can be used to migrate user profiles, application settings, operating system settings, and files. When deciding what to migrate, consider the following:

- Users
- Applications and settings
- Operating system settings
- File types, files, and folders

Consider carefully how to migrate users. You can specify which users to include and exclude on the command line with user options.

Before migration, review the following considerations:

- If local user accounts don't exist on the destination computer, use /lac with the LoadState command. If you don't use this option, USMT will not migrate the accounts.
- You might need to create new user accounts on the destination computer. The /lae option enables the account that was created by using /lac. If you create a disabled local account by using only the /lac option, a local administrator must enable the account on the destination computer.
- Be careful when specifying a password for local accounts. The /lac:[Password] allows you to specify a password when the local user accounts are created. If you create a local account that has a blank password, anyone can sign in to that account on the destination computer. If you create a local account that has a password, the password is available to anyone with access to the folder where you store the USMT command-line tools and accompanying scripts.
- Source and destination computers don't have to be connected to a domain for domain user profiles to migrate.

The following process might help you decide which applications to redeploy and which to discontinue:

1. Create and prioritize a list of applications to migrate.
2. Identify an experienced application owner to provide insight into how the organization installs, configures, and uses the various applications.
3. Identify and locate the application settings to migrate.

4. After you complete the list of applications to migrate, review the list and then work with each application owner to develop a list of settings to migrate.

5. Consider whether the destination version of the application is newer than the source version and whether the existing settings work with the new version. If they do, consider whether they work correctly.

6. Create a custom .xml file to migrate the settings and work with application owners to develop test cases. Typically, you continue to perform migration testing for application settings to determine whether the settings have migrated successfully.

When planning your migration, identify which operating-system settings you want to migrate and to what extent you want to create a new standardized environment. USMT allows you to migrate the settings that you choose and keep the default values for all other operating-system settings. Operating-system settings include the desktop's appearance, such as wallpaper or colors; actions such as double-clicking or single-clicking to open an item; and Internet settings and mail-server connection information.

Consider the following when determining which operating system settings to migrate:

- Any previous migration experiences or the results of any surveys and tests that you conduct.

- The number of help-desk calls related to operating-system settings that you have had in the past and how many you think you will receive in the future.

- How much new operating-system functionality you want to use.

- Which settings to migrate. Divide the settings into three categories: settings that users must have to do their work, settings that enhance the user experience, and settings that might reduce support calls. Migrating these items can increase user productivity and overall satisfaction with the migration process.

When planning your migration, if you are not using MigDocs.xml, identify the file types, files, folders, and settings to migrate. It's important to perform the following steps:

1. Determine the standard file locations on each computer.

2. Identify and locate the nonstandard locations. Consider the file types that you want to include and exclude in the migration, the locations that you want to exclude, and new locations to which you want to migrate files on the destination computer.

3. After verifying which files and file types end users regularly use, locate the files.

Estimating migration store size

You must determine how much space you need to store the data that you want to migrate. Base your calculations on the volume of email, personal documents, and system settings for each user. The best way to estimate these is to survey several computers that are representative for the entire set of computers and then arrive at an average size that you can multiply by the total number of computers.

The amount of space the store will require will vary depending on your organization's local storage strategies. For example, one key element that determines the size of migration data stores is email storage. If your organization stores email centrally, data stores will be smaller. If your organization stores email locally, such as by using .pst files, data stores will be larger. Mobile users will often have larger amounts of data than desktop users. Perform tests and inventory the network to determine the average size of your organization's data stores. During the tests, measure the time that you need to perform the migration. Several companies have had to extend the time to finish migration due to the extended time it takes to copy huge amounts of data to and from the network's shared folder.

If you use a hard-link migration, you don't have to estimate the size of the migration store because files don't move from the local disk. This is only possible in the computer refresh scenario.

Consider the following issues when determining how much disk space you will need:

- **Email** If users manage a large volume of email or keep email on their local computers instead of on a mail server, this email can occupy as much disk space as all other user files combined. Before migrating user data, consider having users who store email locally move their email to the mail server.

- **User documents** The size required for user documents varies greatly depending on the types of files involved. You can use an estimate of 100 to 300 megabytes (MB) as a general average. However, this might differ greatly from company to company. This estimate assumes typical office work such as using word-processing and spreadsheet programs. You should compare this estimate to several sample folders of user documents before performing calculations for storage requirements.

- **User operating-system settings** Five MB usually is a sufficient amount of space in which to save registry settings. However, this requirement can fluctuate based on the number of applications that a user installs on his or her computer.

You can use the ScanState tool to calculate the disk-space requirements of a particular compressed or uncompressed migration. The ScanState tool provides disk-space requirements for the computer's state when the tool is running. The computer's state might change during daily use. Therefore, using the calculations as an estimate when planning your migration is recommended.

To create an XML file that includes an improved space estimate for the migration store, use /p of the ScanState tool. This option creates an XML file in the path that you specify. The following example shows the ScanState command to create this .xml file:

```
ScanState.exe C:\MigrationLocation [additional parameters]
/p:"C:\MigrationStoreSize.xml"
```

The following example shows a sample report:

```xml
<?xml version="1.0" encoding="UTF-8"?>

<PreMigration>

  <storeSize>

    <size clusterSize="4096">11010592768</size>

  </storeSize>

  <temporarySpace>

    <size>58189144</size>

  </temporarySpace>

</PreMigration>
```

The report returns the disk-space requirements in bytes, so in the sample report, the store is estimated to be about 10.5 gigabytes (GB) and a temporary space of 55 MB.

Securing migrated data

One of the most crucial things to keep in mind when using a remote storage location for user state data is security. Security of the migration store is easily overlooked and sometimes poses a security breach that could be easily avoided. Data maintained by users might contain privileged information that should not be accessible to other users.

When designing your user state migration strategy, consider the following:

- **Security of the file server and the deployment server** You must maintain the security of the file and deployment servers. Make sure that the file server where you save the migration store is secure. You also must secure the deployment server to ensure that the user data in the log files is not exposed. Transmitting data over a secure Internet connection, such as a virtual private network (VPN), is recommended.

- **Encrypting the migration store** You can use ScanState with the /encrypt switch and specify a password, or path to a certificate, to be used for the encryption. To recover the user state data, you must use the /decrypt switch with the LoadState command.

Creating a USMT package

If you are using System Center 2012 R2 Configuration Manager, you will notice that there is already a deployment package containing all files needed to run USMT. However, previous versions of Configuration Manager don't contain such a package. If that is your case, you must create a package so you can use USMT in your deployment task sequences.

MORE INFO **TASK SEQUENCES**

Learn more about Configuration Manager task sequences in Chapter 3, "Implement a Zero Touch deployment."

To create a USMT package, perform the following steps:

1. Download and install the Windows Assessment and Deployment Kit (Windows ADK). Although the Windows ADK contains several tools, you only need to install the USMT for this procedure.

NOTE **WINDOWS ASSESSMENT AND DEPLOYMENT TOOLKIT**

You can download the Windows Assessment and Deployment Toolkit from *http://www.microsoft.com/en-us/download/details.aspx?id=39982*.

2. Locate the USMT folder, usually found in C:\Program Files (x86)\Windows Kits\8.1 \Assessment and Deployment Kit\User State Migration Tool, and copy its contents to a network share.

3. Create a new package in Configuration Manager with the contents of the network share you copied the USMT files to.

Thought experiment
Windows 8.1 migration at Contoso Ltd.

Contoso Ltd. wants to migrate 300 existing computers from Windows 7 to Windows 8.1. After all hardware upgrades were made, your new assessment shows all computers are ready to migrate. Users will retain their existing computers after the migration, and their user state data must be maintained while minimizing network traffic and decreasing the time to migrate. You decide to use USMT to migrate the user state data. To help you plan better for user state migration, answer the following questions:

1. Should you perform an online or offline user state migration?

2. Should you use a compressed migration store or a hard-link migration?

3. What tools can you use to automate the process of migrating user state data?

Objective summary

- You can use hard links to increase the performance of user state migration in wipe-and-load scenarios.

- You can use remote storage to migrate user state in side-by-side scenarios.

- You can use ScanState /p to estimate the space requirements for user state migration.

- You can use ScanState /encrypt to encrypt the migration store, and LoadState /decrypt to decrypt the migration store.

- You don't need to create a USMT package in System Center 2012 R2 Configuration Manager because one exists by default.

Objective review

Answer the following questions to test your knowledge of the information in this objective. You can find the answers to these questions and explanations of why each answer choice is correct or incorrect in the "Answers" section at the end of this chapter.

1. You run ScanState /p and review the results. Part of the .xml file returned contains the following text:

   ```
   <storeSize>

     <size clusterSize="4096">11010592768</size>

   </storeSize>
   ```

   You need to report to your manager the amount of necessary space for the migration store. How much space is needed?

   A. 10.5 MB

   B. 10.5 GB

   C. 10.5 TB

   D. 10.5 EB

2. You are upgrading 50 computers from Windows 7 to Windows 8.1. Users will maintain their existing computers after the migration. You need to specify how to migrate the user state data in the minimum amount of time. What approach should you use?

   A. Use a USB drive for the migration store and compress the data.

   B. Use a network share for the migration store and compress the data.

   C. Use a local drive for the migration store.

   D. Use hard links for the migration store.

3. You are upgrading all computers from the sales and IT departments in your company's network from Windows XP to Windows 8.1. The IT users will receive newly purchased computers, and the Sales users will receive the computers IT users were using. You need to select a user state migration approach. Which approach should you use?

   A. Use a hard-link migration store for IT users and a network share migration store for Sales users.

   B. Use a hard-link migration store for Sales users and a network share migration store for IT users.

C. Use a network share migration store for all users.

   D. Use a hard-link migration store for all users.

4. You are upgrading computers from Windows 7 to Windows 8.1. Some computers have a local printer attached, some computers have shared folders, some computers have network printers, and some computers have customized Internet Explorer settings. Which of the following items should you migrate with USMT as part of your upgrade to Windows 8.1?

   A. Local printers, shared folders, network printers, and customized Internet Explorer settings

   B. Only local printers and network printers

   C. Only shared folders and customized Internet Explorer settings

   D. Only network printers and customized Internet Explorer settings

5. You are planning an offline migration. In what state is the ScanState tool supported?

   A. ScanState can be run while the source instance of Windows is running.

   B. ScanState can run while the source instance of Windows is booted into Safe Mode.

   C. ScanState can run while booted into Windows PE.

   D. ScanState can run while booted into recovery mode.

Objective 1.3: Configure the deployment infrastructure

In the next few chapters, you learn how to deploy a new operating system to devices over the network. To achieve that, you must prepare your deployment infrastructure with various tools required to push an operating system image over the network.

In this section, you learn about Windows Deployment Services (WDS), Microsoft Deployment Toolkit (MDT), and Configuration Manager distribution points. These technologies can be used alone or together to deploy an operating system over the network.

> **This objective covers how to:**
> - Configure WDS
> - Install and configure MDT
> - Identify network services that support deployments
> - Select Configuration Manager distribution points
> - Support BitLocker

Configuring Windows Deployment Services

Windows Deployment Services (WDS) is a server role that you can install on computers running Windows Server. WDS enables you to deploy operating systems including, but not limited to Windows 8.1, Windows 8, Windows Server 2012, and Windows Server 2012 R2, to computers over the network. WDS sends these operating systems across the network by using unicast or multicast transmissions. Unicast is the default transmission method. It uses a one-to-one communication method so that each image it deploys to a remote computer requires one-to-one communication. Multicast enables WDS to send an operating system image to multiple computers at the same time, using the same amount of bandwidth required for a single unicast deployment. Multicast can minimize the use of network bandwidth, but mostly only when dealing with large deployments. When you use multicast transmissions, the same amount of traffic crosses the network independently of whether you are deploying Windows 8.1 to one computer at a time or 50 computers at a time.

The following high-level steps describe how to deploy Windows 8.1 by using multicast through WDS:

1. An operating system deployment transmission is prepared on the WDS server.

2. The media access control (MAC) addresses of Preboot Execution Environment (PXE)–compliant network adapters are made available to the WDS server.

3. The computers that are targets of the transmission must boot by using PXE–compliant network adapters.

4. The computers locate the WDS server and begin the operating system setup process. If the WDS server has been provisioned with an answer file, the setup completes automatically. If the WDS server has not been provisioned with an answer file, an administrator must enter setup configuration information.

> **NOTE MULTIPLE WDS SERVERS**
>
> When using the WDS console, you can configure each WDS server to have only one unattended installation file for each processor architecture. To work around this limitation in the GUI, you can use WDSutil to create multiple unattended installation files. In environments in which you frequently perform operating system deployment, consider using System Center 2012 R2 Configuration Manager because it makes the process of configuring automatic operating system deployment for multiple operating system types and roles easier.

The installation defaults for WDS are suitable when you deploy the role in small environments. If you are deploying WDS in larger environments and don't choose to implement System Center 2012 R2 Virtual Machine Manager for server operating system deployments, you might want to configure the options discussed in the following sections, which are available by editing the properties of the WDS server in the Windows Deployment Services console.

PXE response settings

With PXE response settings, you can configure how the WDS server responds to computers. As Figure 1-11 shows, you can configure WDS not to respond to any client computers (effectively disabling WDS), to respond to known client computers, or to respond to all computers but require an administrator manually to approve an unknown computer. Known computers are computers that have *prestaged computer accounts* in Active Directory. To create a prestaged computer, you need one of the following identifiers:

- **Globally unique identifier (GUID) of the computer**   This is a 32-digit, alphanumeric string that uniquely identifies a computer. You can find the GUID in the BIOS, on the computer as a sticker, or by using Windows PowerShell to query for the ObjectGUID property. For example, if you want to find the GUID of Computer01, you would run the `Get-ADComputer Server01 -Properties ObjectGUID | Select ObjectGUID` Windows PowerShell command.

- **MAC address of the network interface card (NIC) that the computer uses**   You can find the MAC address on a sticker on the NIC, on the computer as a sticker, or by running the `ipconfig /all` command and looking for the physical address. Using a MAC with the GUI-based creation can be tricky because the GUI-based wizard in Active Directory Users And Computers only asks for the GUID. If you enter just the MAC address, the Next button remains dimmed, and you can't proceed. Instead, you must use twenty zeros in front of the MAC address. For example, if your computer's MAC address is C6-50-00-DE-BF-83, you would need to use 00000000000000000000C65000DEBF83 in the wizard.

To create the prestaged computer accounts, first add the AD DS Tools feature Remote Server Administration Tools. Perform the following high-level steps:

1. Launch Active Directory Users And Computers from the WDS server.

2. Create a new computer object.

3. Select the This Is A Managed Computer check box during the new computer object creation.

4. Enter the GUID (without dashes) or the MAC address (without dashes and preceded by twenty zeros) in the computer's unique ID (GUID/UUID) text box.

5. Select the option to use any remote installation server or select a specific remote installation server.

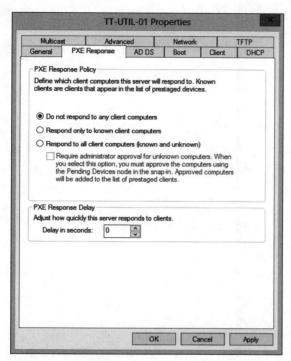

FIGURE 1-11 WDS Server Properties, PXE Response tab

You use the PXE Response Delay setting when you have more than one WDS server in an environment. You can use this setting to ensure that clients receive transmissions from one WDS server over another, giving the server configured with the lowest PXE response delay priority over other WDS servers with higher delay settings.

EXAM TIP

Make sure you know the benefits of only responding to known client computers: higher security, less risk, more control for administrators—and know the downsides: more administrative overhead and slower computer deployment cycle. In addition, know the benefits of responding to all client computers: faster computer deployment cycle, less administrative overhead. Finally, know the downsides of responding to all client computers: less secure, less control, more risk.

Client naming policy

A client naming policy enables you to configure how computers deployed from WDS will be named if you aren't using deployment options that perform the action. You can also use the settings on the tab, shown in Figure 1-12, to configure domain membership and the OU location to use for newly created computer accounts.

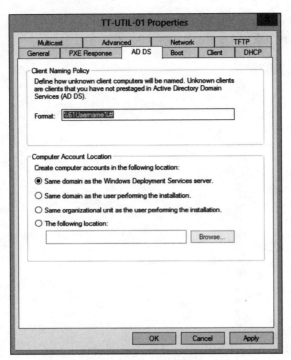

FIGURE 1-12 WDS Server Properties, AD DS tab

WDS boot options

On the Boot tab of the WDS server's properties dialog box, shown in Figure 1-13, you can configure when or whether clients continue with a PXE boot. The settings enable you to configure known clients and unknown clients independently. One of the common options available is to require the F12 key to be pressed to continue the PXE boot. You can also configure a default boot image for each architecture that WDS supports. By default, after a client has connected to a WDS server, you must press the F12 key to continue deploying the operating system. In environments in which you are performing a large number of simultaneous deployments, requiring this level of manual intervention might slow down the deployment process.

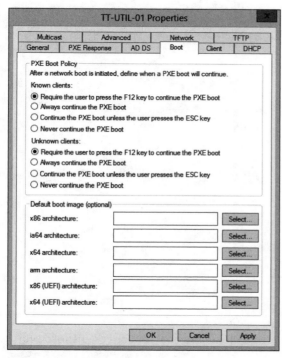

FIGURE 1-13 WDS Server Properties, Boot tab

Multicast options

The default settings of WDS cause all computers that join a *multicast transmission* to receive the installation image at the same speed. If you frequently deploy operating systems, you are aware that sometimes one or two computers have network adapters that slow a transmission that should take only 15 minutes into one that takes hours. The slowest multicast client dictates the transmission speed for the rest of the multicast clients.

To avoid this issue, you can configure the transfer settings on the Multicast tab, shown in Figure 1-14, so that clients are partitioned into separate sessions, depending on how fast they can consume the multicast transmission. Those slow computers will still take a long time to receive the image, but the other computers connected to the transmission can complete the deployment more quickly without having to wait for the slower computers.

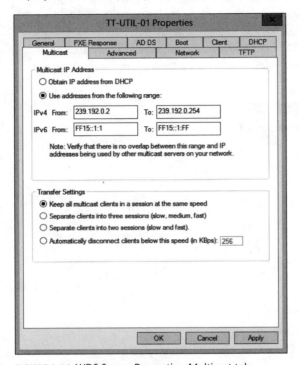

FIGURE 1-14 WDS Server Properties, Multicast tab

Other options

Although you are less likely to need them, you can configure other options on the following tabs:

- **Advanced tab** You can configure WDS to use a specific domain controller and Global Catalog (GC) server. You can also configure whether WDS is authorized in Dynamic Host Configuration Protocol (DHCP). DHCP authorization occurs automatically when you install the WDS role.

- **Network tab** You can specify a User Datagram Protocol (UDP) port policy to limit when UDP ports are used with transmissions. You can also configure a network profile to specify the speed of the network, minimizing the chance that WDS transmissions will slow the network down.

- **TFTP tab** You can specify maximum block size and Trivial File Transfer Protocol (TFTP) window size.

Installing and configuring MDT

MDT consists of free guidance material and free tools to help produce repeatable and scalable client computer deployment solutions based on Lite Touch Installation (LTI) and, when combined with Configuration Manager, zero-touch installation (ZTI) technologies. Throughout the planning phase, this solution package can assist you in understanding the requirements, best practices, and methods you can use to implement an efficient and cost-effective deployment strategy.

Install MDT 2013

MDT 2013 is the newest version of MDT that supports Windows Server 2012 R2 and Windows 8.1. It requires the Windows ADK to run. Both applications have a straightforward installation process, which is not covered in this book.

> **MORE INFO   DOWNLOAD MDT 2013 AND THE WINDOWS ADK**
>
> You can download MDT 2013 from *http://www.microsoft.com/en-us/download/details*
> *.aspx?id=40796*. You can also find the necessary installation instructions on the same page, under *Install Instructions*.
>
> You can download the Windows ADK for Windows 8.1 Update from *http://www.microsoft*
> *.com/en-us/download/details.aspx?id=39982*. You can also find the necessary installation instructions on the same page, under *Install Instructions*.

Configure MDT 2013

After MDT is installed, you must create a deployment share to host boot images, install images, device drivers, task sequences, and other settings. To create a deployment share, perform the following steps:

1. On the computer on which you installed MDT 2013, from the Start screen, type **Deployment**.

2. In the search results, click Deployment Workbench.

The Deployment Workbench window appears, as shown in Figure 1-15.

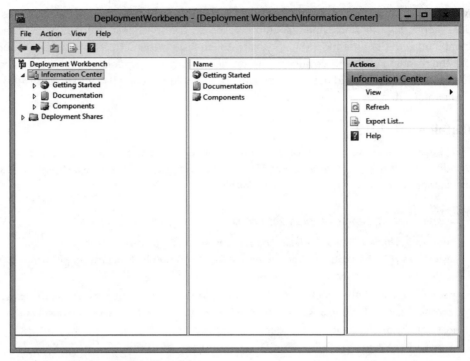

FIGURE 1-15 Deployment Workbench

3. Right-click Deployment Shares and then click New Deployment Share.

4. In the New Deployment Wizard, in the Deployment Share Path text box, type the path to the new deployment share and then click Next.

5. On the Share page, in the Share Name text box, type the name of the new share.

   It's recommended to use a hidden share (hidden share names end with the $ character, as in DeploymentShare$).

6. Click Next.

7. On the Descriptive Name page, in the Deployment Share Description text box, type a description for the deployment share and then click Next.

8. On the Options page, enable the deployment settings that you want to use and then click Next. The following options are available:

   A. Ask If A Computer Backup Should Be Performed. This option displays a message to the user during the installation, asking whether a backup should be done prior to installing the new operating system.

B. Ask For A Product Key. This option displays a message to the user when deploying from the MDT deployment share, asking for the product key of the operating system being installed.

C. Ask To Set The Local Administrator Password. This option displays a message to the user, asking for a password to be used for the local administrator account.

D. Ask If An Image Should Be Captured. This option displays a message to the user when starting a deployment, asking whether MDT should capture an image from the computer to use as an install image.

E. Ask If Bitlocker Should Be Enabled. This option displays a message to the user, asking whether BitLocker should be enabled after the operating system is installed.

9. On the Summary page, click Next and then, on the Confirmation page, click Finish.

> **MORE INFO   MDT 2013**
>
> Learn more about configuring and using MDT in Chapter 2, "Implement a Lite Touch deployment."

Identifying network services that support deployments

Besides the different tools and services you have learned about so far, operating system deployment over a network requires standard network services such as:

- **DNS**   Devices that connect to MDT or Configuration Manager must be able to resolve names to connect to shares and add their computer accounts to Active Directory.

- **DHCP**   Devices that use the PXE service must be allocated an IP address. To avoid manually assigning IP addresses, you should use DHCP.

- **AD DS**   If the device on which you are deploying an operating system will be part of a domain, you need access to AD DS to create the computer account for the device.

- **PXE service**   If you are installing the operating system on a bare-metal system over the network, you must boot the devices by using PXE.

- **WDS**   You can use WDS to deploy images to devices over the network. WDS is usually integrated with MDT for LTI deployments and Configuration Manager for ZTI deployments.

- **Configuration Manager**   You can use Configuration Manager to deploy images to devices over the network. Configuration Manager is usually integrated with MDT for ZTI deployments.

- **Configuration Manager distribution point**   A distribution point is a server in the Configuration Manager infrastructure that integrates with WDS to provide PXE services and access to images and task sequences used to deploy an operating system.

- **Configuration Manager state migration point**   A state migration point is a server in the Configuration Manager infrastructure that USMT can use to migrate user state data.

Selecting Configuration Manager distribution points

Configuration Manager distribution points store the images that you can deploy to destination computers. The distribution point also stores any other content that the task sequence references, such as applications, software updates, or packages. Furthermore, a distribution point can be integrated with WDS to provide PXE service and multicasting.

When selecting which distribution points to use for operating system deployment, you must consider the proximity of the distribution point to the device on which you want to deploy an operating system. Install images are large and can consume a lot of bandwidth if they are delivered over a wide area network (WAN). For that reason, it's recommended to have at least one distribution point for each physical network location, which enables you to deploy operating systems locally over the local area network (LAN).

To add a distribution point to an existing Configuration Manager infrastructure, perform the following steps:

1. In the Configuration Manager console, click Administration.

2. In the Administration workspace, expand Site Configuration and click Servers And Site System Roles.

3. Right-click Servers And Site System Roles and choose Create Site System Server.

The Create Site System Server Wizard appears, as shown in Figure 1-16.

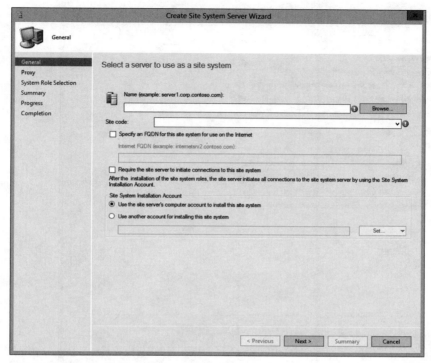

FIGURE 1-16 Create Site System Server Wizard

4. In the Name text box, type the name of the computer to be used as a distribution point and, in the Site Code list, select your site code. Click Next.

5. On the Proxy page, click Next.

6. On the System Role Selection page, click Distribution Point and then click Next.

7. On the Summary page, click Next and then, on the Completion page, click Close.

To configure a distribution point to use PXE and multicasting, perform the following steps:

1. In the Administration workspace, expand Site Configuration and click Distribution Points.

2. Right-click the distribution point you want to configure and then click Properties.

3. In the Properties dialog box, click the PXE tab.

The PXE properties appear, as shown in Figure 1-17.

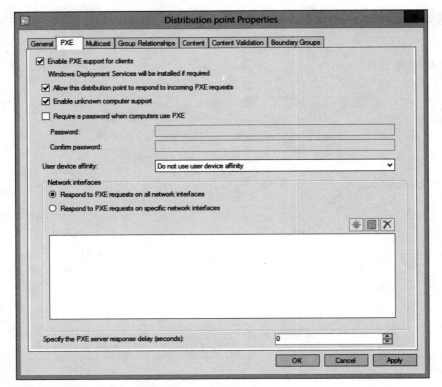

FIGURE 1-17 Distribution Point Properties, PXE tab

4. Ensure that Enable PXE Support For Clients is selected to enable PXE. Selecting this check box automatically installs the WDS role on the server in question after the dialog box is closed.

5. Specify which settings to use based on your needs according to the following list:

■ Allow This Distribution Point To Respond To Incoming PXE Requests. This activates the PXE boot services on this server.

■ Enable Unknown Computer Supports. This allows computers that don't have a record in Configuration Manager to use PXE services.

■ Require A Password When Computers Use PXE. This requires a user to type a password when booting a system by using PXE and connecting to this distribution point.

■ Specify The PXE Server Response Delay (Seconds). This value dictates the number of seconds before a system continues its normal boot process. If the task sequence advertisement is not mandatory, you must press F12 at boot to begin the Windows PE boot process.

6. Click the Multicast tab.

The Multicast properties appear, as shown in Figure 1-18.

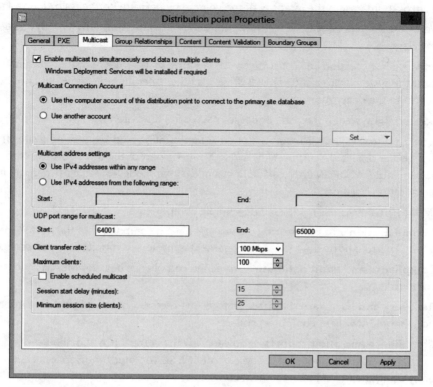

FIGURE 1-18 Distribution Point Properties, Multicast tab

7. Ensure that the Enable Multicast To Simultaneously Send Data To Multiple Clients option is selected and then click OK.

> **MORE INFO** **CREATING DISTRIBUTION POINTS**
>
> For more information about how to designate a distribution point in Configuration Manager, see *http://technet.microsoft.com/en-us/library/bb681012.aspx*.

Supporting BitLocker

When you protect a logical volume with BitLocker, it encrypts the entire volume. BitLocker typically is used to encrypt the system volume to help prevent unauthorized access to the operating system and associated files.

Implementing BitLocker in an enterprise environment has several prerequisites for both client systems and the infrastructure that must support them. BitLocker can run on any computer that supports Windows Vista or a newer operating system. However, using hardware with a motherboard that supports TPM 1.2 or newer has several advantages. TPM support enables BitLocker to ensure the integrity of the volume by performing the following tasks:

- Verifying that the early boot files have not been compromised, such as with a virus or malware.
- Enhancing protection against software-based attacks. If someone were to attempt to start the system from a DVD or USB drive, his other operating system would not have access to the decryption keys.
- Locking the system if the early boot files have been tampered with.

You can use a tool called Microsoft BitLocker Administration And Monitoring (MBAM) to support BitLocker on a large corporate network. MBAM is part of the Microsoft Desktop Optimization Pack (MDOP). MBAM can work in stand-alone mode, or you can integrate it with Configuration Manager.

The MBAM architecture is composed of multiple components:

- **Administration and monitoring server**   The main component of the MBAM installation. This role hosts the MBAM management console and monitoring web services.
- **Compliance and audit database**   Stores the compliance data for MBAM client computers.
- **Recovery and hardware database**   Stores the recovery data and hardware information that MBAM client computers collect.
- **Compliance and audit reports**   You can view the compliance and audit reports by using a browser to connect to the Microsoft SQL Server Reporting Services (SSRS) site or by using the MBAM management console
- **Self-service portal**   Provides a self-service portal so that users can retrieve recovery keys when necessary.
- **Policy template**   The Group Policy template that specifies the MBAM settings.

The MBAM client agent is responsible for

- Enforcing BitLocker settings configured in Group Policy.
- Collecting the recovery keys for the three BitLocker data drive types—operating system drives, fixed data drives, and removable data drives—and transferring them to the recovery and hardware database.
- Collecting recovery and hardware information about the client computer and transferring it to the recovery and hardware database.
- Collecting compliance data for the computer and transferring the data to the reporting system.

MBAM 2.5 supports integration with Configuration Manager 2007, Configuration Manager 2012, and Configuration Manager 2012 R2. Integration with Configuration Manager eliminates the stand-alone MBAM compliance infrastructure and uses the Configuration Manager infrastructure. If you use Configuration Manager, you can now view the compliance status in the Configuration Manager console and inspect reports to view individual computers.

Integration with Configuration Manager is in the form of a configuration pack that installs:

- The MBAM configuration items and a configuration baseline.
- An MBAM collection that includes clients that support MBAM.
- Four compliance reports.

> **MORE INFO** **MBAM**
>
> For more information about MBAM, see *http://technet.microsoft.com/en-us/library/hh826072.aspx.*

Thought experiment
Windows 8.1 migration at Contoso Ltd.

Contoso Ltd. wants to migrate 300 existing client computers from Windows 7 to Windows 8.1. After hardware upgrades were completed, you performed an assessment and discovered that all computers are ready to migrate. All computers to be migrated are System Center Configuration Manager clients. Configuration Manager is currently used only for hardware and software inventory. You decide to use Configuration Manager to migrate to Windows 8.1. To help you prepare better for the migration, answer the following questions:

1. Which Configuration Manager site system roles must be configured to allow images to be deployed by using multicast?

2. What must be enabled in distribution points to allow a bare-metal computer to deploy an operating system image from Configuration Manager?

3. If Configuration Manager were not available, which tool should you use to deploy client computer images with multicasting?

Objective summary

- MDT 2013 requires Windows ADK for Windows 8.1 Update.
- MDT can be used with WDS for LTI deployments.
- MDT can be used with Configuration Manager for ZTI deployments.
- Deployment shares contain boot images, install images, drivers, and task sequences used to deploy an operating system.

Objective review

Answer the following questions to test your knowledge of the information in this objective. You can find the answers to these questions and explanations of why each answer choice is correct or incorrect in the "Answers" section at the end of this chapter.

1. You are configuring WDS so you can use it to deploy computers that will run the Windows 8.1 operating system. All the computers in your organization have PXE-compliant network cards. Which of the following images must you add in WDS to perform a basic operating system deployment? (Choose all that apply.)

   A. Boot image

   B. Install image

   C. Capture image

   D. Discover image

2. You decide to use LTI deployment to deploy Windows 8.1 to devices on your network. Which services or tools are required to use LTI deployment over PXE? (Choose two. Each correct answer forms part of a complete solution.)

   A. WDS

   B. MDT

   C. WINS

   D. VMM

3. You decide to use ZTI deployment to deploy Windows 8.1 to devices on your network. Which services or tools are required to use ZTI deployment over PXE? (Choose three. Each answer forms part of a complete solution.)

   A. WDS

   B. MDT

   C. WINS

   D. Configuration Manager

4. You are prestaging a computer object in Active Directory. You obtained the MAC address of the target computer. However, when you enter it as part of the prestaging computer object creation process, you cannot click Next. You need to proceed in the process and ensure that the computer can be imaged in WDS. What should you do?

   A. Add 20 zeros to the end of the MAC address.

   B. Add 20 zeros to the beginning of the MAC address.

   C. Add the IP address of the computer to the end of the MAC address.

   D. Add the IP address of the computer to the beginning of the MAC address.

5. You must implement BitLocker on 2,500 computers. Which tool can you use to simplify the enforcement of BitLocker and ensure its compliance through reports and policy?

   A. ADK

   B. WDS

   C. MBAM

   D. MAP

Objective 1.4: Configure and manage activation

As part of maintaining an infrastructure of Windows-based computers, you must determine how to handle Windows operating system activation. Activation is a requirement of the Windows 8.1 operating system and requires validation for each Windows 8.1 license through an online activation service, by phone, through the Key Management Service (KMS), or through Active Directory–based activation. In this section, you learn how activation works and about the volume activation models to consider for an effective Windows 8.1 deployment.

> **This objective covers how to:**
> - Identify the appropriate activation tool
> - Configure KMS
> - Configure Active Directory–based activation
> - Configure MAK

Identifying the appropriate activation tool

Enterprise environments use three types of volume activation models. You can use any or all of the options associated with these models, depending on your organization's needs and network infrastructure.

- **Key Management Service**   A service that enables organizations to activate systems within their network from a computer on which a Key Management Service (KMS) host has been installed. KMS enables IT professionals to complete activations on their local network, eliminating the need for individual computers to connect to Microsoft for product activation. KMS does not require a dedicated system, and it can coexist on a system that provides other services. By default, volume editions of Windows 8.1 and Windows Server 2012 R2 connect to a system that hosts the KMS service to request activation. No action is required from the user. KMS usage is recommended for managed environments where more than 25 physical or virtual Windows client operating systems are connected consistently to the organization's network or in environments with five or more servers.

- **Active Directory–based activation**   A service that enables you to use AD DS to store activation objects, which can greatly simplify the maintenance of volume-activation services for a network. Active Directory–based activation is new for Windows 8 and Windows Server 2012. Therefore, if you need to activate older operating systems such as Windows 7 or Windows Server 2008 R2, use KMS or another activation method. To support Active Directory–based activation, the schema must be updated to the Windows Server 2012 or Windows Server 2012 R2 schema level. You do not need to set the forest or domain functional level to Windows Server 2012 or later. When you use Active Directory–based activation, you don't need a host server, and activation requests process during client computer startup. Any computer that is running Windows 8.1 with a generic Volume License Key (VLK) and is connected to the domain will activate automatically and transparently. Computers will stay activated as long as they remain members of the domain and maintain periodic contact with a domain controller. Activation takes place after the licensing service starts. When the service starts, the computer running Windows 8.1 connects to AD DS automatically, receives the activation object, and activates without user intervention.

- **MAK activation**   Uses product keys that activate a specific number of computers. If you don't control the use of VLKs, excessive activations can result in the depletion of the activation pool. You don't use MAKs to install Windows 8.1 but, rather, to activate after installation. You can use MAKs to activate any Windows 8.1 volume edition.

The biggest task you will face when setting up volume activation is the decision about which tool or tools to use. You can use KMS, AD DS, MAKs, or any combination of these, depending on your needs. To understand better when to use each technology, consider the following:

- **When to use KMS**   KMS is the default key for volume activation clients, independent of the Windows version in use. If your network has multiple versions of Windows client and server operating systems, you will probably want to use KMS to activate them. KMS is used routinely in large enterprise networks to reduce the administrative overhead of activation.

- **When to use Active Directory–based activation**   Active Directory–based activation is only available for Windows 8, Windows Server 2012, and newer Windows operating systems. Although it provides better control of activation by enabling an administrator to set permissions on activation objects in Active Directory, this activation method can't be used for computers running older operating systems. Although Active Directory–based activation is still fairly new, it's likely to become the standard activation method in the future because it offers reduced administrative overhead as well as enhancements to KMS.

- **When to use MAKs**   Both KMS and Active Directory–based activation require computers to be connected periodically to a company network that provides those services. MAK can be used to activate computers that are being used in remote locations without access to corporate network resources. On smaller networks, use of MAKs is more common because activation isn't as much of an administrative burden as it would be on large enterprise networks.

Configuring KMS

You can use KMS to perform local activations for computers in a managed environment without connecting each computer to Microsoft. You can enable KMS functionality on a physical computer or virtual machine that runs Windows Server 2012 R2, Windows Server 2012, Windows Server 2008, Windows 7, Windows 8, or Windows 8.1.

Windows Server 2012, Windows 8, and newer versions include KMS host services. After you initialize KMS, the KMS activation infrastructure is self-maintaining.

A single KMS host can support an almost unlimited number of KMS clients. Most organizations can operate with just two KMS hosts for their entire infrastructure: one main KMS host and a backup host for redundancy.

To enable KMS functionality, you install a KMS host key on the KMS host and then activate it on the phone or by using an online web service. You can use a single KMS host key six times, so if you are installing seven or more KMS hosts, you must purchase another host key. Start the command prompt window on the host computer by using elevated privileges and then run the cscript C:\windows\system32\slmgr.vbs -ipk <KmsKey> command.

During installation, a KMS host will automatically publish its existence and location in DNS in the form of a service (SRV) record. This enables both domain members and stand-alone computers to locate the KMS infrastructure.

Client computers can also locate the KMS host by using connection information manually configured in the registry. Client computers then use information returned from the KMS host to self-activate.

> **MORE INFO**   **KMS**
>
> For more information about how KMS works, see *http://technet.microsoft.com/en-us /library/ff793434.aspx*.

Configuring Active Directory–based activation

Active Directory–based activation greatly simplifies the process of activating clients that are running Windows 8, Windows 8.1, Windows Server 2012, or Windows Server 2012 R2. To use Active Directory–based activation, your forest and domain must be at the Windows Server 2012 or Windows Server 2012 R2 functional level.

Although you can't edit activation objects directly, you can use advanced AD DS tools to view each activation object, and you can configure security ACLs for the activation objects to restrict access as needed. If necessary, you can delete activation objects. On a local client computer, a user with read/write permission for an activation object can use the command prompt to perform the functions.

> **NOTE**   **ACTIVE DIRECTORY–BASED ACTIVATION AND KMS**
>
> If an environment will continue to have older versions of volume-licensed operating systems and Microsoft Office applications, administrators need a KMS host to maintain activation status in addition to enabling Active Directory–based activation for clients that are running Windows 8 and Windows Server 2012 or newer versions.

The high-level process for enabling Active Directory–based activation is as follows:

1. Install the Volume Activation Services role on a domain controller.

2. Configure Volume Activation Services by selecting Active Directory–based activation as the activation method and entering the KMS host key.

3. Activate the KMS host key with Microsoft-hosted activation services by using the Volume Activation Tools console.

4. When a domain-joined computer running Windows Server 2012 R2 or Windows 8.1 with a generic VLK starts, the licensing service on the client automatically queries the domain controller for licensing information.

5. If the licensing service on the client finds a valid activation object, activation proceeds silently without requiring any user intervention. The same renewal guidelines apply to both Active Directory–based activation and KMS activation.

6. If the licensing service on the client does not find volume licensing information in AD DS, clients that are running Windows Server 2012 R2 and Windows 8.1 look for a KMS host and then attempt activation by following the KMS activation process.

> **MORE INFO**   **ACTIVE DIRECTORY–BASED ACTIVATION**
>
> For more information about Active Directory–based activation, see *http://technet .microsoft.com/en-us/library/dn613828.aspx*.

Configuring MAK

You can use a multiple activation key (MAK) in organizations that have a volume licensing agreement but don't meet the requirements to operate a KMS or prefer a simpler approach. A MAK also enables activation of computers that are isolated from a corporate network.

A MAK is simply a product key that you can use to activate Windows on multiple computers. Each MAK can be used a specific number of times. You can use the Volume Activation Management Tool (VAMT) to track the number of activations that have been performed with each key and how many activations remain. The VAMT tool is covered in detail in Chapter 5, "Prepare and deploy the application environment."

If a client computer is not connected to the Internet, or is in a remote or highly secure location that is not connected to the Internet, you can use another MAK validation option called a MAK proxy activation, which performs the following tasks:

1. Installs a MAK product key on the client computer.

2. Retrieves the installation ID from the client computer.

3. Transmits the installation ID to Microsoft on behalf of the client.

4. Obtains a confirmation ID.

5. Activates the client computer by applying the confirmation ID.

Objective summary

- You can use MAK, KMS, Active Directory–based activation, or a combination of any of these solutions to activate computers.

- You can use Active Directory–based activation only for computers running Windows 8, Windows Server 2012, and newer operating systems.

- Active Directory–based activation requires the Active Directory schema to be updated with the Windows Server 2012 schema extensions.

- KMS can be used to manage activation for newer Windows versions such as Windows 8.1 and Windows Server 2012 as well as for older Windows versions, including Vista and Windows Server 2003.

- A MAK can be used to activate any Windows operating system and acts as a regular product license that can be reused.

Objective review

Answer the following questions to test your knowledge of the information in this objective. You can find the answers to these questions and explanations of why each answer choice is correct or incorrect in the "Answers" section at the end of this chapter.

1. You have 100 client computers that were configured with a MAK. The computers are connected to the corporate network. You want to avoid communication between these computers and the Internet for activation purposes. What should you do?

A. Implement KMS.

B. Implement Active Directory–based activation.

C. Implement Volume Activation Services.

D. Implement a MAK proxy.

2. You have 250 client computers that were upgraded to Windows 8.1. You need to manage activation for these computers and enable an administrator to remove the activation for a given computer if necessary. Which activation technology should you use?

A. KMS

B. Active Directory–based activation

C. MAK

D. MAK proxy

3. Which activation technologies can you use to manage activation for Windows 7 and Windows Server 2008? (Choose all that apply.)

A. KMS

B. Active Directory–based activation

C. MAK

D. MAK proxy

4. Your existing environment consists of domain controllers that run Windows Server 2012. The domain and forest functional level are set to Windows Server 2008 R2. Client computers run Windows 8. You plan to use Active Directory–based activation. What should you do first?

A. Upgrade the domain controllers to Windows Server 2012 R2.

A. Upgrade the client computers to Windows 8.1.

B. Update the domain and forest functional levels to Windows Server 2012.

C. Update the domain and forest functional levels to Windows Server 2012 R2.

5. Your sales team is made up of 250 people, and each has a portable computer. On average, 50 of the computers connect to the corporate network. The remaining 200 computers are offsite and rarely connect to the corporate network. Some of the computers are not joined to the domain. Which activation method would best suit the computers to avoid activation reminders while also allowing activation?

A. MAK Proxy

B. Active Directory-based activation

C. KMS

D. MAK

Answers

This section contains the solutions to the thought experiments and answers to the lesson review questions in this chapter.

Objective 1.1

Thought experiment

1. Windows-based and Linux/UNIX computers. Because the environment consists of multiple operating systems, you must select multiple scenarios to match.

2. AD DS for the Windows-based computers; IP range, manual list, or file import for Linux computers. Because the environment consists of multiple operating systems, you must select multiple discovery methods to ensure that you assess all the computers.

3. WMI for Windows-based computers, SSH for Linux computers. MAP can use multiple methods to assess computers, based on the operating system.

Objective review

1. **Correct answers:** A and C

   A. **Correct:** Hardware inventory is used to retrieve WMI data related to hardware requirements.

   B. **Incorrect:** Software inventory returns information about files found on a computer.

   C. **Correct:** Asset Intelligence enables you to run reports to see which computers don't support installing a given software or operating system.

   D. **Incorrect**: Compliance settings are used to check if settings are enabled on a computer.

2. **Correct answer:** C

   A. **Incorrect:** Configuration Manager requires an agent.

   B. **Incorrect:** ACT verifies app compatibility issues.

   C. **Correct:** MAP uses WMI to gather inventory without using an agent.

   D. **Incorrect:** WDS is used to deploy an operating system image, not to gather inventory data.

3. **Correct answers:** B and C

   A. **Incorrect:** WMI is used to gather inventory data; it is not a method for discovery.

   B. **Correct:** Network protocol can be used to find computers on the network.

   C. **Correct:** AD DS can be used to discover computer accounts.

   D. **Incorrect:** SNMP is used to manage network devices.

4. **Correct answer**: B

    A. **Incorrect:** MAP does not integrate with Operations Manager.

    B. **Correct:** By integrating MAP with Configuration Manager, you can rely on existing data that Configuration Manager gathers.

    C. **Incorrect:** MAP does not integrate with App Controller.

    D. **Incorrect:** MAP does not integrate with Service Manager.

5. **Correct answers:** B and D

    A. **Incorrect:** RDP is not a protocol that MAP requires.

    B. **Correct:** MAP requires network access.

    C. **Incorrect:** MAP does not require the Configuration Manager client to be installed for inventory to be collected.

    D. **Correct:** You must provide MAP with a known service account that can connect to the target computers.

Objective 1.2

Thought experiment

1. Online. By using an online migration, you meet the requirements of minimizing network traffic and decreasing time to migrate. In this scenario, you would likely use a hard-link migration or a removable disk drive.

2. Hard-link migration. A hard-link migration leaves the data where it is, which is the fastest method. A compressed migration store copies the data off to a file server or to a removable disk drive, which slows the process down.

3. System Center Configuration Manager, MDT, or logon scripts. There are multiple methods for automation, and each can reduce or eliminate the time an IT administrator would have to spend migrating user state data.

Objective review

1. **Correct answer:** B

    A. **Incorrect:** 10.5 MB. ScanState returns the amount of space required in bytes. Thus, for most situations, you must divide the returned number by 1048576 to view the required space in megabytes or by 1048576000 to view the required space in gigabytes.

    B. **Correct:** 10.5 GB. ScanState returns the amount of space required in bytes. Thus, for most situations, you must divide the returned number by 1048576 to view the required space in megabytes or by 1048576000 to view the required space in gigabytes.

C. **Incorrect:** 10.5 TB. ScanState returns the amount of space required in bytes. Thus, for most situations, you must divide the returned number by 1048576 to view the required space in megabytes or by 1048576000 to view the required space in gigabytes.

D. **Incorrect:** 10.5 EB. ScanState returns the amount of space required in bytes. Thus, for most situations, you must divide the returned number by 1048576 to view the required space in megabytes or by 1048576000 to view the required space in gigabytes.

2. **Correct answer:** D

A. **Incorrect:** Using a USB drive for the migration store and compressing the data copies the data, which is unnecessary when upgrading the same computer.

B. **Incorrect:** Using a network share for the migration store and compressing the data copies the data, which is unnecessary when upgrading the same computer.

C. **Incorrect:** Using a local drive for the migration store copies the data, which is unnecessary when upgrading the same computer.

D. **Correct:** Using hard links for the migration store keeps the data on the computer and is faster than the other options.

3. **Correct answer:** C

A. **Incorrect:** Using a hard-link migration store for IT users and a network share migration store for sales users is incorrect. None of the users will reuse the same computer. Hard links can't be used.

B. **Incorrect:** Using a hard-link migration store for sales users and a network share migration store for IT users is incorrect. None of the users will reuse the same computer. Hard links can't be used.

C. **Correct:** Use a network share migration store for all users. None of the users will reuse the same computer, so the data needs to be moved off the computers. Hard links can't be used.

D. **Incorrect:** Using a hard-link migration store for all users is incorrect because hard links can't be used, and none of the users will reuse the same computer.

4. **Correct answer:** D

A. **Incorrect:** USMT does not migrate local printers or shared folders.

B. **Incorrect:** USMT does not migrate local printers.

C. **Incorrect:** USMT does not migrate shared folders.

D. **Correct:** USMT migrates network printers and customized Internet Explorer settings.

5. **Correct answer:** C

A. **Incorrect:** Offline migrations cannot be completed while the source instance of Windows is running.

B. **Incorrect:** Offline migrations cannot be completed while the source instance of Windows is running.

C. **Correct:** Offline migrations require the source instance of Windows to be shut down. Windows PE enables access to the source operating system without having it running.

D. **Incorrect:** ScanState is not supported under recovery mode.

Objective 1.3

Thought experiment

1. Distribution point. A distribution point is where the operating system images are stored. In addition, multicast is configured as part of the distribution point configuration.

2. PXE support. A bare-metal computer does not have an operating system, so it must boot over the network. This requires PXE.

3. WDS. Besides Configuration Manager, WDS also supports multicast deployments. In environments without Configuration Manager, MDT integrated with WDS is the next best solution.

Objective review

1. **Correct answers:** A and B

   A. **Correct:** A boot image is required to boot from PXE.

   B. **Correct:** An install image is required to install an operating system.

   C. **Incorrect:** A capture image is used to capture an operating system from a reference computer.

   D. **Incorrect:** A discover image is used for booting from a removable device.

2. **Correct answers:** A and B

   A. **Correct:** WDS is required for PXE boot.

   B. **Correct:** MDT is required for an LTI deployment.

   C. **Incorrect:** WINS is used for NetBIOS name resolution, which is not a requirement for LTI deployments.

   D. **Incorrect:** VMM is used to manage virtual machines, services, and virtualization hosts.

3. **Correct answers:** A, B, and D

   A. **Correct:** WDS is installed on distribution points with PXE enabled.

   B. **Correct:** MDT is used to create task sequences integrated to Configuration Manager for ZTI deployments.

C.   **Incorrect:** WINS is used for NetBIOS name resolution, which is not a requirement for ZTI deployments.

D.   **Correct:** Configuration Manager integrates with WDS and MDT for ZTI deployments.

4.   **Correct answer:** B

A.   **Incorrect**: Adding 20 zeros to the end of the MAC address will allow you to proceed in the process, but the computer being imaged won't be matched up to the prestaged computer object. When using a MAC address in place of a GUID in a prestaged computer object, you must use 20 zeros at the beginning of the MAC address.

B.   **Correct:** Adding 20 zeros to the beginning of the MAC address will allow you to complete the creation of the prestaged computer object and image the computer. When using a MAC address in place of a GUID in a prestaged computer object, you must use 20 zeros at the beginning of the MAC address.

C.   **Incorrect:** Adding the IP address of the computer to the end of the MAC address will not allow you to proceed. The prestaging of a computer object requires a GUID or a MAC address with 20 zeros prepended. Until the appropriate length is reached, the new computer creation wizard will not allow you to click Next.

D.   **Incorrect:** Adding the IP address of the computer to the beginning of the MAC address will not allow you to proceed. The prestaging of a computer object requires a GUID or a MAC address with 20 zeros prepended. Until the appropriate length is reached, the new computer creation wizard will not allow you to click Next.

5.   **Correct answer:** C

A.   **Incorrect:** The Assessment and Deployment Kit does not offer the necessary tools required for large-scale BitLocker deployments and management.

B.   **Incorrect:** Windows Deployment Services does not offer the necessary tools required for large-scale BitLocker deployments and management.

C.   **Correct:** Microsoft BitLocker Administration and Monitoring is the correct tool for managing large-scale BitLocker deployments.

D.   **Incorrect:** MAP is an assessment planning tool unrelated to BitLocker management.

Objective 1.4

Thought experiment

1.   KMS is the correct choice because Windows Server 2008 and Windows Server 2008 R2 must be supported. For server-based operating systems, Active Directory–based activation handles only Windows Server 2012 and Windows Server 2012 R2.

2. Active Directory–based activation offers the best overall solution if you are activating Windows 8, Windows 8.1, Windows Server 2012, or Windows Server 2012 R2. For example, with Active Directory–based activation, you don't need to meet a minimum threshold before activation can occur. In addition, the activations are indefinite as long as the computer remains actively joined to the domain. With KMS, a KMS host is required, periodic check-ins with the KMS host are required, and activations are valid for 180 days at a time.

3. When computers are mostly or always disconnected from the corporate network, using a MAK is the most appropriate method because it doesn't require connectivity to the corporate network.

Objective review

1. **Correct answer:** D

   A. **Incorrect:** KMS does not work with MAKs.

   B. **Incorrect:** Active Directory–based activation does not work with MAKs.

   C. **Incorrect:** Volume Activation Services are used for KMS and AD DS.

   D. **Correct:** MAK proxies access the Microsoft licensing services on behalf of MAK clients.

2. **Correct answer:** B

   A. **Incorrect:** KMS does not allow removing a license from a given computer.

   B. **Correct:** Active Directory–based activation allows an administrator to remove an activation object from Active Directory.

   C. **Incorrect:** A MAK does not allow an administrator to remove the activation.

   D. **Incorrect:** A MAK proxy does not allow an administrator to remove the activation.

3. **Correct answers:** A, C, and D

   A. **Correct:** KMS can be used with older versions of Windows.

   B. **Incorrect:** Active Directory–based activation can only be used with Windows 8, Windows Server 2012, and newer.

   C. **Correct:** A MAK can be used with older versions of Windows.

   D. **Correct:** A MAK proxy can be used with older versions of Windows.

4. **Correct answer:** C

   A. **Incorrect:** Upgrading the domain controllers to Windows Server 2012 R2 isn't necessary because Active Directory–based activation is supported on Windows Server 2012, which is already being used on the existing domain controllers.

   B. **Incorrect:** Upgrading the client computers to Windows 8.1 isn't necessary because Active Directory–based activation is supported for Windows 8 client computers, which are already being used in the existing environment.

C. **Correct:** Updating the domain and forest functional levels to Windows Server 2012 will enable you to begin using Active Directory–based activation immediately and without any substantial changes to the environment.

D. **Incorrect:** Updating the domain and forest functional levels to Windows Server 2012 R2 isn't necessary because it would require an update of all the domain controllers first. In addition, by just updating the domain and forest functional levels to Windows Server 2012, you'll be ready to use Active Directory–based activation with the existing environment.

5. **Correct answer:** D

A. **Incorrect:** Using a MAK proxy would require all of the computers to come back to your proxy server before activating. This adds an unnecessary step to the activation and uses the company network for all activations. Instead, for remote computers, you should use a MAK key without a proxy so that they can go directly to the Microsoft service and activate.

B. **Incorrect:** Active Directory-based activation requires computers to be joined to the domain. In this scenario, some computers are not joined to the domain, so using a MAK key would be a better choice.

C. **Incorrect:** KMS is best suited for computers that are consistently connected to your corporate network on the internal LAN. Communication occurs over RPC, which isn't supported over the Internet directly. (Instead, it is often encapsulated in HTTP or HTTPS.)

D. **Correct:** There are two reasons to use a MAK key without a proxy. One reason is that the computers are remote and have limited contact with the corporate network. The other reason is that not all the computers are joined to the domain. Using a MAK key without a proxy allows successful activations without introducing complexities or unnecessary steps.

CHAPTER 2

Implement a Lite-Touch deployment

When you automate your first operating system deployment, it can be rather exciting. Often, your first automated deployment is nothing more than an answer file. Soon, administrators realize that additional areas of automation are possible. Many administrators begin testing additional automation tools such as Windows Deployment Services (WDS) and Microsoft Deployment Toolkit (MDT) and exploring automation options to reduce the administrative overhead of deploying operating systems. The keys to implementing a Lite-Touch deployment infrastructure successfully are knowing the available tools and capabilities, understanding the pros and cons of the configuration settings, and being able to implement the tools to meet your requirements.

Objectives in this chapter:

- Objective 2.1: Install and configure WDS
- Objective 2.2: Configure MDT
- Objective 2.3: Create and manage answer files

Objective 2.1: Install and configure WDS

WDS is a foundation for many automated deployment infrastructures, especially as an infrastructure for Lite-Touch installation (LTI) deployments. WDS is often one of the first technologies you deploy when you build out your deployment infrastructure. You need to understand how to install it and configure it for an LTI deployment so that you can ensure a high-performing and trouble-free deployment infrastructure.

> **This objective covers how to:**
> - Configure unicast and multicast deployment methods
> - Add images to WDS
> - Configure scheduling
> - Restrict who can receive images

Configuring unicast and multicast deployment methods

WDS has two methods to deploy images to computers—unicast and multicast. You must become intimately familiar with both of these methods and understand environments and situations in which one would be superior to the other.

With unicast, the WDS server sends one network transmission to one computer. Thus, if you are deploying an operating system image to five computers, the WDS server sends five network transmissions, as shown in Figure 2-1.

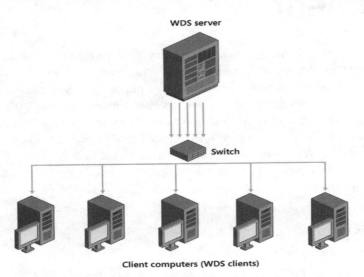

FIGURE 2-1 Unicast deployment diagram

Familiarize yourself with the following characteristics of unicast:

- Unicast is the easiest method to use for deploying computers because it doesn't require additional network setup as multicast does. Unicast works right out of the box.

- Unicast uses more network bandwidth than multicast when deploying operating system images to several computers or more.

- Although unicast uses more network bandwidth, it isn't necessarily slower when deploying to several computers at one time than the same deployment by using multicast. It just means that it takes up more network bandwidth. The performance differences often aren't visible until you try to image many computers at a time with unicast.

With multicast, the WDS server sends one network transmission to multiple computers, as shown in Figure 2-2.

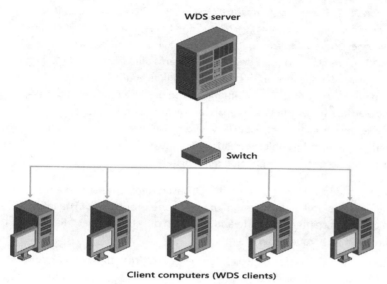

FIGURE 2-2 Multicast deployment diagram

You should be familiar with the following characteristics of multicast:

- Your network team must enable Internet Group Management Protocol (IGMP) snooping on your network devices. This ensures that multicast transmissions are not broadcast to every computer on the subnet, which can cause network flooding.

- You must create a multicast transmission before you can deploy images by using multicast. The process to create a multicast transmission is shown later in this chapter.

- Multicast is best suited for environments where you will deploy images to several or more computers simultaneously. If you are only deploying images to one or two computers at a time, opt for unicast instead.

Before you deploy images by using multicast, look at the default multicast configuration to ensure that it meets your needs. The following settings represent the default multicast settings in WDS:

- Multicast IP addresses are allocated from a static pool. For IPv4, the range is from 239.192.0.2 to 239.192.0.254. For IPv6, the range is from FF15::1:1 to FF15::1:FF. Talk to your network team to ensure that this range won't conflict with any existing multicasting on your network.

- The multicast transfer settings ensure that all multicast clients operate at the same speed during the multicast transmission. In such a situation, if you have an older computer with a slow network interface card (NIC) and a new computer with a fast NIC, the multicast transmission will operate at the speed of the slow NIC, which degrades

I worked on a project to reimage client computers for a school district. As part of the project, I implemented WDS. The plan was to image a classroom of 20 or 30 computers at a time. There were a lot of computers to reimage, so I decided to test unicast and multicast deployments to see whether one would prove better for the situation. One big factor was that school was out for the summer, so there weren't any concerns about bandwidth—nobody was working or using the network. In this case, testing indicated that unicast performed faster for imaging classrooms. This might have been due to a faulty router or switch or other factors. Because it takes time to prepare an environment for multicast, it might not always make sense for a project, especially if you have to involve additional teams for network configuration and troubleshooting. In this situation, unicast was the appropriate choice and enabled us to begin imaging immediately.

When you are ready to proceed with your first multicast-based deployment, make sure you have an existing image group and an installation image. Image groups and installation images are discussed in detail in Chapter 4, "Create and maintain desktop images." Perform the following steps to proceed with your deployment:

1. In the Windows Deployment Services console, right-click Multicast Transmissions and then click Create Multicast Transmission.

2. On the Transmission Name page, as shown in Figure 2-3, enter a descriptive name for the transmission and then click Next.

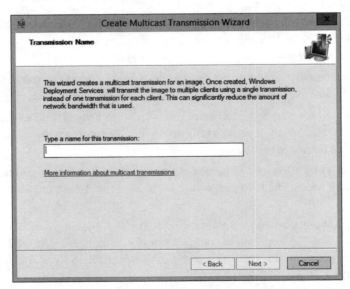

FIGURE 2-3 Multicast transmission creation process, Transmission Name page

3. On the Image Selection page, as shown in Figure 2-4, ensure that the image group that contains your installation image is selected, click the image you want to transmit, and then click Next.

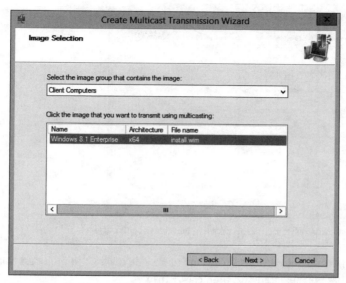

FIGURE 2-4 Multicast transmission creation process, Image Selection page

4. On the Multicast Type page, as shown in Figure 2-5, select when the transmission will start.

You can use the default setting, which starts the transmission when the first multicast client makes a request, or you can opt to start the transmission on a schedule. An Auto-Cast transmission starts when the first client requests the image while subsequent clients join the existing transmission. Clients that join a transmission after it has started will download the missed parts of the transmission after the initial transmission completes. Scheduled-Cast transmission is one that starts after a specified number of clients have requested the image or at a specified date and time. If you are imaging a classroom full of computers and plan to walk around and manually power them up, you should opt for a scheduled cast and start it 15 minutes out or after a specific number of computers have joined the transmission. This enables all the computers to start and finish at the same time.

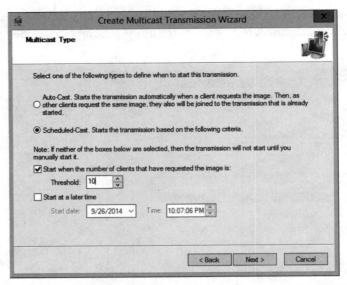

FIGURE 2-5 Multicast transmission creation process, Multicast Type page

5. On the Operation Complete page, as shown in Figure 2-6, review the multicast transmission settings that you selected and then click Finish.

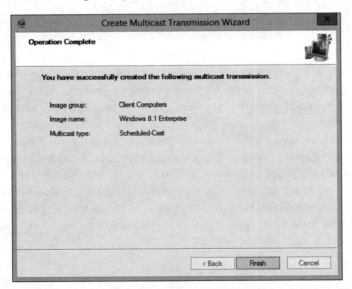

FIGURE 2-6 Multicast transmission creation process, Operation Complete page

6. After you create the multicast transmission, view the status of the transmission in the WDS console, as shown in Figure 2-7. You can view the transmission speed for active clients by looking at the Transfer Rate column. You can disconnect a client by right-

clicking a client and then clicking Disconnect. Alternatively, you can also force a specific client to use unicast by right-clicking the client and then clicking Bypass Multicast.

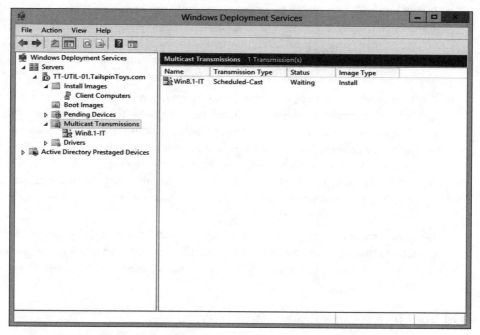

FIGURE 2-7 Multicast transmission status

EXAM TIP

This exam objective specifically calls out installing and configuring WDS. Although the typical methods of configuring WDS are covered here, familiarize yourself also with WDSutil, which is a command-line utility that can handle most aspects of WDS management. Prior to Windows PowerShell functionality for WDS, WDSutil was the primary command-line tool for administration. See *http://technet.microsoft.com/en-us/library /cc771206.aspx* for a breakdown of the command-line options for WDSutil.

Adding images to WDS

One of the primary operational tasks you will perform in WDS is adding images. Before you learn about the planning and operational tasks of adding images to WDS, review the four images that you will work with in WDS:

- **Boot images**   You use a boot image to boot a WDS client computer before selecting an install image to deploy to it. A boot image contains Windows PE, which is used to boot a WDS client computer, and the WDS client, which is used to select the install image to deploy. For the vast majority of deployments, you will use the boot.wim file available as part of the Windows installation media. You can find boot.wim in the \Sources\ folder in the root of the Windows installation media.

- **Install images**   You use an install image to deploy an operating system to WDS client computers. Usually, the install image is created from a reference computer that is configured to meet your company requirements. However, it can also be the install.wim file that is part of the Windows installation media. The install.wim file is located in the \Sources\ folder in the root of the Windows installation media.

- **Capture images**   You use a capture image to create an install image from a reference computer. A capture image is a customized boot image. After you configure a reference computer to use for your install image, you should restart the reference computer and boot to a capture image. A capture image is made up of Windows PE and a WDS image capture wizard. After the reference computer is captured, a .wim file is created. As part of the capture, you have the option to upload the image automatically to WDS. Don't forget, before capturing a computer with a capture image, you must run Sysprep and generalize the computer.

- **Discover images**   A discover image is a customized boot image that you use for computers that don't support Preboot Excecution Environment (PXE). A discover image facilitates such computers in booting up, finding a WDS server, and having an install image deployed.

Add boot images to WDS

There isn't much planning to do for boot images in WDS. Often, you just need to add boot images for the operating systems, such as Windows, that you are planning to deploy with WDS. On the operational side, adding boot images from the WDS console is straightforward. You just right-click Boot Images in the left pane of the WDS console, click Add Boot Image, browse to the location of boot.wim (located in the \Sources\ folder in the root of the Windows installation media), and enter a name and description (or use the default name and description). From an exam perspective, there really isn't much to test. One exception is adding boot images by using Windows PowerShell. New for Windows Server 2012 R2 is a WDS module that includes 33 functions. To use Windows PowerShell to add a boot image from the Windows 8.1 installation media mounted on the D:\ drive, run the following Windows PowerShell command.

```
Import-WdsBootImage –Path D:\sources\boot.wim –NewImageName "Windows 8.1" –NewFileName
"Win8.1.wim"
```

After running the command, you should see output similar to running a Get-WdsBootImage command, as shown in Figure 2-8.

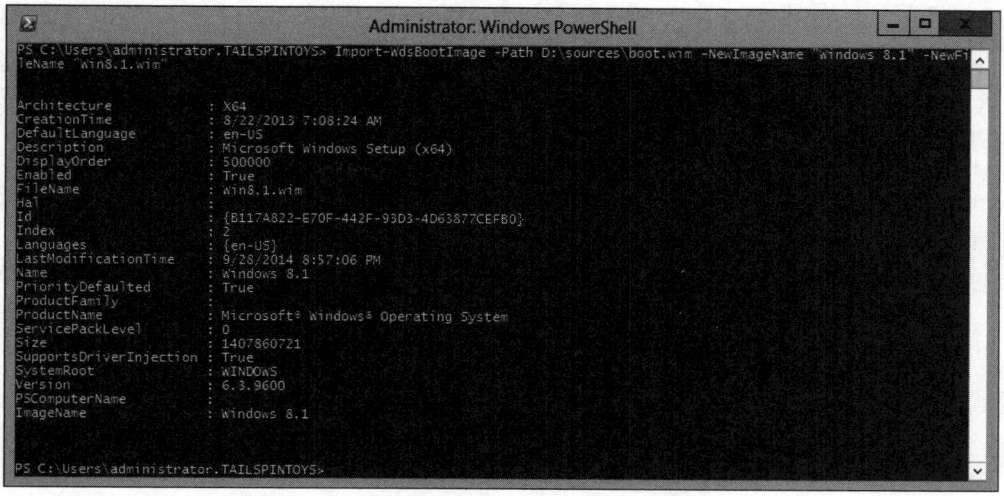

FIGURE 2-8 Adding a boot image by using Windows PowerShell

Add install images to WDS

Of all the images that you'll work with in WDS, the install image is the most important one. It is the image that your computers will run, so a mistake in your reference computer, and thus your install image, could be spread across all your computers. You should be familiar with two types of install images for the exam:

- **Default Windows install images** A default Windows install image is just an image of the Windows installation media. If you deploy a default Windows install image to a computer, the result would be the same as if you had inserted the Windows installation DVD in the computer and performed a manual installation of Windows. Each Windows installation medium has an install.wim file that you can use as an install image. It is located in the \Sources\ directory at the root of the installation media. Often, a default Windows install image is used to perform initial testing of a new WDS deployment. Thereafter, most organizations choose to create a customized install image by capturing a reference computer.

- **Custom install image** A custom install image is one that is built to meet company requirements. It often contains a core set of applications such as Microsoft Office and antivirus software. It is typically customized to adhere to company standards. Many companies customize the theme, background, and support information to help standardize the look of their computers. Custom install images require a capture image to be created first. Without the capture image, you would have no way to capture the reference computer to an install image.

In Chapter 4, in the "Capture an image to an existing or new WIM file" section, you walk through the process of capturing an image for use as an install image.

Add capture images to WDS

Before you can create a custom install image, you must have a capture image, and before you can create a capture image, you must have a boot image. This information is important for the exam. You must understand how all the images work together, which images require which other images, and the order in which to perform core WDS tasks. In this section, you create a capture image.

Before beginning, ensure that you have a boot image; those steps were covered earlier in this chapter. To create a capture image, perform the following steps.

1. In the WDS console, click Boot Images in the left pane.

2. In the right pane, right-click your boot image and then click Create Capture Image. The Create Capture Image Wizard window appears.

3. On the Metadata And Location page, enter an image name, image description, and location of the .wim file, as shown in Figure 2-9. It is recommended to use a descriptive word such as *capture* in the name so that administrators can differentiate capture images from install images when booting to PXE. Click Next to continue.

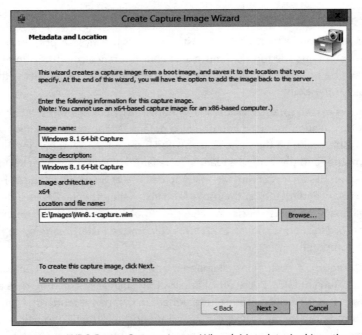

FIGURE 2-9 WDS Create Capture Image Wizard, Metadata And Location page

4. On the Task Progress page, as shown in Figure 2-10, wait until the capture image creation completes, click Add Image To The Windows Deployment Server Now, and then click Finish.

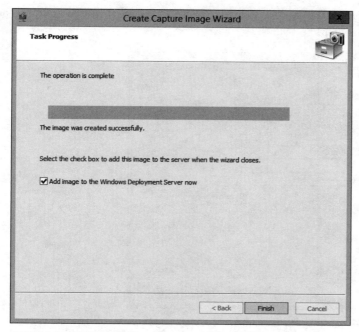

FIGURE 2-10 WDS Create Capture Image Wizard, Task Progress page

5. The Add Image Wizard starts automatically. On the Image File page, as shown in Figure 2-11, verify the location that you saved the capture image to and then click Next.

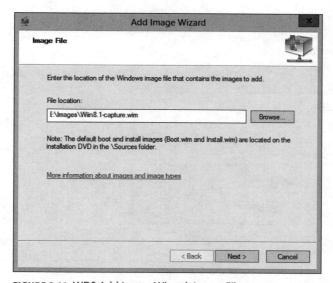

FIGURE 2-11 WDS Add Image Wizard, Image File page

6. On the Image Metadata page, as shown in Figure 2-12, click Next to accept the name and description entered previously.

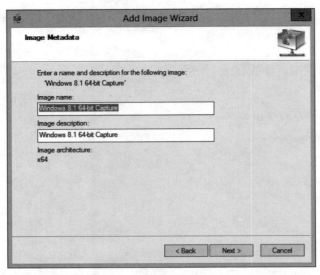

FIGURE 2-12 WDS Add Image Wizard, Image Metadata page

7. On the Summary page, shown in Figure 2-13, click Next.

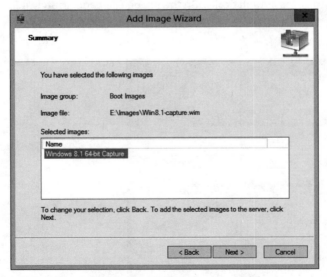

FIGURE 2-13 WDS Add Image Wizard, Summary page

On the Task Progress page, the creation progress appears.

8. When the image is successfully added to the server, as shown in Figure 2-14, click Finish.

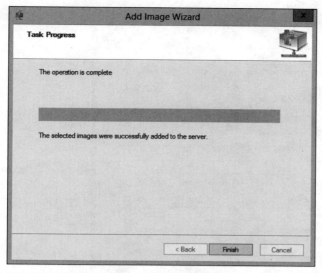

FIGURE 2-14 WDS Add Image Wizard, Task Progress page

Add discover images to WDS

Of all the images you'll work with in WDS, the discover image is probably the least used. However, it is still important to know how to create a discover image in WDS. To do so, you need an existing boot image. To create a discover image in WDS, perform the following steps.

1. In the WDS console, in the left pane, click Boot Images.

2. In the right pane, right-click a boot image and then click Create Discover Image.

   The Create Discover Image Wizard window appears.

3. On the Metadata And Location page, as shown in Figure 2-15, type an image name, an image description, a location and file name, and the name of the WDS server that the discover image will use.

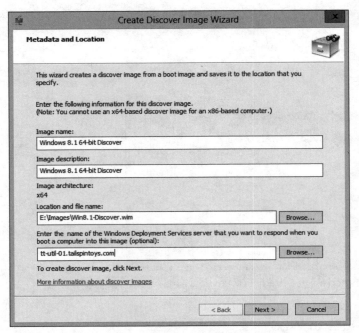

FIGURE 2-15 WDS Create Discover Image Wizard, Metadata And Location page

On the Task Progress page, the progress appears. When it's finished, a message appears indicating that the image was successfully created, as shown in Figure 2-16.

4. Click Finish to complete the process.

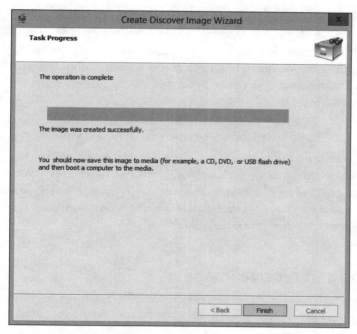

FIGURE 2-16 WDS Create Discover Image Wizard, Task Progress page

> **MORE INFO** **NEW FEATURES AND FUNCTIONALITY**
>
> Certification exams often cover new and enhanced functionality as well as deprecated technology. See *http://technet.microsoft.com/en-us/library/dn281955.aspx* for more detail.

Configuring scheduling

WDS offers limited scheduling capabilities. All the available scheduling capabilities are available for multicast deployments only. Although scheduling was touched on briefly earlier when discussing multicast deployment, the scheduling options are examined in greater detail here. The skills measured on the exam specifically call out the configuration of scheduling.

In WDS, when scheduling a multicast deployment, you are creating a Scheduled-Cast transmission. When configuring a Scheduled-Cast transmission, two options are available:

- Start when the number of clients that have requested the image meets a specified threshold. For this option, you specify a threshold, and when that threshold is met, the multicast transmission begins. Often, this option is useful when you image a group of computers and you want the imaging process to complete at the same time for all of them. If you don't schedule the transmission, multicast clients can join the transmission at any time. For clients that join late, the beginning part of the transmission will have to be re-sent after the initial transmission completes.

- **Start at a later time.** Instead of waiting for a specific number of multicast clients to join a transmission, you can choose a date and time to start the transmission. This option is often used when an organization doesn't want to saturate a network link during business hours. In such cases, you would select a time after business hours. The benefit of this approach is that the prep work can be performed during business hours, and the deployment can take place later.

MICROSOFT VIRTUAL ACADEMY **WINDOWS 8.1 DEPLOYMENT JUMP START**

The Microsoft Virtual Academy offers free online courses delivered by industry experts, including a course relevant to this exam. Look at the available MVA training that is relevant to areas you don't have a lot of experience in, starting with the Windows 8.1 Deployment Jump Start. You can access the course at *http://www.microsoftvirtualacademy.com /training-courses/windows-8-1-deployment-jump-start*.

Restricting who can receive images

An important but often overlooked aspect of automated operating system deployments is security. Consider some security considerations to take into account during your deployment planning.

- **Licensed software**   Some of your images will contain licensed software. Often, the license keys are stored on the computer that makes them available to users. For images that contain licensed software, you should plan to prevent standard users from deploying your image with licensed software to their computer.
- **Minimizing accidents or mistakes**   With a fully automated operating system deployment infrastructure, you run a risk of someone accidentally booting a computer to the network and the computer being reimaged. For a client computer, this might be a minor inconvenience for an employee. However, for a critical server, this could result in a major outage for the entire organization.
- **Network**   Deploying images over the network takes a lot of bandwidth. If you have a WDS server in Los Angeles, you do not want an administrator in Shanghai to reimage a computer by using the WDS server in Los Angeles.

Fortunately, WDS offers multiple ways to restrict who can access WDS images. You should use one or more of the following methods to enhance the security of your company images:

- **Authentication**   You must be able to authenticate to the domain to which the WDS server is joined to use WDS images. Although this opens up WDS images to all authenticated users by default, it also prevents anonymous users from using WDS images.
- **Filters**   You can use filters to narrow down the computers that can use an install image. By default, not many filters are applied, and any computer can use any image as long as the appropriate permissions are in place. Filters can be inclusive so that only the computers that match a filter can use an install image. In addition, filters can

exclude computers that match a filter so that only computers that do not match the filter can use an install image. You can add filters based on the following computer characteristics:

- Manufacturer
- Model
- BIOS vendor
- BIOS version
- Chassis type
- UUID
- Device group

- **Permissions**   There are two places to configure permissions. You can configure permissions on the User Permissions tab of an image's properties, as shown in Figure 2-17, or you can configure permissions in an image group's security settings. By default, authenticated users have Read and Read & Execute permissions, which allow them to access WDS images. The advanced permissions, which show more granular permission entries, show that authenticated users have the following permissions:

- Traverse Folder/Execute File
- List Folder/Read Data
- Read Attributes
- Read Extended Attributes
- Read Permissions

- **Multiple WDS servers**   For environments in which you need to restrict WDS imaging to local IT administrators, you can create geographically based security groups and configure the WDS images so that only the local group can deploy images. In such cases, you should deploy a WDS server in each geographic location that plans to use automated operating system deployments. Although not related to restricting who can receive images, it is important to know that WDS servers do not communicate with each other or share a common configuration. Thus, setting up and maintaining an infrastructure with multiple WDS servers requires extra administrative effort when compared to solutions such as MDT with linked deployment shares.

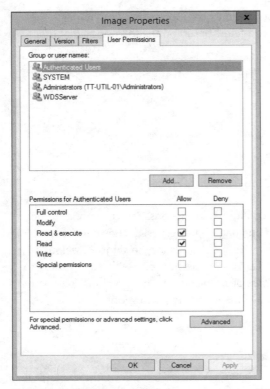

FIGURE 2-17 WDS image permissions

Finally, don't forget about enhancing security indirectly. For example, as discussed earlier in this chapter, you can configure the PXE response so that WDS responds only to prestaged computers, or you can configure WDS to respond to all computers but then require an administrator to approve unknown computers manually. If you configure the PXE response so that an administrator must approve unknown computers, the administrator will have three options in the WDS console for the unknown devices:

- **Approve**   By approving a pending device, the administrator enables the deployment process to continue.

- **Name And Approve**   An administrator can specify a host name for the computer and approve it so that the deployment process continues.

- **Reject**   By rejecting a pending device, an administrator cancels the deployment.

Often, in high-security environments, you should take advantage of most or all of the WDS security options. Combining multiple security methods in your solution is known as a layered security approach.

Thought experiment

Windows 8.1 deployment at Tailspin Toys

Tailspin Toys has two offices. One office is in San Francisco and the other office is in New York. The offices are connected by a 10-megabit (Mb) network. Each office has about 300 client computers, half of which are portable computers. All client computers run Windows 7 Enterprise.

The company plans to upgrade all portable computers to Windows 8.1. The management team wants to automate the installation process. To minimize disruption, users will be reimaged independently, a couple of computers at a time. You decide to use WDS to automate the deployments. To help you assess your knowledge, answer the following questions:

1. To which office should you deploy WDS?

2. Should you use a unicast or multicast method for the deployments?

3. What should you do to ensure that WDS can image only portable computers?

Objective summary

- A unicast deployment sends one network transmission to each WDS client.
- A multicast deployment sends one network transmission to multiple WDS clients, which reduces network bandwidth.
- A boot image is used to boot a WDS client computer to Windows PE and a WDS client prior to beginning the imaging process.
- You use an install image to deploy a customized version of Windows or a default installation of Windows. A customized install image is captured from a reference computer.
- A capture image is used to create an install image from a reference computer. You should capture the reference computer after it is configured and after you run Sysprep /Generalize /OOBE.
- A discover image is used to boot a computer that cannot boot to PXE so that you can deploy a WDS install image.
- You can configure scheduling of multicast deployments by choosing a date and time or setting a threshold for the number of computers that have to join a transmission before it starts.
- You can restrict access to WDS images by using filters and permissions. Permissions can be set on an individual image or on an image group.

Objective review

Answer the following questions to test your knowledge of the information in this objective. You can find the answers to these questions and explanations of why each answer choice is correct or incorrect in the "Answers" section at the end of this chapter.

1. You have a WDS server running on Windows Server 2012 R2. You need to automate some WDS configuration tasks. Which solution should you use? (Choose all that apply.)

   A. Windows PowerShell WDS module

   B. WDSutil.exe

   C. WDSdiag.exe

   D. WDSmgmt.msc

2. You are attempting to capture an image of a reference computer. When you boot to the capture image, the WDS Image Capture Wizard does not see the system volume. What should you do?

   A. Reboot to Windows and then run the Sysprep /Generalize /OOBE /Shutdown command.

   B. Press Shift+F10 to open a Windows PE command prompt and then run the Sysprep /Generalize /OOBE /Reboot command.

   C. Reboot to Windows and then grant the SYSTEM account Full Control on the system drive.

   D. Press Shift+F10 to open a Windows PE command prompt and then use XCALCS to grant the SYSTEM account Full Control on the system drive.

3. You are running a default installation of WDS on Windows Server 2012 R2. Your immediate need is to create a discover image. What should you do first?

   A. Create a capture image.

   B. Create an install image.

   C. Add a boot image.

   D. Import the Windows PowerShell WDS module.

4. You are planning to image 100 client computers by using WDS. The network team has asked that the imaging take place after business hours, so you need to set up the imaging to take place at a future time. What should you do?

   A. Use unicast and schedule a transmission for a future time.

   B. Use multicast and schedule a transmission for a future time.

   C. Use unicast and a WDS filter.

   D. Use multicast and a WDS filter.

5. Your company has recently switched from Dell to HP for its laptop computers. A new batch of HP EliteBook 840 G1 laptops has arrived for imaging, but an advisory was sent out that recommends that all laptops of this model running a BIOS prior to F03 be

updated before using. You need to ensure that your image is only installed on the HP laptops running the F03 bios. Which WDS filters should you apply?

A. UUID and BIOS Version

B. BIOS Vendor and BIOS Version

C. Model and BIOS Version

D. Model and BIOS Vendor

Objective 2.2: Configure MDT

The Microsoft Deployment Toolkit (MDT) provides you with the ability to prepare and customize various aspects of the deployment process. MDT enables administrators to automate deployments and minimize the time that is required to complete a deployment.

> **This objective covers how to:**
> - Configure deployment shares
> - Manage the driver pool
> - Configure task sequences
> - Configure customsettings.ini

Configuring deployment shares

Deployment shares are folders that contain images and files such as drivers, applications, and scripts for use in an LTI deployment. Deployment shares can be located in a variety of locations, including:

- Local drives
- Network shared folders
- Standalone Distributed File System (DFS) folder

Deployment shares hold data that is needed for part of the deployment process, including:

- Operating systems
- Packages
- Applications
- Device drivers
- Task sequences

There are two methods of creating a deployment share. First, after MDT has been installed, you can use the Deployment Workbench, which has a built-in wizard that creates a shared folder as a deployment share. By default, the share will be hidden and thus end with a dollar sign. The wizard will ask for the path that the folder should reside in and accepts local and network paths, as shown in Figure 2-18. If a local path is specified, the share name can also be customized. If a network path is specified, a UNC path must be used.

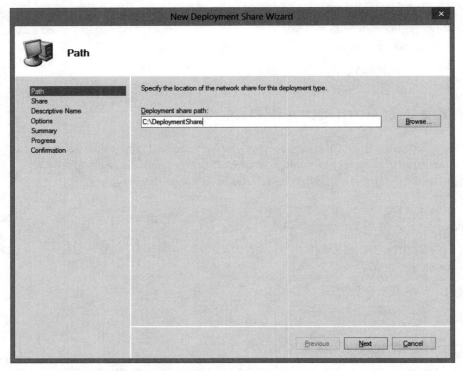

FIGURE 2-18 MDT New Deployment Share Wizard, Path page

When you create deployment shares, you have a number of configuration options, which include:

- Ask If A Computer Backup Should Be Performed
- Ask For A Product Key
- Ask To Set The Local Administrator Password
- Ask If An Image Should Be Captured
- Ask If Bitlocker Should Be Enabled

The computer backup, image capture, and BitLocker options are enabled by default when using the wizard. All, none, or any combination of options can be configured when completing the wizard, which is shown in Figure 2-19. The options can be changed later. See the "Configuring customsettings.ini" section later in this chapter for additional detail.

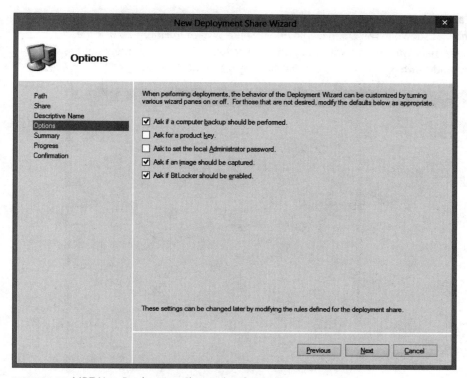

FIGURE 2-19 MDT New Deployment Share Wizard, Options page

Alternatively, if a shared folder already exists, you can use Windows PowerShell to create a deployment share. However, before using Windows PowerShell, add the BDD snapin manually by running the Add-PSSnapIn Microsoft.BDD.PSSnapIn command. Business Desktop Deployment (BDD) is the original name for early versions of MDT, and its name is still displayed in a few places in the MDT product. The cmdlet to use to create a deployment share manually, Add-MDTPersistentDrive, requires a Windows PowerShell drive to exist, which can then be used from the Deployment Workbench. Deployment shares that are configured through Windows PowerShell are stored in a user's profile and will automatically be opened by the Deployment Workbench. The following command is an example of a Windows PowerShell method to configure both a drive and a deployment share:

```
New-PSDrive -Name "DS001" -PSProvider "MDTProvider" -Root "C:\DeploymentShare"
-Description "MDT Deployment Share" -Force -Verbose | Add-MDTPersistentDrive -Verbose
```

 EXAM TIP

When using Windows PowerShell to add a deployment share, you do not specifically create or share a directory. You only configure the Deployment Workbench to use an existing share.

After a deployment share has been created, it can be used from within the Deployment Workbench, as shown in the Open Deployment Share Wizard in Figure 2-20. If the deployment share was created with the previous version of MDT, the contents of the share can be upgraded when opened for the first time by using MDT 2013.

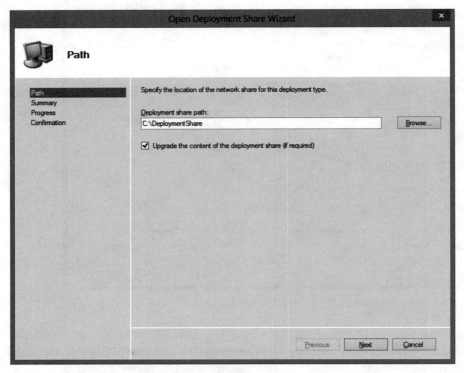

FIGURE 2-20 Open Deployment Share Wizard, Path page

After a deployment share has been created or opened within the Deployment Workbench, your next steps include copying data to the share, such as:

- Operating systems
- Applications
- Packages
- Drivers

If you plan to perform multicast deployments by using MDT and WDS, enable multicast for the deployment share. To do so, perform the following steps:

1. Open the MDT Deployment Workbench.
2. Right-click the MDT Deployment Share in the left pane and then click Properties.

3. In the MDT Deployment Share Properties window, on the General tab, click Enable Multicast For This Deployment Share (requires Windows Server 2008 R2 Windows Deployment Services).

4. Click OK.

When adding an operating system in MDT, as shown in Figure 2-21, you have a few choices for the type of operating system that you are adding:

- A full set of source files such as those found on the installation media
- A custom image file that has been deployed and captured
- All existing images available on the WDS server

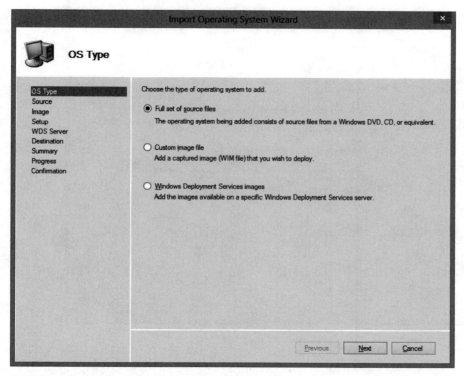

FIGURE 2-21 Import Operating System Wizard, OS Type page

Operating systems can also be imported by using Windows PowerShell. To import the operating system named Windows 8 Enterprise x86 with source files that are located on the E:\ drive, run the following command:

```
Import-MDTOperatingSystem -Path "DS001:\Operating Systems" -SourcePath "E:\"
-DestinationFolder "Windows 8 Enterprise x86"
```

You can also add applications and configure the type of application to add, as shown in Figure 2-22. The options include:

- Application with source files, as typically used with a local installation.
- Application without source files, or elsewhere on the network, as typically used with network installations.
- Application bundle, which installs the application and the dependencies of the application.

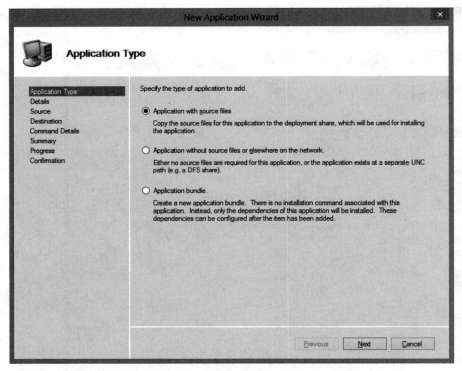

FIGURE 2-22 New Application Wizard, Application Type page

You can also deploy applications by using Windows PowerShell. To import a package named App1 that is located on the E:\ drive and requires the command-line switch "-q", run the following command:

```
Import-MDTApplication -Path "DS001:\Applications" -enable "True" -Name "App1" -ShortName
"App1" -CommandLine "-q" -WorkingDirectory ".\Applications\App1" -ApplicationSourcePath
"E:\" -DestinationFolder "App1"
```

Packages are defined as Windows packages that contain software features, updates, or hotfixes. Packages will have either a .cab or .msu file extension. You can add packages to the Deployment Workbench, as shown in Figure 2-23, for use with images and task sequences to enhance and customize a deployment further.

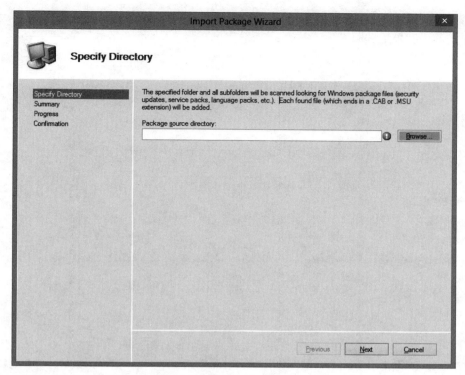

FIGURE 2-23 Import Package Wizard, Specify Directory page

You can also import packages by using Windows PowerShell. You can run the following command to import packages that are located in the E:\Data folder and all folders under the Data folder:

```
Import-MDTPackage -Path "DS001:\Packages" -SourcePath "E:\Data"
```

Deployment shares can also be configured to support specific platforms, or reconfigured for a different local or network path, as shown in Figure 2-24.

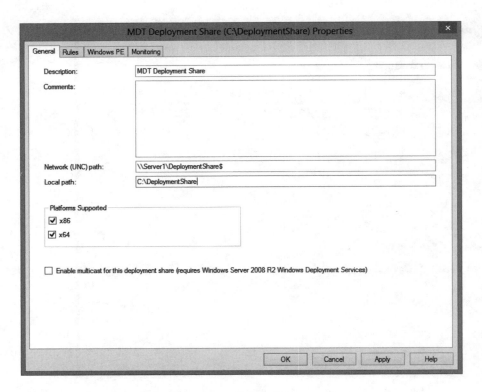

FIGURE 2-24 MDT Deployment Share Properties, General tab

> *MORE INFO* **MICROSOFT DEPLOYMENT TOOLKIT 2013**
>
> For more information about MDT 2013, see *http://technet.microsoft.com/en-us/windows /dn475741.aspx.*

Managing the driver pool

MDT includes a systematic approach for managing and deploying device drivers. In large environments that support multiple platforms, driver management can be a big challenge. With MDT, drivers can now be imported into the driver pool for easy sorting, versioning, and injection, ensuring that the target hardware is fully functional after the image has been deployed. Device drivers could be required to use specific hardware on a computer to which an image is being deployed or, optionally, for printers and peripherals that might be installed in the future. The Import Driver Wizard loads the drivers as specified in the associated .inf file types.

MDT will scan a specified directory for drivers, as shown in Figure 2-25.

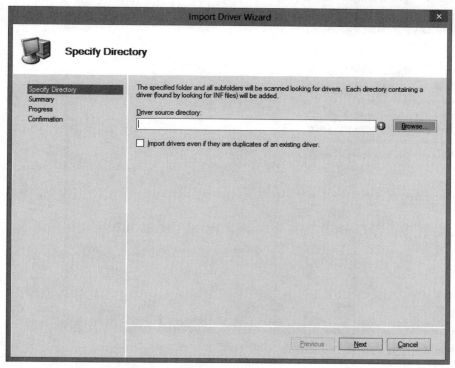

FIGURE 2-25 Import Driver Wizard, Specify Directory page

You can also import device drivers by using Windows PowerShell. You can run the following command to import a driver that is located on the E:\Data drive:

```
Import-MDTDriver -Path "DS001:\Out-of-Box Drivers" -SourcePath "E:\Data"
-ImportDuplicates
```

You can customize the Windows PE boot images for x86 and x64 platforms with drivers that have been loaded into the Deployment Workbench, as shown in Figure 2-26. You can configure the Windows PE image to include all drivers from the configured selection profile or any combination of the following settings:

- Include All Network Drivers In The Selection Profile
- Include All Mass Storage Drivers In The Selection Profile
- Include All Video Drivers In The Selection Profile
- Include All System-Class Drivers In The Selection Profile

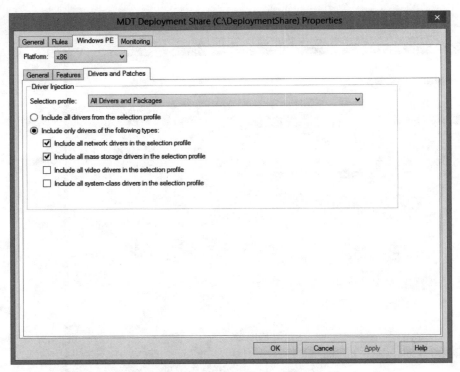

FIGURE 2-26 MDT Deployment Share Properties, Windows PE tab

Configuring task sequences

Task sequences are the steps that will be taken in order as part of an LTI deployment. An MDT task sequence uses the same task sequence engine as System Center Configuration Manager, although Configuration Manager is not required to run MDT task sequences. MDT includes a New Task Sequence Wizard, as shown in Figure 2-27, which walks you through creating a new task sequence.

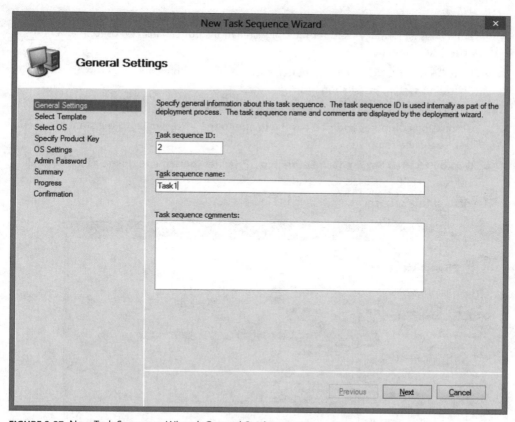

FIGURE 2-27 New Task Sequence Wizard, General Settings page

MDT 2013 has the following nine default task sequence templates:

- **Sysprep and Capture** Runs Sysprep on a reference computer and then captures the image of that computer.

- **Standard Client Task Sequence** Creates and deploys reference images for computers.

- **Standard Client Replace Task Sequence** Runs the User State Migration Tool (USMT) backup and the optional full Windows Images backup actions. This sequence can also be used to perform a secure wipe of a computer that will be removed from the network.

- **Custom Task Sequence** Can be customized to meet your requirements. It has one default task, which is for an application installation.

- **Standard Server Task Sequence** Has default sequence for deploying server operating systems. The difference between this template and the client template is that the server template does not use USMT.

- **Litetouch OEM Task Sequence** Preloads operating system images onto the computer. This is normally used for factory installations but can also be used in an enterprise environment.

- **Post OS Installation Task Sequence** Contains tasks that should be run after the operating system installation has completed.

- **Deploy to VHD Client Task Sequence** Creates a virtual hard disk (VHD) on the destination computer and deploys the image to the VHD, similar to the standard client task sequence template.

- **Deploy to VHD Server Task Sequence** Provides the same template as the VHD client template but is used for servers.

The default task sequences are shown in Figure 2-28.

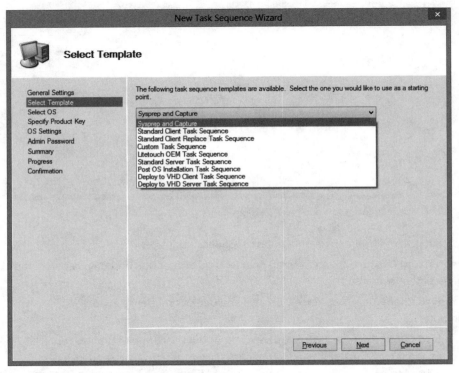

FIGURE 2-28 New Task Sequence Wizard, Select Template page

The template that you choose determines which pages of the wizard are shown to you. For example, if you select the Custom Task Sequence template, it will take you directly to the summary screen to create the task. However, if you select the Standard Client Task Sequence template, it prompts you to select the operating system, product key, operating system settings, and password. Figure 2-29 shows the Specify Product Key page of the wizard.

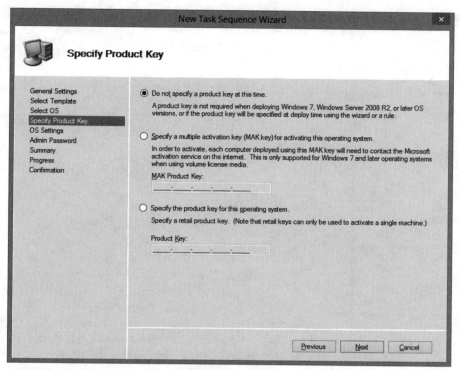

FIGURE 2-29 New Task Sequence Wizard, Specify Product Key page

MORE INFO **CREATE A TASK SEQUENCE WITH MDT**

For more information about creating a task sequence, see the article at *http://technet .microsoft.com/en-us/library/dn744302.aspx*.

Configuring customsettings.ini

MDT 2013 is highly customizable by using a settings configuration file. The configuration file, named customsettings.ini, contains information that will be used during an LTI deployment. To automate deployments as much as possible, you must work with the customsettings.ini file. Otherwise, you must answer several installation questions manually during deployments. A customsettings.ini file contains

- Sections
- Properties
- Settings

The following is a sample customsettings.ini file:

```
[Settings]

Priority=Default, MACAddress

Properties=CustomProperty


[Default]

OSInstall=Y

ScanStateArgs=/v:5 /o /c

LoadStateArgs=/v:5 /c /lac

UserDataLocation=NONE


[00:0F:20:35:DE:AC]

CustomProperty=TRUE
```

When customizing a customsettings.ini file, the only section that is required is Settings. All the other sections in the file are optional. The optional settings can set the configuration for either an individual computer, as identified by the MAC address, or a group of computers, as identified by a specified characteristic such as the make, model, or geographic location.

The properties that can be defined in the customsettings.ini file are predefined in the ZTIGather.wsf file, which is used for both Zero Touch Installation (ZTI) and LTI deployments, and automatically sets the values for properties that can be defined. You can run the ZTIGather.wsf script on computers, which then outputs a very large amount of data about the computers, to ensure that you use the right values for properties in the customsettings.ini file. When customizing a customsettings.ini file, ensure that all the properties you use are considered customizable.

Although the way properties are used for both ZTI and LTI deployments are similar, some properties are unique for each deployment scenario. In an LTI deployment, most of the properties relate to the deployment wizard, such as

- SkipadministratorPassword
- SkipCapture
- SkipUserData

There are more than 300 customizable properties that you can use in customsettings.ini. Although you don't need to be familiar with all of them for the exam, you should look at the complete list and familiarize yourself with some of them. On a computer on which MDT is installed, you'll find the Microsoft Deployment Toolkit Documentation Library. In the documentation library, expand Toolkit Reference and then look at Properties.

Thought experiment

Going to LDI deployments at Fabrikam

You are the system administrator for Fabrikam. You, along with three other IT administrators, handle all aspects of the computing environment. Fabrikam is a small organization with one main office and 350 client computers. You are preparing to deploy WDS and MDT as part of a project to bring LTI operating system deployments to your organization.

You need to prepare the infrastructure for LTI deployments. To help you plan better for the project, answer the following questions:

1. MDT is deployed, but WDS isn't yet. Where should you put the operating system images that you want to deploy?

2. You just finished configuring a computer to use as a reference computer. Now, you want to use the computer to create the installation image. Which MDT task sequence should you use?

3. You are preparing to add some packages to your deployment share. Which file extensions are valid for packages?

Objective summary

- Deployment shares store information used during a deployment.
- Deployment shares can have operating systems, packages, applications, and device drivers.
- Windows PowerShell can be used to configure components of a deployment share.
- You can use packages, applications, and device drivers to streamline the update process of an operating system deployment.
- Device drivers can be used with specific Windows PE selection profiles.
- Task sequences can be used to customize a deployment.
- Nine task sequence templates are available to customize a deployment.
- The customsettings.ini file provides additional customization capabilities, which can help automate more of the deployment process.

Objective review

Answer the following questions to test your knowledge of the information in this objective. You can find the answers to these questions and explanations of why each answer choice is correct or incorrect in the "Answers" section at the end of this chapter.

1. MDT task sequences use the same engine as which other product?

    A. Windows Server 2012

    B. System Center 2012 R2 Configuration Manager

    C. Exchange Server 2013

    D. SharePoint Server 2013

2. You need to automate several aspects of a deployment to minimize the number of manual deployment steps required. Which file should you use?

    A. Bootstrap.ini

    B. Customsettings.ini

    C. Deploy.xml

    D. Settings.xml

3. You have an existing MDT deployment share. You deploy a new MDT server. You need to add the existing share to the new MDT server. What should you do?

    A. In the MDT console, create a new deployment share and specify the path to the existing deployment share.

    B. In the MDT console, open the existing deployment share.

    C. Run the Add-MDTPersistentDrive Windows PowerShell command.

    D. Run the Get-MDTPersistentDrive Windows PowerShell command.

4. Which storage locations can a deployment share be located on? (Choose all that apply.)

    A. Network share

    B. Local storage

    C. Microsoft Access database

    D. SQL Server database

5. You are attempting to run the Get-MDTDeploymentShareStatistics command on your MDT server, but an error message appears. The error is "Get-MDTDeploymentShareStatistics : The term 'Get-MDTDeploymentShareStatistics' is not recognized as the name of a cmdlet, function, script file, or operable program." You need to be able to run MDT Windows PowerShell commands. What should you do?

    A. Run the Import-Module Microsoft.BDD.PSSnapIn command.

    B. Run the Add-PSSnapIn Microsoft.BDD.PSSnapIn command.

C. At the Windows PowerShell prompt, change the directory to C:\Windows\System32.

D. Open the Windows PowerShell prompt as Administrator.

Objective 2.3: Create and manage answer files

Answer files are a crucial part of implementing an LTI deployment method with the MDT. Answer files are XML files that contain settings and responses to virtually all aspects of the Windows setup process. Answer files can be used with any type of deployment image and can include settings about items such as:

- User accounts
- Display settings
- Product key
- Time zone

Many other settings can also be configured with an answer file.

> **This objective covers how to:**
> - Identify the appropriate location for answer files
> - Identify the required number of answer files
> - Identify the appropriate setup phase for answer files
> - Configure answer file settings
> - Create Autounattended.xml answer files

Identifying the appropriate location for answer files

Before implementing an unattended installation using answer files, you should be familiar with how Windows Setup interprets the files. First, to ensure that an answer file is read and interpreted during the Windows Setup process, it must be stored in the appropriate working directory. In some cases, answer files must also have specific names. The files can be located in a number of locations, and each location has a different precedence. The answer file that has the highest precedence is used for the customization of that installation. Second, the Windows Setup process starts by taking an inventory of all valid answer files based on the order of precedence. The files are validated and cached to the local computer. During the WindowsPE and offlineServicing passes, valid answer files are cached to $Windows.~BT\Sources\Panther. After the image has been extracted to the local disk, answer files are cached to %WINDIR%\panther. The following table lists the valid locations for an answer file.

TABLE 2-1 Answer file precedence table

Precedence	Location	Notes
1	Registry: HKLM\System\Setup!UnattendFile This entry is created inside the registry of the image that you are deploying.	This registry entry specifies the location of your answer file. Using this option gives you the flexibility to use a preferred path as opposed to the pre-defined locations that Windows Setup references.
2	%WINDIR%\Panther\Unattend This directory is located in the image that you are deploying.	This location is used for custom installations only and is not searched for installations that start with Windows PE. The file name of the answer file must be Unattend.xml or Autounattend.xml.
3	%WINDIR%\Panther This directory is located in the image that you are deploying. Answer files within this directory should not be overwritten.	This location is used by Windows Setup to cache valid answer files.
4/5	Removable media This refers to the Windows Setup DVD in conjunction with an answer file stored on one of the various types of removable media.	Answer files for removable media must be stored at the root of the media drive. The filename of the answer file must be Unattend.xml or Autounattend.xml.
6	For windowsPE and offlineServicing passes: \Sources of the installation media All other passes: %WINDIR%\System32\Sysprep within the image you are deploying.	For the windowsPE and offlineServicing passes, discussed in detail in the upcoming "Identifying the appropriate setup phase for answer files" section, the answer file must be named Autounattend.xml. For all other passes, the file name must be Unattend.xml.
7	%SYSTEMDRIVE% This directory path is located within the image you are deploying.	The file name of the answer file must be Unattend.xml or Autounattend.xml.

EXAM TIP

Be expected to know the difference between Unattend.xml and Autounattend.xml, including the locations that specifically require one file name or the other.

Identifying the required number of answer files

Theoretically, you could place an answer file in all seven of the locations specified in Table 2-1. However, the installation process will only use answer files that have valid configuration data for the configuration pass it is currently working in. As a good practice, you should use the minimum number of answer files that are needed for your deployment. From an exam perspective, the best way to identify the required number of answer files is to understand the answer files and what they do, where they are stored, and how they are processed. You might be presented with an exam scenario to meet a specified set of deployment requirements and then be asked to figure out which answer file(s) are required. The following sections in this chapter discuss the details of answer files and their role in automated deployments.

Identifying the appropriate setup phase for answer files

An answer file is composed of seven configuration passes, each representing a different phase within the Windows Setup procedure. Within each configuration pass, you are given a series of components that can be added to your answer file and manipulated to meet the needs of your image deployment. It is important to note that these components are not always unique to a specific configuration pass. In some cases, the same component can be referenced across multiple passes.

You should be familiar with the Windows Setup procedure and how each configuration pass is used. The following are the seven configuration passes:

- windowsPE
- offlineServicing
- generalize
- specialize
- auditSystem
- auditUser
- oobeSystem

Although there are seven configuration passes, only the windowsPE, specialize, and oobeSystem passes are used for every deployment. The other configuration passes are used only as needed. The windowsPE configuration pass, as shown in Figure 2-30, configures settings that are specific to the preinstallation environment as well as to installation settings. The Windows Setup settings that can be configured include:

- Disk drive partitions and formatting
- Windows image location and credentials
- Destination partition
- Windows product key
- Local Administrator account password
- Specific commands that must run during setup

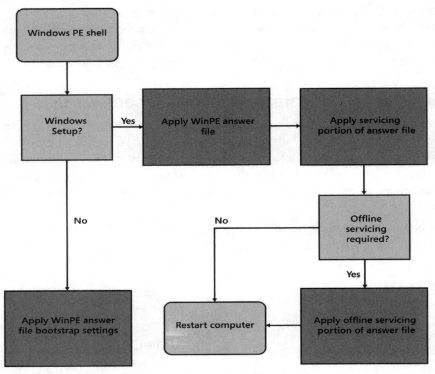

FIGURE 2-30 The windowsPE configuration pass logical order

You can use the offlineServicing pass of the configuration to apply Windows Setup settings to an offline Windows image. During this pass, packages can be added to the offline Windows image. The offlineServicing pass uses Package Manager (Pkgmgr.exe) to apply packages.

The generalize pass of the configuration, shown in Figure 2-31, is used to create a custom image of a Windows installation that can then be deployed to multiple computers. Settings defined in the generalize pass can be used to automate aspects of a deployment of the image. During the generalize pass, specific details of the Windows installation are removed from the image, such as the security identifier (SID) and other hardware-specific settings. The generalize pass is only used when the /generalize switch is provided with the Sysprep command. Other answer file settings are applied to the Windows image before the Sysprep generalization occurs.

> **MORE INFO**   **WHAT IS SYSPREP?**
>
> For more information about Sysprep, see the article at *http://technet.microsoft.com/en-us /library/cc721940(v=ws.10).aspx.*

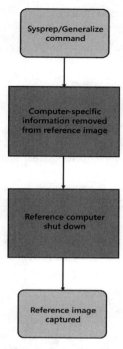

FIGURE 2-31 The generalize pass logical order

The specialize pass of the installation, shown in Figure 2-32, allows settings to be configured for an individual machine. These settings can include:

- Network settings
- International and language settings
- Domain information

The specialize pass can be used to enhance or customize settings further that were made in the generalize pass.

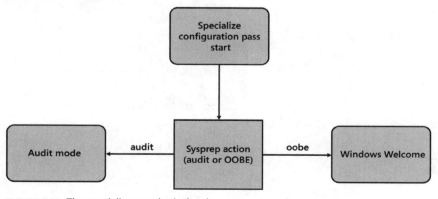

FIGURE 2-32 The specialize pass logical order

The auditSystem pass of the installation is only used if the system has been booted into audit mode. When a computer has been started by using the audit mode, the auditSystem and auditUser passes are processed. The auditSystem pass can be used to add additional drivers to a Windows image.

The auditUser pass of the installation is typically used for RunSynchronous and RunAsynchronous commands that might include scripts, applications, or other executables.

> **MORE INFO** **THE AUDITSYSTEM PASS**
>
> For more information about the auditSystem pass as well as about a detailed decision tree, see *http://technet.microsoft.com/en-us/library/cc749062(v=ws.10).aspx*.

The oobeSystem pass of the installation, as shown in Figure 2-33, configures the settings that are typically used during the first power on for end users, known as Windows Welcome. The oobeSystem settings are applied before the first user logs on to Windows. The out-of-box experience (OOBE) runs the first time an end user powers on a new computer. OOBE runs before the user logs on or runs additional software, and it performs the tasks that are necessary to configure Windows for first use.

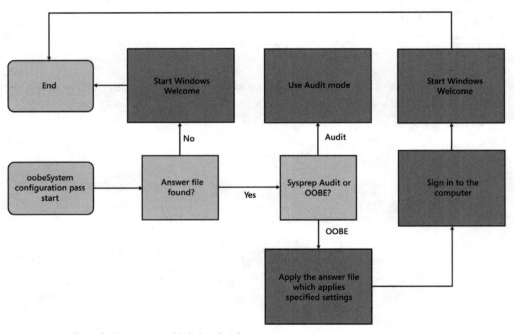

FIGURE 2-33 The oobeSystem pass high-level order

Configuring answer file settings

Each of the components you add to your answer file will include a series of settings that can
be adjusted. Changing the value of these settings is straightforward. You can edit an answer
file by using a text editor or by using Windows System Image Manager (SIM).

One example of a quick edit using a text editor is to include changing the input language
from en-US to fr-FR. To do so, open the existing answer file, search for the <InputLocale> tag,
and replace en-US with fr-FR. You should also confirm that the <settings pass=""> tag is set
to the appropriate pass because <InputLocale> can be modified during pass 4: specialize and
pass 7: oobeSystem.

Settings can also be edited in Windows SIM. SIM includes a detailed description of each
setting and several examples to work from. The following example demonstrates how to use
Windows SIM to make setting changes to your answer file. Refer to Figure 2-34.

1. Add the desired component to your answer file. In this example, you work with
    Microsoft-Windows-International-Core.

2. Select the component within your answer file. The available settings appear in the
    right pane.

3. Click in the field to the right of the setting label and enter your desired value. For a
    better understanding of the setting, right-click the setting label and select Help.

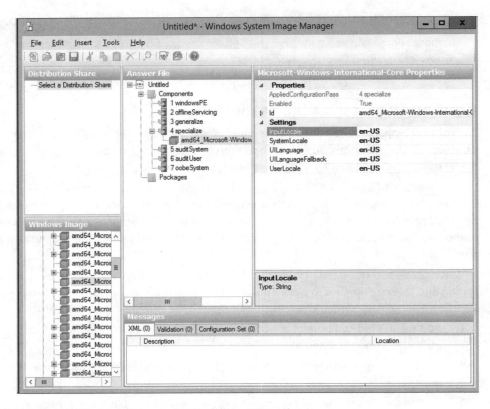

FIGURE 2-34 Windows System Image Manager, setting values

Creating Autounattend.xml answer files

You can create answer files manually or by using the Windows SIM, as shown in Figure 2-35.

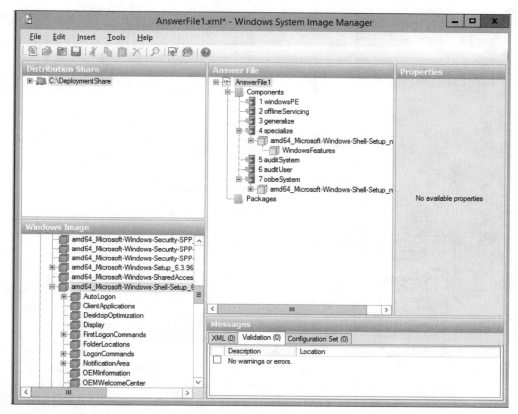

FIGURE 2-35 Windows System Image Manager with a validated answer file

As part of creating an answer file in Windows SIM, you must specify the Windows image file and a catalog file. A catalog file is a binary file that is associated to a specific Windows image file and contains the packages and settings in that WIM file. Often, the WIM file and the catalog file (.clg) are stored in the same folder. Windows SIM prompts you if it cannot locate a catalog file for a specified WIM file. In such a scenario, Windows SIM can create a catalog file. Alternatively, you can create an answer file in advance in Windows SIM. By using Windows SIM, you can verify that the configuration settings within an answer file are valid for the installation. Figure 2-36 shows an answer file that has a validation error.

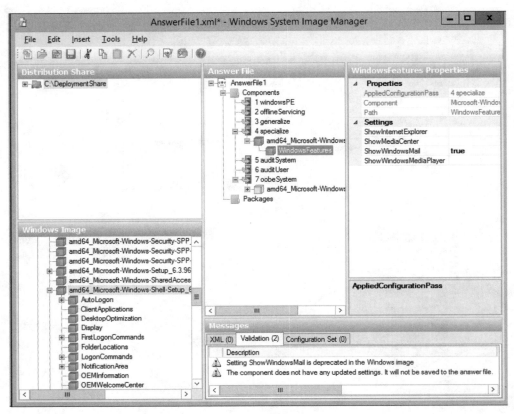

FIGURE 2-36 Windows System Image Manager with a validation error

Answer files can also be created or modified manually. As mentioned earlier, the answer file is an XML file that can be edited by using a text editor. Here is a sample answer file:

```xml
<?xml version="1.0" encoding="utf-8"?>

<unattend xmlns="urn:schemas-microsoft-com:unattend">

    <settings pass="oobeSystem">

        <component name="Microsoft-Windows-Shell-Setup" processorArchitecture="amd64"
publicKeyToken="31bf3856ad364e35" language="neutral" versionScope="nonSxS"
xmlns:wcm="http://schemas.microsoft.com/WMIConfig/2002/State" xmlns:xsi="http://www
.w3.org/2001/XMLSchema-instance">

            <OOBE>

                <HideEULAPage>true</HideEULAPage>

                <HideOEMRegistrationScreen>true</HideOEMRegistrationScreen>

            </OOBE>
```

```
        <UserAccounts>

            <AdministratorPassword>

                <Value>UABAACQAJAB3ADAACgBkAAUAMAcwB3AG8AcgBkAA==</Value>

                <PlainText>false</PlainText>

            </AdministratorPassword>

        </UserAccounts>

    </component>

</settings>

<cpi:offlineImage cpi:source="wim://client01/deploymentshare$/operating%20
systems/windows%208%20enterprise%20x64/sources/install.wim#Windows 8 Enterprise"
xmlns:cpi="urn:schemas-microsoft-com:cpi" />

</unattend>
```

When you create answer files, avoid adding settings that you don't need. Windows SIM will not create empty settings in an answer file, but you can manually introduce empty strings in an answer file. Your goal should be to reduce answer file bloat such as empty strings, which can increase deployment times.

Answer files often contain sensitive data such as the password of the local Administrator account. Windows SIM enables you to obfuscate local computer passwords in answer files. To obfuscate a password in an answer file with Windows SIM, perform the following steps:

1. In Windows SIM, open an answer file that contains a password you want to obfuscate.
2. Click the Tools menu and then click Hide Sensitive Data.
3. Save the answer file and then validate that the password is obfuscated.

Note that you cannot obfuscate domain-based passwords or other sensitive data such as product keys. By default in Windows SIM 6.3, Hide Sensitive Data is enabled by default when you create new answer files.

When you are finished creating an answer file, use Windows SIM to validate the answer file. Validating an answer file is an important step to ensure that everything is in order. If you have a validation error, such as the one displayed in Figure 2-36, you can double-click the validation error to find the exact setting causing the validation error.

Objective summary

- An answer file may be stored in one of several locations. Each answer file location has a precedence value, which determines the answer file that is used.
- An installation might go through seven customization passes when using an answer file:
  - windowsPE
  - offlineServicing
  - generalize
  - specialize
  - auditSystem
  - auditUser
  - oobeSystem
- Windows SIM can be used to create and validate answer files.

Objective review

Answer the following questions to test your knowledge of the information in this objective. You can find the answers to these questions and explanations of why each answer choice is correct or incorrect in the "Answers" section at the end of this chapter.

1. Which tool can you use to create an answer file?

   A. DISM

   B. Windows SIM

   C. Sysprep

   D. Setup.exe

2. Which pass of the Windows Setup process removes the security identifier from a reference computer?

   A. generalize

   B. oobeSystem

   C. specialize

   D. offlineServicing

3. Which pass of the Windows Setup process configures unique settings for different departments?

   A. generalize

   B. oobeSystem

   C. specialize

   D. offlineServicing

4. You are planning to use removable media to store answer files for automating Windows 8.1 deployments. You need to store an answer file to a removable media drive with a drive letter of F:\. What should you name the file and where you should save it?

   A. Name the file Unattend.xml and save it in the F:\Sysprep folder.

   B. Name the file Unattend.xml and save it in the root of the F:\ drive.

   C. Name the file Autounattend.xml and save it in the F:\Panther folder.

   D. Name the file Unattended.xml and save it in the root of the F:\ drive.

5. You are planning to add packages to an offline Windows 8.1 image. Which tool should you use?

   A. Setup.exe

   B. LoadState

   C. Windows SIM

   D. DISM

Answers

This section contains the solutions to the thought experiments and answers to the lesson review questions in this chapter.

Objective 2.1

Thought experiment

1. You should deploy WDS to both offices. It is a good practice to avoid imaging computers over a wide area network (WAN) link because images are often very large and will saturate a WAN link, which will degrade the network. By deploying WDS to both offices, imaging will take place on the local area network (LAN).

2. You should use unicast for the deployments. Because you will image only one or two computers at a time, unicast makes sense because it doesn't require any changes to your existing network.

3. You should use filters in WDS to ensure that WDS can image only portable computers. You can use a Chassis Type filter, Manufacturer filter, or Model filter to target only portable computers.

Objective review

1. **Correct answers:** A and B

   A. **Correct:** The Windows PowerShell WDS module is new for Windows Server 2012 R2, and it can automate configuration tasks.

   B. **Correct:** Prior to the Windows PowerShell WDS module, WDSutil was the only command-line tool for WDS. It can automate configuration tasks for WDS.

   C. **Incorrect:** WDSdiag exists as a .dll, not as a .exe. It cannot automate WDS configuration tasks.

   D. **Incorrect:** WDSmgmt.msc is the WDS graphic user interface console. It is used to perform one-time configuration tasks but isn't used to automate tasks like a script can do.

2. **Correct answer:** A

   A. **Correct:** To ensure that the WDS Image Capture Wizard sees the system volume, generalize the image by using Sysprep.

   B. **Incorrect:** Although Shift+F10 opens a Windows PE command prompt, you can't generalize the existing Windows installation from Windows PE.

   C. **Incorrect:** The permissions on the system volume do not need to be modified from default settings to be seen by the WDS Image Capture Wizard.

   D. **Incorrect:** The permissions on the system volume do not need to be modified from default settings to be seen by the WDS Image Capture Wizard.

3. **Correct answer:** C

   A. **Incorrect:** A capture image is built from a boot image. Thus, a boot image must be created first.

   B. **Incorrect:** An install image can be a default Windows installation or a customized Windows installation. However, an install image is not related to creating a discover image.

   C. **Correct:** A capture image is built from a boot image. Thus, you must first add a boot image before you can create a discover image.

   D. **Incorrect:** You can create images with the WDS console. The Windows PowerShell WDS module is automatically imported when you use cmdlets from the module, so you do not need to import the module manually.

4. **Correct answer**: B

   A. **Incorrect:** Unicast cannot be scheduled at a future time.

   B. **Correct:** Multicast transmissions can be scheduled at a future time by using a Scheduled-Cast transmission.

   C. **Incorrect:** You can use a WDS filter to filter images based on specified computer attributes such as the manufacturer and chassis type. However, you cannot use a filter to schedule future deployments.

   D. **Incorrect:** You can use a WDS filter to filter images based on specified computer attributes such as the manufacturer and chassis type. However, you cannot use a filter to schedule future deployments.

5. **Correct answer:** C

   A. **Incorrect:** Although the BIOS Version is helpful, the UUID will be unique to each computer.

   B. **Incorrect:** Although the BIOS Version is helpful, the BIOS Vendor does not identify the hardware model number.

   C. **Correct:** The BIOS Version and Model will help identify all HP Elitebook laptops running the F03 version of the BIOS.

   D. **Incorrect:** Although the Model information is useful, the BIOS Vendor does not identify the current BIOS version.

Objective 2.2

Thought experiment

1. You should put your operating system images in the deployment share. The deployment share is where your images should be placed when using MDT.

2. You should use the Sysprep and Capture task sequence template. It prepares the reference computer with Sysprep and then captures the image.

3. The valid file extensions for packages are .cab and .msu.

Objective review

1. Correct answer: B

   A. Incorrect: The MDT task sequences use the same engine as Configuration Manager but not the same as Windows Server 2012.

   B. Correct: MDT and Configuration Manager use the same task sequence engine.

   C. Incorrect: The MDT task sequences use the same engine as Configuration Manager but not the same as Exchange Server 2013.

   D. Incorrect: The MDT task sequences use the same engine as Configuration Manager but not the same as SharePoint Server 2013.

2. Correct answer: B

   A. Incorrect: Bootstrap.ini is a file that you can customize to point the deployment wizard to different locations on the network. It is not relevant to the question, which focuses on reducing the manual deployment steps in a deployment.

   B. Correct: The customsettings.ini file controls a wide range of deployment settings that enable you to cut down drastically on manual steps in a deployment.

   C. Incorrect: Deploy.xml is a file that should not be modified because MDT manages it.

   D. Incorrect: Settings.xml is a file that MDT manages and should not be modified.

3. Correct answer: B

   A. Incorrect: When you create a new deployment share, you can't point it to the path of an existing share because the wizard will not allow you to continue.

   B. Correct: By opening the existing deployment share, you add it to MDT.

   C. Incorrect: The Add-MDTPersistentDrive cmdlet is valid only if you have an existing Windows PowerShell drive.

   D. Incorrect: The Get-MDTPersistentDrive cmdlet retrieves information but does not perform any modifications.

4. Correct answers: A and B

   A. Correct: A deployment share can be located on a network share. It can also be located on local storage.

   B. Correct: A deployment share can be located on local storage. It can also be located on a network share.

   C. Incorrect: A deployment share cannot be located in a Microsoft Access database.

   D. Incorrect: A deployment share cannot be located in a SQL Server database.

5. **Correct answer:** B

   A. **Incorrect:** The MDT cmdlets are part of a snap-in, not a module, so you must add a snap-in.

   B. **Correct:** Because the MDT cmdlets are part of a snap-in, adding the snap-in is the correct answer.

   C. **Incorrect:** The path from which you run the command is not relevant.

   D. **Incorrect:** The error message is indicative of a snap-in or module not loaded. Running Windows PowerShell as Administrator will not fix this issue.

Objective 2.3

Thought experiment

1. To automate most operating system deployment tasks while minimizing costs, deploy WDS and MDT. WDS is built into Windows Server as a role, and MDT is a free download. Each tool can stand alone to automate some deployment tasks. However, combining them brings the best results because you can use WDS for PXE to eliminate the need for media.

2. To prevent users from reimaging their own computers, you can set restrictive permissions on each image. Create a security group in Active Directory. Add the IT administrators to the group and then add the group to the image permissions and assign Read and Read & Execute permissions to the group. Finally, remove the Authenticated Users group from the permissions. Do not use deny permissions for Authenticated Users because that will override the allow permissions for IT administrators, which will prevent them from using the image too.

3. To prepare IT administrators to support and maintain the deployment infrastructure, introduce the Deployment Workbench, the WDS console, WDSutil, Windows SIM, Windows ADK, and the WDS commands in Windows PowerShell. In addition, it is a good idea to show the IT administrators the answer files and customization files that are being used.

Objective review

1. **Correct answer:** B

   A. **Incorrect:** DISM is used for other tasks such as adding packages to offline Windows images.

   B. **Correct:** Windows SIM is used to create answer files.

   C. **Incorrect:** Sysprep prepares a reference computer for capturing.

   D. **Incorrect:** Setup.exe is often used for installing applications or a manual installation of a Windows operating system.

2. **Correct answer:** A

   A. **Correct:** The generalize pass is when the security identifier is removed from a reference computer.

   B. **Incorrect:** The oobeSystem pass configures settings that are part of the initial boot of a computer and is not related to removing the security identifier from a reference computer.

   C. **Incorrect:** The specialize pass is used to configure some settings such as language and time zone, but it is not related to removing the security identifier from a reference computer.

   D. **Incorrect:** The offlineServicing pass is used to add packages or updates to an offline image but can't be used to remove the security identifier from a reference computer.

3. **Correct answer:** C

   A. **Incorrect:** The generalize pass is used to configure all computers equally and can't be used to configure different department computers with different settings.

   B. **Incorrect:** The oobeSystem pass is used to configure the initial boot of a computer and is not related to configuring different department computers with different settings.

   C. **Correct:** The specialize pass is often used in addition to the generalize pass to configure unique settings for different department computers.

   D. **Incorrect:** The offlineServicing pass is used to add packages or updates to an offline image but can't be used to configure different department computers with different settings.

4. **Correct answer:** B

   A. **Incorrect:** Although the Unattend.xml file name is valid, the location must be in the root of the removable media drive.

   B. **Correct:** The file must be named Unattend.xml or Autounattend.xml, and the location must be in the root of the removable media drive.

   C. **Incorrect:** Although the Autounattend.xml file name is valid, the location must be in the root of the removable media drive.

   D. **Incorrect:** The file must be named Unattend.xml or Autounattend.xml.

5. **Correct answer**: D

   A. **Incorrect:** Setup.exe is a generic name for an installation file and is not used to add packages to an offline image.

   B. **Incorrect:** LoadState transfers user state data from a migration store to a destination computer but does not add packages to an offline image.

   C. **Incorrect:** Windows SIM creates answer files but does not add packages to an offline image.

   D. **Correct:** DISM adds packages to an offline image.

CHAPTER 3

Implement a Zero-Touch deployment

In the first two chapters, you learned about implementing an operating system deployment (OSD) infrastructure and Lite-Touch deployments. To take further advantage of the technologies discussed in Chapter 1, "Implement an operating system deployment infrastructure," you need to learn about Zero-Touch deployments. A Zero-Touch installation (ZTI) is the most automated installation available and reduces administrative overhead and maintenance for your OSD infrastructure. In this chapter, you learn more about Configuration Manager, including how to configure it for ZTIs and integrate the Microsoft Deployment Toolkit (MDT) and Configuration Manager, which enables new functionality and automation.

Objectives in this chapter:

- Objective 3.1: Configure Configuration Manager for OSD
- Objective 3.2: Configure distribution points
- Objective 3.3: Configure MDT and Configuration Manager integration

Objective 3.1: Configure Configuration Manager for OSD

Configuration Manager enhances the technologies discussed in Chapter 2, "Implement a Lite-Touch deployment," by incorporating all the benefits of end-to-end client management. Tasks such as migrating an enterprise full of Windows 7 devices to Windows 8.1 can now be accomplished through a ZTI deployment, using a single solution, all while gaining the ability to monitor and report on the results. To take advantage of these enhancements, you must understand the various components that make up the deployment process and how they are connected within Configuration Manager.

> **This objective covers how to:**
> - Configure deployment packages and applications
> - Configure task sequences
> - Manage the driver pool
> - Manage boot and deployment images

Configuring deployment packages and applications

Since the introduction of System Center 2012 R2 Configuration Manager, two solutions have become available for distributing content to endpoint devices. These two solutions are deployment packages and applications. Each has its own strengths and weaknesses, but both can be used with OSD. Understand the benefits of each to prepare for your deployment.

Deployment packages

Deployment packages are referred to as packages and programs from within the Configuration Manager console. Deployment packages handle basic distribution and workflow options while giving you the flexibility to do simple and quick deployment or management tasks. The benefits of a deployment package include:

- The ability to deploy a script quickly that initiates a management task on an endpoint device, such as configuring a scheduled task.
- The ability to distribute a payload of files to an endpoint device.
- The ability to run a single command such as an application uninstall.
- The option to use a recurring deployment schedule.
- A simple solution for packaging software and including it in OSDs.

The deployment package life cycle includes the following ordered tasks:

1. Creating the package. A package can contain content such as a payload of files, a script, or a program. Alternatively, a package can be configured without any content and be used to run a simple command such as a registry edit.

2. Distributing the package. Any package that contains content must be distributed to the relative distribution points before it can be deployed to clients. A breakdown about distributing content is covered in more detail in Objective 3.2, "Configure distribution points."

3. Deploying the package. The deployment process oversees which person or device the content will go to, based on Configuration Manager collections. A collection is a grouping of users or computing devices. In Configuration Manager, you can target actions, such as deployments, at collections. Common uses of collections include grouping all client computers, grouping all client computers running a specific operating system, and grouping all laptop computers. In addition, the deployment is configured for a specific date and time and can be a one-time deployment or a recurring scheduled deployment.

4. Monitoring the deployment. You can view success and failure status messages from the Monitoring workspace in the management console or through the built-in reports included with Configuration Manager.

5. Managing the package. Maintenance for a package or deployment is common and easily completed from the Software Library workspace in the management console.

This includes modifying the package contents, updating the run command, and adjusting the deployment schedule.

The prerequisites for creating a deployment package include the following items:

- A functional Configuration Manager server infrastructure and prior implementation of all the related prerequisites for content distribution and client management.

- An understanding of the package or program that you need to deploy. You need to know basic details such as the name, version, and manufacturer as well as the installation requirements and command-line arguments being deployed.

- The target audience you are deploying the package or program to and whether the deployment will be required (known as mandatory in Configuration Manager 2007) or available (known as optional in Configuration Manager 2007).

- The desired schedule for the deployment.

> **MORE INFO** **CONFIGURATION MANAGER PREREQUISITES**
>
> For more information about the supported configurations and server prerequisites, see *http://technet.microsoft.com/en-us/library/gg682077.aspx*.

In the following example, you create a software package by using the management console. For this demonstration, you prepare the HP HotKey software for deployment. This software-based driver is included with most HP EliteBook portable computers and adds additional functionality to the integrated keyboard. When it's complete, this package can be used for distribution to managed devices or included in an operating system deployment.

1. In the Configuration Manager console, click the Software Library workspace.
2. In the left pane, expand Application Management.
3. Right-click Packages and click Create Package.
4. On the Package page, as shown in Figure 3-1, fill in the program Name and other fields if needed for your deployment. Select the This Package Contains Source Files check box.
5. Click Browse to define your package source files.

The site server computer account must have Read permissions to the package source files.

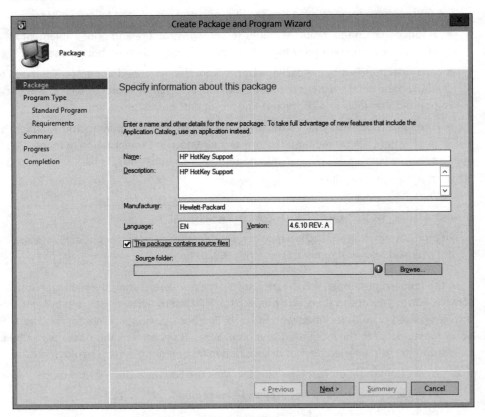

FIGURE 3-1 Create Package And Program Wizard, Package page

6. On the Set Source Folder page, as shown in Figure 3-2, choose the source directory for your program and then click OK.

It is a good practice to use Uniform Naming Convention (UNC) paths. One consequence of not using UNC paths occurs during a migration from an older version of Configuration Manager to a newer version. If you don't use UNC paths, you have to move all your existing packages manually.

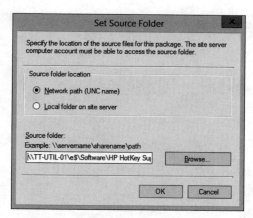

FIGURE 3-2 Create Package And Program Wizard, Set Source Folder dialog box

7. Click Next on the Package page.

8. On the Program Type page, as shown in Figure 3-3, select Standard Program and then click Next.

   You use Program For Device for Windows CE mobile devices. Using Do Not Create A Program would make this a payload package without a run command.

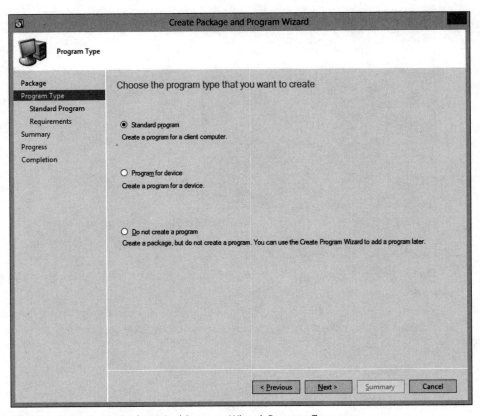

FIGURE 3-3 The Create Package And Program Wizard, Program Type page

9. On the Standard Program page, as shown in Figure 3-4, type a name in the Name text box and a command in the Command Line text box. Be sure to test the install outside of Configuration Manager.

You must ensure that the installation works locally on a client computer and from a UNC path to ensure that it works when you deploy it with Configuration Manager. A fully silent installation is required for OSD. You can set the Run drop-down box to Hidden for a fully silent installation. It is also recommended to halt automatic reboots and add an appropriate log file on supported programs.

10. In the Program Can Run drop-down menu, choose Whether Or Not A User Is Logged On.

The Allow Users To View And Interact With The Program Installation is an optional setting that enables users to interact with the installation program. This is useful when users need to choose an installation option or other configuration setting during an installation. For most deployments, automating the installation and not allowing users to interact with the installation is the preferred choice. Startup Folder enables you to specify the folder that the program runs from.

11. Click Next.

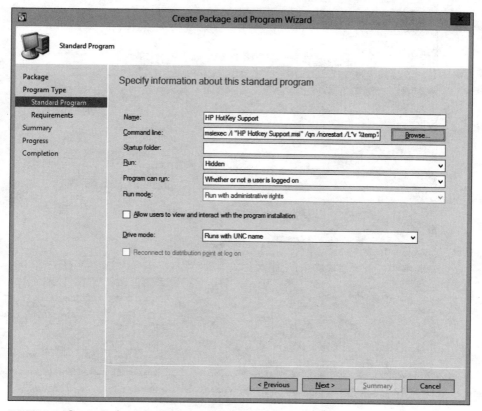

FIGURE 3-4 Create Package And Program Wizard, Standard Program page

The Requirements page, shown in Figure 3-5, contains a few options for tuning your program, none of which is required to be changed. Run Another Program First enables you to run another program prior to this one. You might use this option to make sure a required component, such as the Microsoft .NET Framework, is installed first. The Platform Requirements section enables you to narrow the scope of supported operating systems. Estimated Disk Space is useful because it prevents the program from downloading if disk space is insufficient. Maximum Allowed Run Time prevents a program from running indefinitely in case of a silent failure.

12. Click Next on the Requirements page.

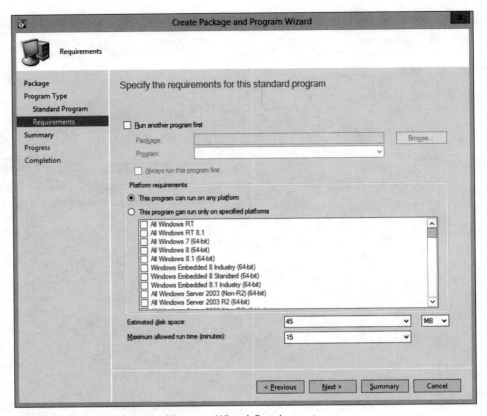

FIGURE 3-5 Create Package And Program Wizard, Requirements page

13. On the Summary page, confirm your configuration and click Next to begin the build process.

14. After the The Create Package And Program Wizard Completed Successfully message appears on the Completion page, click Close.

With the package and program configured, one more item needs to be completed through the console to ensure that the program will run properly in a task sequence.

1. Navigate to the package you created and select the Programs tab in the lower third of the management console. If this section is not visible, click the expansion arrow in the lower right.

2. Right-click the HP HotKey Support program and select Properties.

3. Click the Advanced tab. Click Allow This Program To Be Installed From The Install Package Task Sequence Without Being Deployed, as shown in Figure 3-6. This option allows the package to be used in a task sequence without an active deployment.

4. Click OK to apply the change.

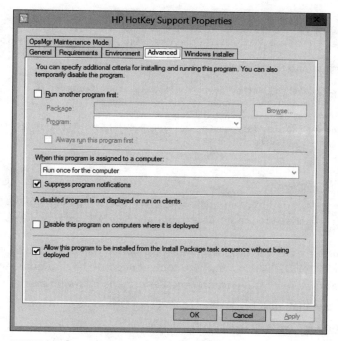

FIGURE 3-6 Program properties window, Advanced tab

At this stage, a new package and corresponding program are available in the management console. Now look at how to complete the same steps by using Windows PowerShell. To create these items, use the New-CMPackage and New-CMProgram cmdlets.

1. Open the management console.

2. Click the drop-down menu in the upper-left corner and select Connect Via Windows PowerShell, as shown in Figure 3-7.

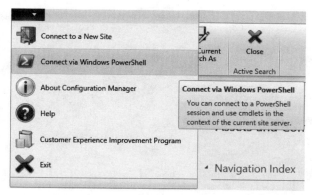

FIGURE 3-7 Management console, Connect Via Windows PowerShell

3. Run the following command to create the HP HotKey package:

```
New-CMPackage –Name 'HP HotKey Support (PS)' –Description 'HP HotKey
Support – Created with PS'' –Version '4.6.10 REV: A' –Manufacturer 'Hewlett
-Packard' –Language 'EN' –Path '\\TT-UTIL-01\e$\Software\WebEx Productivity Tools'
```

4. Run the following command to create the corresponding program:

```
New-CMProgram –PackageName 'HP HotKey Support (PS)' –StandardProgramName
'HP HotKey Support' –CommandLine 'msiexec /i "HP Hotkey Support.msi"
/qn /norestart /L*v %temp%\HPhotkey_install.log' –RunType Hidden
–ProgramRunType WhetherOrNotUserIsLoggedOn –RunMode RunWithAdministrativeRights
–DiskSpaceRequirement 45 –DiskSpaceUnit MB –Duration 15
```

> **MORE INFO** **ADDITIONAL CMDLETS**
>
> Use the Get-CMPackage and Get-CMProgram cmdlets to review the configuration of the
> items. To make additional changes, use the Set-CMPackage and Set-CMProgram cmdlets.

Next, distribute the source files for the program to the distribution point. This is discussed again, briefly, in Objective 3.2 for OSD. Knowing where content needs to be distributed to will depend on the server infrastructure in your environment. Perform the following steps:

1. Right-click the package that must be distributed and click Distribute Content.

2. On the General page, click Next.

3. On the Content Destination page, as shown in Figure 3-8, click the Add button and select Distribution Point from the drop-down menu. Select the preferred distribution point from the list of available servers and click OK.

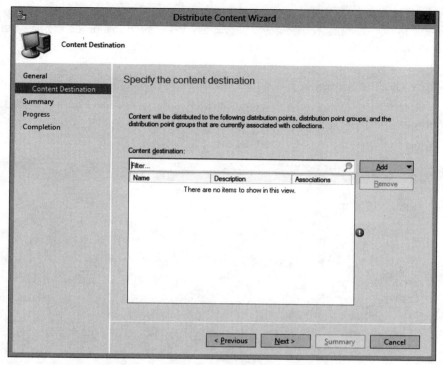

FIGURE 3-8 Distribute Content Wizard, Content Destination page

4. On the Summary page, confirm your selection and then click Next.

5. On the Completion page, click Close.

There are multiple ways to review the status of content after distribution. The first point of interest is the summary tab of the package, shown in the lower third of the management console. Under the Content Status section, you see a pie chart, as shown in Figure 3-9.

Content Status

- Success: 1
- In Progress: 0
- Failed: 0
- Unknown: 0

1 Targeted (Last Update: 10/6/2014 7:32 PM)

FIGURE 3-9 Program summary, content status

A common maintenance task is managing updates or installation changes for your packages. For example, if you decide to change the installation parameters for Office 2013, you might need to update the .msp file, which is part of the source files of the package. When you need to update the source files for a package, redistribute the content so that distribution points have the updated source files. This is a very simple task and can be completed by right-clicking the package and selecting Update Distribution Point.

After you distribute the package contents successfully, you can deploy the package to client devices. In this example, you deploy the program you created to a group of test systems to confirm that the software installs as expected. To deploy the program, perform the following steps:

1. Right-click the package and select Deploy.

2. Next to the Collection text box on the General page, as shown in Figure 3-10, click the Browse button.

3. Select the desired collection and then click OK. Click Next.

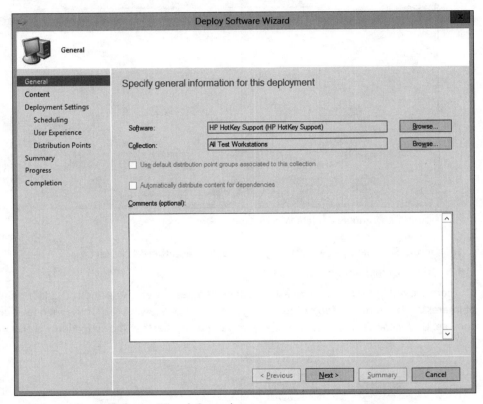

FIGURE 3-10 Deploy Software Wizard, General page

4. On the Content page, confirm that your distribution point is listed in the top section and then click Next.

   Note that you can add other distribution points and distribution point groups on this page.

5. On the Deployment Settings page, as shown in Figure 3-11, click the Purpose drop-down menu, click Available, and then click Next.

By selecting Available in Purpose, you enable users to install the software at their convenience or not at all. If you select Required in Purpose, you are making the software installation mandatory, and users cannot opt out of the installation.

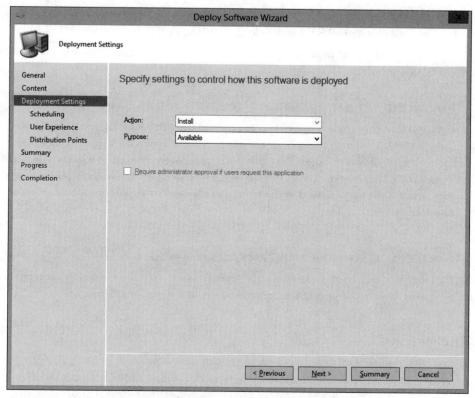

FIGURE 3-11 Deployment Software Wizard, Deployment Settings page

6. On the Scheduling page, enable Schedule When This Deployment Will Become Available. The date and time will align with when you started the wizard.

7. Click Next.

Note the other options on the Scheduling page. Not every setting is covered here, but you should familiarize yourself with the settings as part of your exam preparation.

8. On the User Experience page, click Next.

9. On the Distribution Points page, click Next.

10. On the Summary page, confirm your deployment settings and then click Next.

11. On the Completion page, click Close.

With the deployment active, the devices in the collection will receive the new content the next time they check in. The HP HotKey software will appear in the Software Center application as an optional installation.

With Configuration Manager, you can monitor deployments from within the management console, as follows:

1. Open the management console and navigate to the Monitoring workspace.

2. Select Deployments in the left pane.

3. Type **HP HotKey** in the search field and click Search.

   The filtered results provide a pie chart along with compliance and error messages for troubleshooting.

REAL WORLD **OPERATING SYSTEM DEPLOYMENTS AND PACKAGES**

Packages that only contain source files are commonly used with OSD. Task sequences include their own Run Command action, which can reference a package of source files that you've already distributed. I use this in customer environments to handle tasks such as running a BIOS configuration utility or including a prestart command in a boot image. Packages are still very relevant in Configuration Manager, even with the introduction of Applications.

MORE INFO **LEARN MORE ABOUT PACKAGES AND PROGRAMS**

For more information about creating, deploying, monitoring, and managing packages and programs, see *http://technet.microsoft.com/en-us/library/gg699369.aspx*.

Applications

With a better understanding of how packages and programs are structured you can now move on to applications. The application framework is a new addition supported in Configuration Manager 2012 and Configuration Manager 2012 R2 and offers a much more robust solution for deploying, tracking, and remediating applications. The benefits of an application include:

- Install and uninstall triggers. Use these to uninstall software easily that was previously deployed.

- True dependency support. Ensure that all the proper updates or software prerequisites are installed in their given order.

- Enhanced system requirements. Set a requirement to check for free disk space or available memory.

- Ability to supersede applications with new updates.

- Ability to publish your application to the web-based Application Catalog.

- A variety of detection methods to ensure that your application installed or uninstalled successfully.

- State-based Application model. This takes the conventional Programs model to a new level, incorporating dependencies and requirements for more granular application management and distribution. You can use state-based deployments to determine whether an application is already installed on a computing device. If it is, the content is not downloaded to that computing device. In addition, you can use rules to limit the targeting of a deployment. For example, you could limit the installation of Office 2013 to computing devices with at least 1 GB of RAM.

- Configuration Manager 2012 with a more user-centric focus. New features have been introduced, such as User Device Affinity, which can help you associate users to one or more devices. Application deployments are now user focused rather than device focused. Moving a user from one device to another can now offer a seamless transition.

The application life cycle shares many similarities with the deployment package but expands the capabilities:

1. Creating the application. An application will always contain content. The creation process includes a completely new model and workflow.

2. Distributing the application. Similar to a package, content must be distributed to distribution points after the application has been created.

3. Deploying the application.

4. Monitoring the deployment.

5. Managing the application. The application model is more complex, and, because of this, several more knobs can be tuned to perfect your deployment.

The prerequisites for creating an application are summarized as follows:

- A working Configuration Manager 2012 server infrastructure and all related prerequisites for content distribution and client management.

- A working Application Catalog for self-service capabilities.

- An understanding of the package or program that you need to deploy. This includes basic details, such as the name, version, and manufacturer, as well as the installation requirements and command-line arguments being deployed.

- The target audience that you are deploying the package or program to and whether the deployment will be required or available.

- The desired schedule for the deployment.

> **MORE INFO   APPLICATION CATALOG PREREQUISITES**
>
> For more information about the prerequisites for application management, see
> *http://technet.microsoft.com/en-us/library/gg682145.aspx.*

In the following process, you see the creation of an application by using the management console. In this example, you prepare the WebEx Productivity Tools for a self-service installation. This gives users the ability to browse the application catalog, find the software they need, and install it at their convenience. You should keep OSD in mind to ensure that this same package can be used in the task sequence.

1. In the Configuration Manager console, click the Software Library workspace.
2. In the left pane, expand Application Management.
3. Right-click Applications and click Create Application.
4. On the General page of the Create Application Wizard, as shown in Figure 3-12, fill in the Location field by using the full UNC path to the MSI file or other supported file type that you select and then click Next.

Note that Configuration Manager 2012 R2 supports the following file types: Windows Installer (.msi), Windows app package (.appx or .appxbundle), Windows app package in the Windows Store, App-V v4, App-V v5, Windows Phone app package (.xap), Windows Phone app package in the Windows Phone store, Windows Mobile Cabinet, app package for iOS (.ipa), app package for iOS from App Store, app package for Android (.apk), app package for Android on Google Play, Nokia SIS file, Mac OS X, and Web Application. The wizard reads the MSI file and creates the basic application for you.

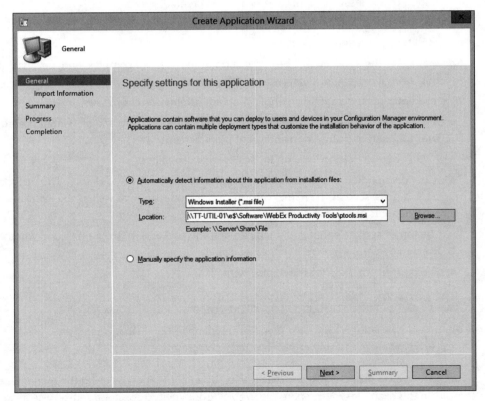

FIGURE 3-12 Create Application Wizard, General page

5. On the Important Information page, confirm the configuration and then click Next.

6. On the General Information page, as shown in Figure 3-13, fill in the application details.

   For this deployment, you update the default Installation program argument to add some additional functionality such as MSI logging. The install behavior also changes to Install For System, which ensures that the application installs by using the local system account. Alternatively, you can use Install For User, which runs the application as the current user. In this example, the application will be included in the imaging task sequence.

7. Click Next when you are ready to proceed.

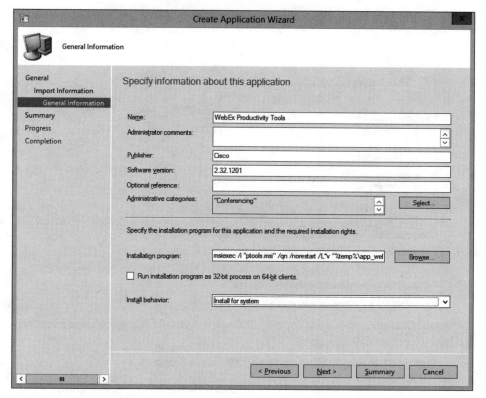

FIGURE 3-13 Create Application Wizard, General Information page

8. On the Summary page, confirm the configuration and click Next.

9. On the Completion page, click Close.

The application is now built, but before distributing it, a few more options are available.

1. Right-click the application and click Properties.

2. On the General Information tab, choose Allow This Application To Be Installed From The Install Application Task Sequence Action Without Being Deployed.

3. On the Deployment Types tab, select WebEx Productivity Tools and then click Edit.

4. On the Requirements tab, click Add.

5. On the Create Requirement page, as shown in Figure 3-14, change the condition to Operating System and select Windows 7, Windows 8, and Windows 8.1. Click OK to save the requirement.

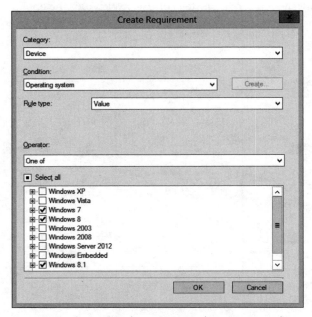

FIGURE 3-14 Create Requirement, operating system requirement

6. Click OK to save the deployment type.

7. Click OK to save the application.

This application is now ready for distribution. Perform the following steps to distribute the content to your distribution point:

1. Right-click the application and select Distribute Content.

2. On the General page of the Distribute Content Wizard, click Next.

3. On the Content page, click Next.

4. On the Content Destination page, click Add and then click Distribution Point. Select the distribution point and then click OK. Click Next.

5. On the Summary page, review your selections and then click Next.

6. On the Completion page, click Close.

7. Monitor your distribution by using the Content Status summary.

With the application content distributed, you can move on to the deployment.

1. Right-click the application and select Deploy.

2. On the General page of the Deploy Software Wizard, as shown in Figure 3-15, click the Browse button next to the Collection text box. You want this application to appear in the catalog, so choose the All Users collection and click OK. (Mobile devices do not support the catalog.) Click Next.

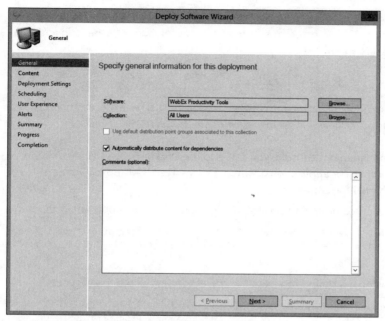

FIGURE 3-15 Deploy Software Wizard, General page

3. On the Content page, confirm that your distribution point is listed in the top section and then click Next.

4. On the Deployment Settings screen, leave Action set to Install and Purpose set to Available.

   Note that you can require an administrator to approve user requests by selecting Next. Approval requests are handled under the Approval Requests section in the left pane of the Software Library workspace. Leave this option as is for your deployment.

5. Click Next.

6. On the Scheduling page, click Next.

   The default time makes this application available immediately.

7. On the User Experience page, click Next.

   The default user notification settings display a confirmation window after the installation completes.

8. On the Alerts page, click Next.

You can trigger an alert if the deployment reaches a specific failure rate. These alerts appear on the Overview screen when you launch the management console.

9. On the Summary page, confirm your deployment settings and then click Next.

10. On the Completion screen, click Close.

The WebEx Productivity Tools are now readily available to all users through the Application Catalog. This empowers users to install the software they need in a familiar app store environment.

> **MORE INFO** **LEARN MORE ABOUT THE APPLICATION CATALOG**
>
> For more information about the Application Catalog, user experience, and configuration options, see *http://technet.microsoft.com/en-us/library/hh489603.aspx*.

Besides the management console, you can also use Windows PowerShell to improve your automation workflow. For application creation, use the New-CMApplication and Add-CMDeploymentType cmdlets.

Run the following command to create the WebEx Productivity Tools application:

```
New-CMApplication -Name "WebEx Productivity Tools (PS)" -Description "WebEx Productivity
Tools - created with PS" -Publisher "Cisco" -SoftwareVersion "2.32.1201" -AutoInstall
$true
```

Run the following command to create the corresponding deployment type:

```
Add-CMDeploymentType -ApplicationName "WebEx Productivity Tools (PS)"
-InstallationFileLocation "\\TT-UTIL-01\e$\Software\WebEx Productivity Tools\ptools
.msi" -MsiInstaller -AutoIdentifyFromInstallationFile -ForceForUnknownPublisher $true
-InstallationBehaviorType InstallForSystem -InstallationProgram 'msiexec /i "ptools.msi"
/qn /norestart /L*v "%temp%\app_webexpt_install.log"'
```

After re-creating the application and deployment type by using Windows PowerShell, you can review their configuration by using the Get-CMApplication and Get-CMDeploymentType cmdlets.

Run the following command to review the application configuration:

```
Get-CMApplication -Name "WebEx Productivity Tools"
```

Run the following command to review the deployment type configuration:

```
Get-CMDeploymentType -ApplicationName "WebEx Productivity Tools"
```

Configuring task sequences

Task sequences are an ordered list of steps or actions that take place on the client computer at the command-line level without requiring user intervention. Task sequences are commonly used for LTI and ZTI operating system deployments but also offer a wide range of options in other areas such as migrating a user from one computer to another.

MDT uses the same task sequence engine and can be integrated with Configuration Manager to provide a more robust workflow. MDT integration is covered in Objective 3.3.

MORE INFO **GETTING STARTED WITH TASK SEQUENCES**

For more information about how to manage task sequences, see *http://technet.microsoft .com/en-us/library/hh273490.aspx.*

Configuration Manager 2012 introduced an updated version of the Create Task Sequence Wizard, as shown in Figure 3-16. Now you have four task sequence templates to choose from, one of which creates a blank task sequence.

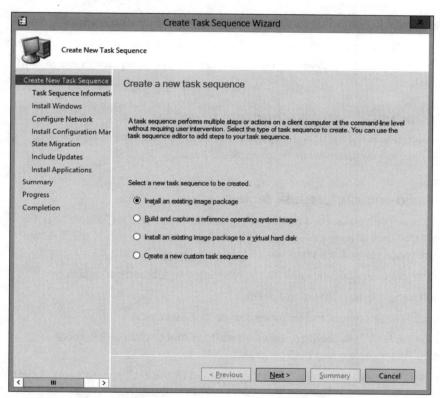

FIGURE 3-16 Create Task Sequence Wizard, Create New Task Sequence page

The template you choose determines which pages appear in the wizard. The following task sequence templates are available by default:

- **Install An Existing Image Package** This option creates a basic task sequence that uses an existing image package. Before using this option, import and capture an image into the console.

- **Build And Capture A Reference Operating System Image** This option creates a task sequence to assist in capturing your first reference image or to update your preexisting reference image.

- **Install An Existing Image Package To A Virtual Hard Disk** This option creates a task sequence to assist in creating a VHD, which can then be published to Virtual Machine Manager.

- **Create A Custom Task Sequence** This option creates a blank task sequence.

Before proceeding with the following build and capture task sequence steps, you should be familiar with the following OSD prerequisites:

- You must be running Configuration Manager 2012 R2 to deploy Windows 8.1.
- If you intend to use PXE, make sure it is enabled on your distribution point.
- Create and distribute your boot images or distribute the Windows default boot images.
- Add your Windows 8.1 install.wim to the list of available operating system images and distribute it.

> **MORE INFO** **OPERATING SYSTEM DEPLOYMENT PREREQUISITES**
>
> For more information about the operating system prerequisites for Configuration Manager, see *http://technet.microsoft.com/en-us/library/gg682187.aspx*.

Create the build and capture task sequence

In the following example, you create a build and capture task sequence for Tailspin Toys. If a reference image does not already exist, the build and capture task sequence is the first step to take. This task sequence builds a Windows 8.1 reference image.

1. In the Configuration Manager console, click the Software Library workspace.
2. In the left pane, expand Operating Systems.
3. Right-click Task Sequences and then click Create Task Sequence.
4. On the Create New Task Sequence page, select Build And Capture A Reference Operating System Image and then click Next.
5. On the Task Sequence information page, as shown in Figure 3-17, enter a name in the Task Sequence Name text box and then select your boot image. Click Next.

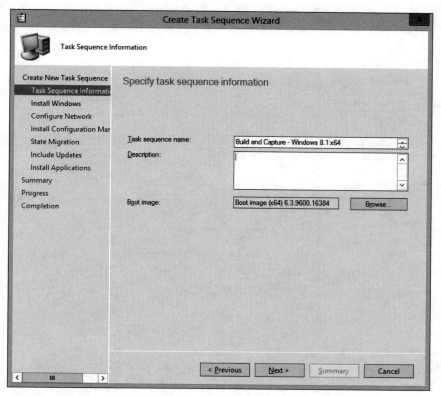

FIGURE 3-17 Create Task Sequence Wizard, Task Sequence Information page

6. On the Install Windows page, as shown in Figure 3-18, click Browse and select the Windows 8.1 operating system image that you imported. Under Specify The Licensing Information For The Windows Installation, enter your product key.

In this example, the Windows 8.1 KMS key has been entered. The last section on this page deals with the local administrator account. The password has been randomly generated and the account disabled. Instead of using the built-in Administrator account, you should create a new local administrator account with a different name, which you can do later in your deployment task sequence.

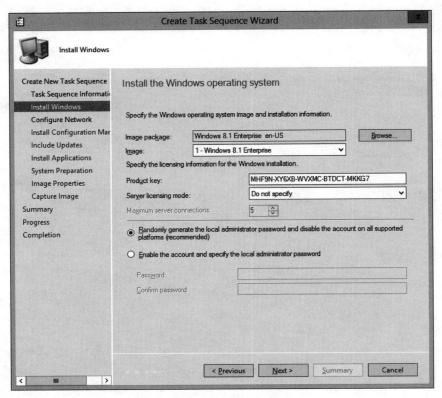

FIGURE 3-18 Create Task Sequence Wizard, Install Windows page

7. On the Configure Network page, select Join A Workgroup and type **workgroup** as the name.

   If your deployment will be captured, you should not join a domain at this time. Joining a domain might alter the operating system configuration because the computer will then be subject to any applicable Group Policy Objects (GPOs). Click Next.

8. On the Install Configuration Manager page, leave the default package and click Next.

9. On the Include Updates page, select Do Not Install Any Software Updates and then click Next.

10. On the Install Applications page, add any applications that you want to include in the reference image. For this example, don't install any applications. Click Next.

11. On the System Preparation page, click Next.

12. On the Image Properties page, fill in the requested criteria and then click Next.

13. On the Capture Image page, as shown in Figure 3-19, specify the UNC path, including the name of the image file where the image capture will be saved, along with an account that has permission to write to this directory. Click Next.

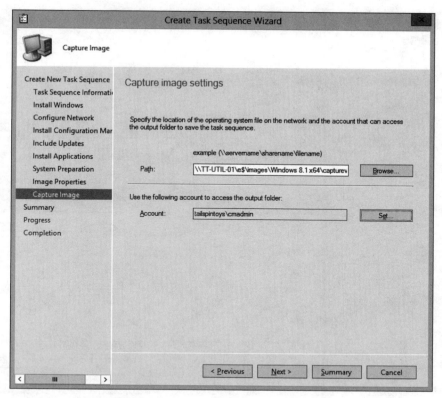

FIGURE 3-19 Create Task Sequence Wizard, Capture Image page

14. On the Summary page, confirm the configuration and then click Next.

15. On the Completion page, click Close.

Deploy the build and capture task sequence

Next, you must deploy the task sequence to a reference computer so the image can be installed, captured, and saved to the path provided in the preceding steps. Perform the following steps to deploy the task sequence:

1. Right-click the new task sequence and click Deploy.

2. On the General page of the Deploy Software Wizard, as shown in Figure 3-20, browse to the collection that contains your reference computer. If your reference computer has not been added to Configuration Manager, you can target the All Unknown Computers collection. Click Next.

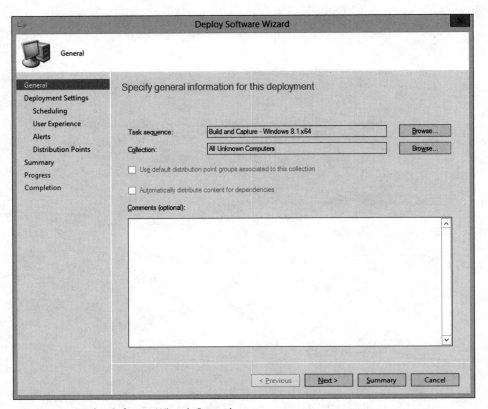

FIGURE 3-20 Deploy Software Wizard, General page

3. On the Deployment Settings page, as shown in Figure 3-21, set Purpose to Available. Set Make Available To The Following to Only Media And PXE.

These changes ensure that the deployment is not required and is only available to clients booting from the network or local media. This can help prevent accidental reimaging of client computers.

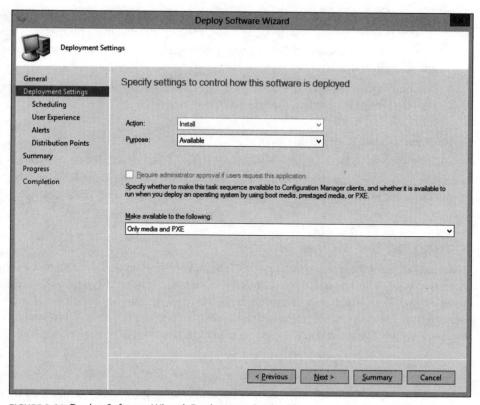

FIGURE 3-21 Deploy Software Wizard, Deployment Settings page

4. On the Scheduling page, click Next. This makes the deployment available immediately.

5. On the User Experience page, click Next.

   The default options are suitable for a build and capture.

6. On the Alerts page, click Next.

7. On the Distribution Points page, click Next.

   The default options are suitable for a build and capture.

8. On the Summary page, confirm the configuration and then click Next.

9. On the Completion page, click Close.

Run the build and capture task sequence

At this stage, your build and capture task sequence has been deployed. You can now boot your reference computer by using PXE or local media. After the computer boots into the Create Task Sequence Wizard, the workflow will consist of the following steps:

1. Select the Build And Capture task sequence and click Next.

The Windows 8.1 operating system will be downloaded and installed on the reference computer, along with the settings, updates, and applications that you specified when creating the task sequence. Configuration Manager captures the reference computer and uploads the .wim file to the provided UNC path.

2. When uploaded, you can use the Create Task Sequence Wizard again to create another task sequence for installing the new reference image.

> **MORE INFO** **UNDERSTANDING TASK SEQUENCE VARIABLES**
>
> Task sequence variables are a powerful addition to any deployment, enabling you to store relative information and call it when needed. For more information about the available task sequence variables, see *http://technet.microsoft.com/en-us/library/gg712685.aspx*.

Managing the driver pool

Device drivers are a key component to any ZTI deployment, and Configuration Manager is a tool that excels at managing drivers. The driver pool, also referred to as the driver catalog, stores all your hardware drivers in a single location. By using category assignments and some basic Windows Management Instrumentation (WMI) filters, you can ensure that your task sequence assigns the appropriate drivers to each of the hardware models you support.

The device driver life cycle includes the following items:

- **Retrieving the drivers**   First and foremost, you need access to the raw hardware drivers. Most manufacturers today offer precompiled driver packages. Alternatively, you can look at third-party solutions for extracting drivers from an active host.

- **Importing the drivers**   The drivers must be imported into the driver catalog. Configuration Manager needs the drivers in the database before you can do anything with them.

- **Assigning categories**   Categories are an administrative tool in Configuration Manager that you can use to organize and manage drivers. You can assign categories during the driver import, or you can assign and manage categories after drivers are imported. Assigning information such as the hardware model number can help with building driver packages and maintaining a manageable driver catalog.

- **Creating driver packages**   Driver packages contain a set of predefined drivers based on your selections. A good practice is to create a driver package based on hardware model.

- **Updating boot images**   After the drivers are in the database, you might need to add some to your boot image, such as a network card driver or a storage driver. Without these drivers in your boot image, you might experience issues using the boot image on certain hardware.

- **Updating the task sequence** Start integrating those hardware drivers with your task sequence.
- **Managing the drivers** Over time, you will want to add, update, or remove drivers.

Importing device drivers and creating packages

In the following example, you import a new set of hardware drivers for an HP EliteBook 8470p portable computer. These drivers were captured from one of Tailspin Toys' client computers. The drivers will be imported, added to a package, and included in a preexisting Windows 8.1 task sequence.

1. In the Configuration Manager console, click the Software Library workspace.
2. In the left pane, expand Operating Systems.
3. Right-click Drivers and then click Import Driver.
4. On the Locate Driver page of the Import New Driver Wizard, enter the full UNC path to the drivers that you are importing, as shown in Figure 3-22. Leave the default option for duplicate drivers enabled and then click Next.

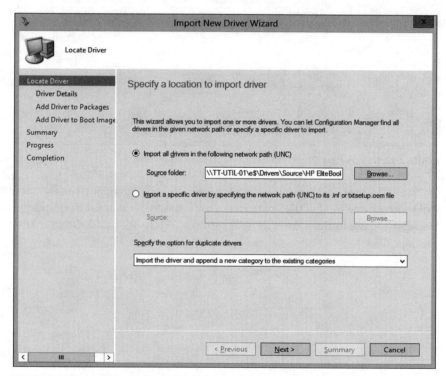

FIGURE 3-22 Import New Driver Wizard, Locate Driver page

5. On the Driver Details page, confirm that the drivers you want to import are listed in the top section.

6. Click the Categories button to create a new category for the drivers you are importing.

7. Click Create and type the name for the new driver category. Refer to Figure 3-23 for the driver import summary and click Next.

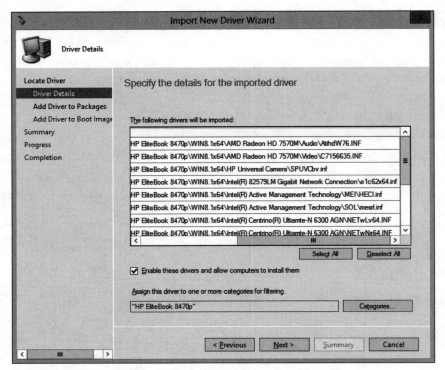

FIGURE 3-23 Import New Driver Wizard, Driver Details page

8. On the Add Driver To Packages page, click New Package. Name the package accordingly and provide the full UNC path to the packages folder that Configuration Manager will use to store the drivers, as shown in Figure 3-24. Click OK to create the package. Click Next.

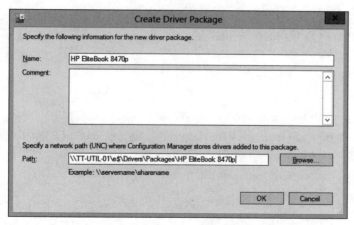

FIGURE 3-24 Import New Driver Wizard, Create Driver Package window

9. On the Add Driver To Boot Image page, click Next.

In this example, these drivers do not need to be added to boot images.

10. On the Summary page, confirm your configuration and then click Next.

11. On the Completion page, click Close.

> **NOTE IMPORT DRIVERS WITH WINDOWS POWERSHELL**
>
> Use the Import-CMDriver cmdlet to import new drivers by using Windows PowerShell. For example, to import a new USB driver, run the following command.
>
> ```
> Import-CMDriver -UncFileLocation "\\TT-CONFIGMGR-01\E$\Source Files\Drivers
> \Source\USB3\iusb3xhc.inf" -ImportDuplicateDriverOption OverwriteCategory
> -EnableAndAllowInstall $True"
> ```

After the process completes, the following items should now appear in the Configuration Manager console:

- The new hardware drivers are recorded in the catalog. They are visible when selecting the Drivers node in the left pane.

- A corresponding category is assigned to the new hardware drivers, also visible from the Drivers node. As more drivers are added, these categories keep things organized.

- A new driver package is created that includes the drivers you imported. Packages are visible when selecting the Driver Packages node in the left pane.

> **MORE INFO PLANNING A DEVICE DRIVER STRATEGY**
>
> For more information about managing your device driver strategy, see *http://technet .microsoft.com/en-us/library/gg712674.aspx*.

Distributing driver packages

Distribute the driver package to your distribution point so you can start using these drivers in your task sequence.

1. Select the Driver Packages node in the left pane.

2. Right-click the new driver package and then click Distribute Content.

3. On the General page of the Distribute Content Wizard, click Next.

4. On the Content Destination page, click Add and then click Distribution Point. Select the desired distribution point and then click OK. Click Next.

5. On the Summary page, confirm your selections and then click Next.

6. On the Completion page, click Close.

Managing drivers

The steps in the previous section demonstrated how to import new drivers into your environment. Now you need to understand how to manage existing drivers, as shown in the following tasks:

- **Updating driver packages and boot images**   This includes adding and removing drivers to and from packages and boot images.

- **Updating categories**   Categories are a key tool for keeping drivers organized and manageable.

- **Removing drivers from the catalog**   Over time, drivers need to be updated. Leaving outdated drivers in the catalog adds unwanted bloat and makes things difficult to navigate.

- **Enabling and disabling drivers**.

To update existing driver packages, perform the following steps:

1. Select the Drivers node in the left pane.

2. Locate the desired driver by using the search field or filtering options in the main window of the management console.

3. Right-click the driver, highlight Edit, and then click Driver Packages. Refer to Figure 3-25 for reference.

4. Locate the driver package that you need to update.

    - Selecting the box for that package adds the driver.

    - Clearing the box removes the driver.

    - Clicking the New Package button prompts you to create a new package.

    - Choosing the Update Distribution Points check box immediately pushes these changes to all the corresponding distribution points for this driver package.

5. Click OK to apply the changes.

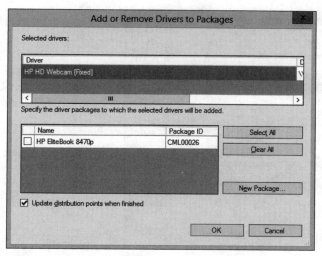

FIGURE 3-25 Add Or Remove Drivers To Packages dialog box

To update boot images, perform the following steps:

1. Click the Drivers node in the left pane.

2. Locate the desired driver by using the search field or filtering options in the main window of the management console.

3. Right-click the driver, highlight Edit, and select Boot Images. Refer to Figure 3-26 for reference.

4. Locate the boot image you need to update.

   - Selecting the box for that boot image adds the driver.

   - Clearing the box removes the driver.

   - Selecting the Update Distribution Points check box immediately pushes the changes to all the corresponding distribution points for this boot image.

5. Click OK to apply the changes.

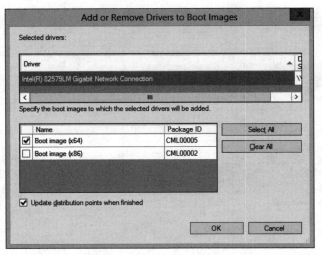

FIGURE 3-26 Add Or Remove Drivers To Boot Images dialog box

To update driver categories, perform the following steps:

1. Click the Drivers node in the left pane.

2. Locate the desired driver by using the search field or filtering options in the main window of the management console.

3. Right-click the driver, highlight Categorize, and then click Manage Categories. See Figure 3-27 for reference.

4. Locate the category you need to update and take the appropriate actions:

   - Selecting the check box for that category adds the driver.

   - Clearing or not selecting the check box removes the driver.

   - Clicking Create prompts you to create a new category.

   - Clicking Rename enables you to rename an existing category.

   - Clicking Delete deletes a current category and all driver associations.

5. Click OK to apply the changes.

FIGURE 3-27 Manage Administrative Categories dialog box

To remove drivers from the catalog, perform the following steps:

1. Click the Drivers node in the left pane.
2. Locate the desired driver by using the search field or filtering options in the main window of the management console.
3. Right-click the driver and then click Delete.
4. On the Delete Driver page, click the Show Reference button to reveal any associations with existing driver packages and/or boot images. Click OK to confirm the deletion.

   The selected driver will be removed from any corresponding categories, packages, and boot images.

To enable and disable drivers, perform the following steps:

1. Click the Drivers node in the left pane.
2. Locate the desired driver by using the search field or filtering options in the main window of the management console.
3. Right-click the driver.

   - Click Disable to prevent further use.
   - Click Enable to resume usage.

Alternatively, use the Enable-CMDriver and Disable-CMDriver cmdlets to complete enabling and disabling drivers by using Windows PowerShell. For example, you can run the Enable-CMDriver -Name "iusb3xhc.inf" command to enable the USB driver or the Disable-CMDriver -Name "iusb3xhc.inf" command to disable the USB driver.

Managing boot and deployment images

Configuration Manager has OSD built into its framework. Part of this framework deals with image building, distribution, and deployment. As an OSD administrator, it will be your responsibility also to manage the images. There are two basic types of images to manage:

- **Boot images**   Used to boot a client computer into Windows PE. Windows PE provides a lightweight environment, separate from whatever is installed on the local disk. This enables you to complete system-wide changes such as reformatting a system and installing Windows 8.1. In Configuration Manager, two boot images come preloaded during the initial product installation, specifically x86 and x64. Boot images are usually identified as boot.wim files. The out-of-box images are stored under \Microsoft Configuration Manager\OSD\boot and will be visible in the management console.

- **Deployment images**   Complete operating system images, whether direct from the installation media or a reference image that has been imported. Deployment images are called from within a task sequence by using Apply Operating System Image. The image is then downloaded from the local distribution point and installed on the client computer.

With every major release of Configuration Manager, the built-in boot images are upgraded to the latest available version. You will experience issues trying to deploy Windows 8.1 with an incompatible boot image.

- Configuration Manager 2012 includes Windows PE 3, which supports deploying Windows 7.

- Configuration Manager 2012 SP1 includes Windows PE 4, which supports deploying Windows 8.

- Configuration Manager 2012 R2 includes Windows PE 5, which supports deploying Windows 8.1.

Add a boot image

As mentioned previously, the boot images are preloaded in Configuration Manager as part of the product installation. Use the following steps if you ever need to re-add the boot images.

1. In the Configuration Manager console, click the Software Library workspace.
2. In the left pane, expand Operating Systems.
3. Right-click Boot Images and then click Add Boot Image.
4. On the Data Source page of the Add Boot Image Wizard, specify the path to the boot. wim file, select the x86 or x64 architecture for your environment, select the boot image, and then click Next.
5. On the General page, enter a name, version, and comments relevant to the boot image. Click Next.
6. On the Summary page, confirm your selection and then click Next.
7. On the Completion page, click Close.

You can also use New-CMBootImage, Get-CMBootImage, Set-CMBootImage, and Remove-CMBootImage to manage boot images by using Windows PowerShell. For example:

- To create a new boot image named WinPE Boot Image, run the following command:

```
New-CMBootImage -Path "\\TT-CONFIGMGR-01\E$\SMS_SFO\osd\boot\i386\boot.wim" -Index
1 -Name "WinPE Boot Image" -Version 1.0 -Description "WinPE Boot Image x86"
```

- To retrieve the detailed properties of a boot image named WinPE Boot Image, run the following command:

```
Get-CMBootImage -Name "WinPE Boot Image"
```

- To rename a boot image named WinPE Boot Image to WinPE Boot Image (x86), run the following command:

```
Set-CMBootImage -Name "WinPE Boot Image" -NewName "WinPE Boot Image (x86)"
```

- To remove a boot image named WinPE Boot Image (x86), run the following command:

```
Remove-CMBootImage -Name "WinPE Boot Image (x86)" -Confirm
```

Distribute a boot image

Boot images need to be distributed to all relative distribution points, the same as a standard package does.

1. Click Boot Images in the left pane.
2. Right-click the boot image in the main window and then click Distribute Content.
3. On the General page of the Distribute Content Wizard, click Next.
4. On the Content Destination page, click Add and then click Distribution Point. Mark the desired distribution point(s) and then click OK. Click Next.
5. On the Summary page, confirm your selections and then click Next.
6. On the Completion page, click Close.

Modify a boot image

After a boot image is created, additional configuration options become available. These items are accessible through the properties page of the target boot image, as shown in Figure 3-28.

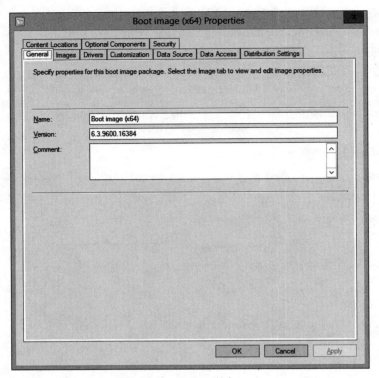

FIGURE 3-28 Boot Image (x64) Properties window

Following are a few of the property pages applicable to boot images:

- **Images** Use this tab to change the description.
- **Drivers** Use this tab to inject any drivers available in the driver catalog.
- **Customization** Use this tab for the following:
  - **Enable Prestart Command** This can be a single command with the option to include files from a package. You might use a prestart command if you want to run a script or prompt for information from the Windows PE environment.
  - **Windows PE Background** This enables you to customize the default background image.
  - **Windows PE Scratch Space (MB)** Scratch space is temporary space Windows PE uses to store data such as log files. In previous versions of Windows PE, before version 5.0, scratch space was set to 32 MB by default, and that often wasn't enough space. It was often necessary to configure scratch space by setting it to 128 MB or more. Now, with Windows PE 5.0 and later, scratch space is dynamically allocated based on the amount of RAM in the computer. For computers with 1 GB or more of RAM, the scratch space is set to 512 MB.

- **Enable Command Support**　This feature enables you to access a command prompt while inside Windows PE by pressing F8. Enabling command support is highly recommended for simplifying troubleshooting.
- **Data Source**　This tab deals with the original file source and how it is distributed. The available options include the image path, image index, distribution point update schedule, and distribution options such as persisting content in the client cache, enabling binary differential replication, and enabling automatic deployment of the boot image to PXE-enabled distribution points.
- **Optional Components**　Use this tab to add additional components to the boot image, making them available in Windows PE. Some examples include Windows PowerShell and Microsoft .NET.

Add a deployment image

The first operating system image that you import into Configuration Manager will likely be from the Windows installation media. If you already have a built image, perhaps from another platform, such as Windows Deployment Services (WDS) or MDT, you can import that .wim file as well. The process is very similar to boot images, as shown in the following steps:

1. In the Configuration Manager console, click the Software Library workspace.
2. In the left pane, expand Operating Systems.
3. Right-click Operating System Images and then click Add Operating System Image.
4. On the Data Source page of the Add Operating System Wizard, specify the path to the .wim file and then click Next.
5. On the General page, enter an appropriate name and fill in the version and comments if desired. Click Next.
6. On the Summary page, confirm the selections and then click Next.
7. On the Completion page, click Close.

Distribute a deployment image

Boot images need to be distributed to all relative distribution points, just like a standard package.

1. Click Operating System Images in the left pane.
2. Right-click the operating system image in the main window and then click Distribute Content.
3. On the General page of the Distribute Content Wizard, click Next.
4. On the Content Destination page, click Add and then click Distribution Point. Mark the desired distribution point and click OK. Click Next.
5. On the Summary page, confirm the selections and then click Next.
6. On the Completion page, click Close.

Modify a deployment image

After an operating system image is imported, additional configuration options become available. These items are accessible through the Properties page of the target image, as shown in Figure 3-29.

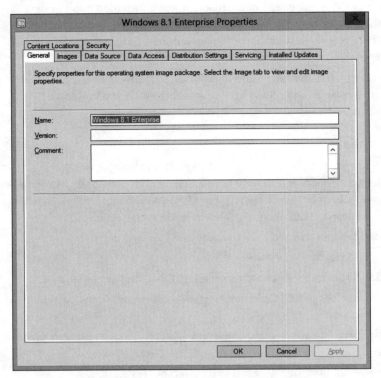

FIGURE 3-29 Operating system Properties window, General tab

Following are a few of the property pages unique to operating system images:

- **Images**   Gives you the ability to change Description, Created By, and Image Version.
- **Data Source**   Deals with the original file source and how it is distributed. The available options include the image path, image index, distribution point update schedule, and distribution options such as persisting content in the client cache, enabling binary differential replication, and enabling automatic deployment of the boot image to PXE-enabled distribution points.
- **Servicing**   Shows you a read-only view for any associated servicing schedules. Software updates can be scheduled to install automatically, and those entries are recorded here.
- **Installed Updates**   Provides a read-only view of the updates that have been installed using the scheduled updates feature.

Thought experiment

Windows 8.1 deployment at Tailspin Toys

Tailspin Toys has one office. The company has approximately 3,000 client computers, half of which are portable computers. There are several hardware vendors and multiple platforms. All client computers run Windows 7 Enterprise. A reference computer has been built and is ready for use.

The company plans to upgrade all client computers to Windows 8.1. In addition, the company is planning to roll out some new productivity applications to all employees. You plan to use the existing deployment infrastructure consisting of Configuration Manager, MDT, and WDS. To help you assess your knowledge, answer the following questions:

1. For the applications that you will deploy, you've specified a command to install the application. What else should you specify?

2. To simplify management of the drivers, what should you do?

3. Which task sequence template should you use to create your reference image?

Objective summary

- Boot images offer some unique customization options, such as command-line support for advanced troubleshooting.
- Deployment images offer some unique customization options such as automated Windows Update servicing.
- There are two options for deploying content to client devices: deployment packages or applications.
- Deployment packages can be set up to distribute a payload of files, run a command, or both.
- Applications require both an install and a detection method.
- Windows PowerShell can be used to create, view, and modify programs, packages, applications, and deployment types.
- The build and capture template is the first step to create a reference image.
- Task sequences are commonly used for deploying operating systems but are also capable of simple management tasks such as uninstalling a software update.
- The operating system image that you deploy must be compatible with the boot image that you are using. For example, if you are deploying the 32-bit version of Windows 8.1, use a 32-bit boot image.
- The driver catalog uses categories to organize content.
- Driver packages can be created and modified through the Import Driver Wizard or on a per-driver basis through the driver catalog.

Objective review

Answer the following questions to test your knowledge of the information in this objective. You can find the answers to these questions and explanations of why each answer choice is correct or incorrect in the "Answers" section at the end of this chapter.

1. You are beginning a large migration to Windows 8.1. The deployment will be automated by using Configuration Manager and WDS. You want to simplify the troubleshooting process if any issues arise during deployments. What should you do?

   A. Adjust the Windows PE scratch space.

   B. Enable command support.

   C. Import the WDS module for Windows PowerShell.

   D. Run a prestart command to launch cmd.exe.

2. You are preparing to enhance an existing Windows 8.1 deployment in Configuration Manager. You need to repartition the disks of client computers automatically before your image is deployed on them. What should you do?

   A. Run a prestart command.

   B. Enable command support.

   C. Upon boot, press F8 and then manually repartition the disks.

   D. Use an operating system install package.

3. You've just updated the source files for a package. You need to ensure that the updated files are used. What should you do?

   A. Validate the content on the distribution point.

   B. Set the content validation job to run at the highest priority.

   C. Redistribute the content on the distribution point.

   D. Run the Add-Content Windows PowerShell command.

Objective 3.2: Configure distribution points

Distribution points are a foundational technology of Configuration Manager. Without them, most of the functionality in Configuration Manager is not available. To prepare for the exam and administer Configuration Manager, you must understand the role of distribution points, the different functions a distribution point can perform, and how and when to group distribution points. Finally, you have to understand how to configure distribution points based on specific organizational requirements.

> **This objective covers how to:**
> - Configure unicast/multicast
> - Configure PXE
> - Configure deployments to distribution points and distribution point groups

Configuring unicast and multicast

Chapter 2 covered unicast and multicast in detail. In this chapter, you configure unicast and multicast from a Configuration Manager viewpoint. Although the underlying technologies work in the same way, the configuration is completely different.

Configure unicast

The default network deployment protocol in Configuration Manager is unicast. Unlike multicast, unicast doesn't have a dedicated configuration area in Configuration Manager. Instead, you configure settings related to deployment, and those settings are applicable to unicast and multicast. For a refresher on unicast, see the "Configuring unicast and multicast deployment methods" section in Chapter 2.

Configure multicast

From a purely protocol perspective, you learned the differences between unicast and multicast in Chapter 2. You also learned when multicast makes sense, such as in deployments that will handle a large number of simultaneous installations. In this section, you walk through the configuration tasks related to multicast.

> **MORE INFO**   **MULTICAST VERSUS BROADCAST**
>
> Broadcast traffic is sent to all hosts on a network. Multicast traffic is sent only to specific hosts on a network. In the case of operating system deployments, multicast traffic only goes to multicast clients that have joined a multicast transmission.

The first step in configuring multicast in Configuration Manager is the enabling step. By default, multicast is not enabled. Walk through the Multicast tab that is on the Distribution point Properties page as shown in Figure 3-30.

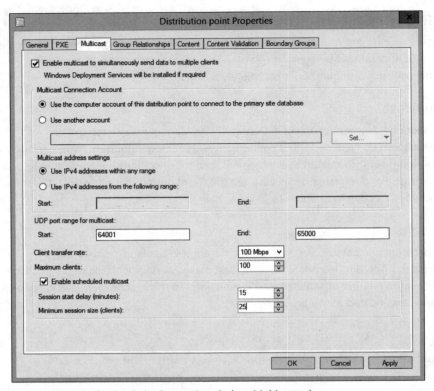

FIGURE 3-30 Distribution Point Properties window, Multicast tab

There are several configurable areas of the Multicast tab, as follows:

- **Enable Multicast**   Enable this option first. By doing so, you unlock the rest of the configurable settings. Note that if WDS is not already installed on the server, it will be automatically added when multicast is enabled.

- **Multicast Connection Account**   By default, the computer account of the distribution point server connects to the primary site database. You can configure another account, such as a user account, instead. However, it is a good practice to leave this at the default setting because the only time this account is needed is when communicating with a remote site database in an untrusted forest.

- **Multicast Address Settings**   By default, IP addresses will be used within any multicast range. The multicast range is 239.0.0.0 to 239.255.255.255. However, if you have other multicasting activities on your network, you can narrow the IP address range so that there aren't any conflicts.

- **UDP Port Range for Multicast**   The default starting port is 64001, and the default ending port is 65000. Unless these ports are conflicting with other network activity on your network, you should keep the port range at the default setting.

- **Client Transfer Rate** The client transfer rate is set to 100 megabits per second by default. You can customize this setting to a value that is appropriate for your environment.

- **Maximum Clients** By default, up to 100 multicast clients can participate in a multicast stream. You can adjust this up or down, based on your use case. If you plan to image a large number of computers simultaneously, you should test some deployments while monitoring your network and distribution point server performance. After you've gathered the performance data, you can adjust the maximum number of clients to a level that allows the service to operate at maximum performance.

- **Enable Scheduled Multicast** Similar to WDS Scheduled-Cast, you can schedule a multicast deployment. You can choose to wait for a specific number of clients before starting, or you can wait a specific amount of time before starting.

In addition to the Multicast tab, you must also configure your operating system images for multicast deployment, as shown in Figure 3-31.

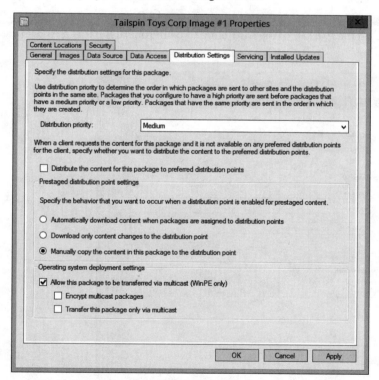

FIGURE 3-31 Operating system image Properties, Distribution Settings tab

After you've enabled Allow This Package To Be Transferred Via Multicast (WinPE Only) on an image, there are two import settings that you should be aware of when configuring an operating system image for multicast:

- **Encrypt Multicast Packages**   You can encrypt multicast packages. This option is useful in high-security environments where confidential or sensitive information is present in your operating system image.

- **Transfer This Package Only Via Multicast**   You can limit the use of the package to just multicast. This prevents the image from being deployed outside of a multicast deployment.

Configuring PXE

Preboot Execution Environment (PXE) is an industry-standard method to boot computers from the network instead of by the traditional approach of booting computers to a locally installed operating system. PXE is most often used as a way to deploy operating system images to computers over the network without using media. You can take advantage of PXE in WDS deployments and in Configuration Manager deployments. By default, PXE is not enabled on distribution points.

To use PXE for your deployments, enable PXE and configure the PXE options. You can enable and configure PXE on the PXE tab of the Distribution Point Properties page, as shown in Figure 3-32.

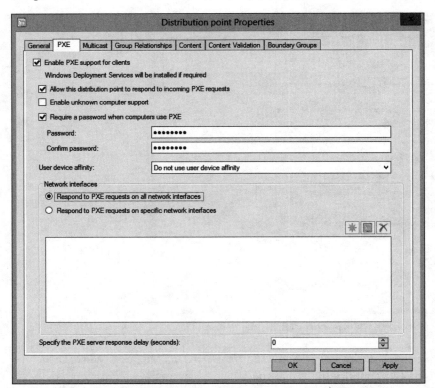

FIGURE 3-32 Distribution Point Properties window, PXE tab

There are several configuration items on the PXE tab, as follows:

- **Enable PXE Support For Clients** Select this option to enable PXE. This is the first step in your PXE configuration because the rest of the PXE configuration items are not modifiable until PXE is enabled. Note that WDS, if not already installed, will be automatically installed when PXE is first enabled.

- **Allow This Distribution Point To Respond To Incoming PXE Requests** Use this setting to halt PXE responses temporarily on a distribution point. Alternatively, you can disable PXE support.

- **Enable Unknown Computer Support** Use this option to enable deployments to computers that are not managed by Configuration Manager. If you plan to deploy only to computers that are already managed by Configuration Manager, you should not enable unknown computer support. Enabling unknown computer support reduces the security of your environment because it opens up the imaging process potentially to any computer and any users, depending on the configured permissions. In most environments, only authorized IT staff should perform computer imaging.

- **Require A Password When Computers Use PXE** By default, you can boot to PXE without specifying a password. However, to restrict PXE functionality only to those who know a password, you can enable the option to require a password for PXE. This setting is most often used in high-security environments.

- **User Device Affinity** Use user device affinity to associate users with specific computers. You can then deploy applications to users instead of to computers. This improves the administrator user experience. There are three options for user device affinity for PXE:

  - **Do Not Use User Device Affinity (Default)** With this option, you do not use user device affinity.

  - **Allow User Device Affinity With Manual Approval** With this option, you have to approve user device affinity manually.

  - **Allow User Device Affinity With Automatic Approval** With this option, Configuration Manager automatically approves user device affinity.

- **Network Interfaces** Listen for PXE requests on all network interface cards (NICs) or just specific NICs. This setting is useful if you have a multihomed server and want to restrict PXE to a specific NIC.

- **Specify The PXE Server Response Delay** Use this setting when there is more than one PXE server and they are both servicing the same subnets. By adding a small delay, you can ensure that a specific PXE server handles the majority of PXE requests.

EXAM TIP

Although there are multiple ways to perform tasks in Configuration Manager, this book primarily shows you how to perform tasks in the Configuration Manager console. Instances will be pointed out when, for example, Windows PowerShell is a good alternative or even a better method. For the exam, expect some questions to ask you how to perform a task and the answer choices to present only Windows PowerShell methods. To prepare, see the Configuration Manager cmdlet reference at *http://technet.microsoft.com/library /jj821831(v=sc.20).aspx*. Don't spend time memorizing all the cmdlets, though. Instead, try using a few of them to perform routine configuration tasks.

Configuring deployments to distribution points and distribution point groups

To build and maintain an effective Configuration Manager environment, spend time planning for and configuring distribution points. Distribution points store packages. Packages contain items such as drivers, applications, operating system images, boot images, and task sequences. For this exam objective, this section is focused on OSD, so it focuses on distribution points for OSD.

Distribute operating system images to distribution points

First, walk through distributing an operating system image to a distribution point. Before you begin, make sure that you have added an existing operating system image in Configuration Manager.

1. In the Configuration Manager console, click the Software Library workspace. In the left pane, expand Operating Systems and then click Operating System Images.

2. In the right pane, right-click your operating system image and then click Distribute Content.

The Distribute Content Wizard launches, as shown in Figure 3-33.

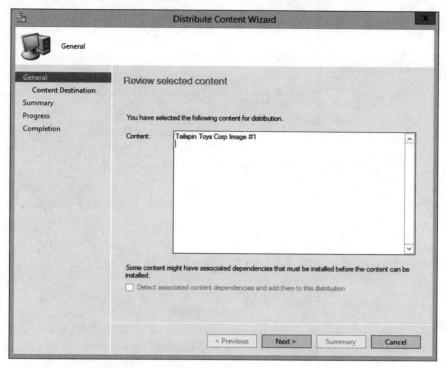

FIGURE 3-33 Distribute Content Wizard, General page

3. On the Content Destination page, as shown in Figure 3-34, click Add and then click Distribution Point.

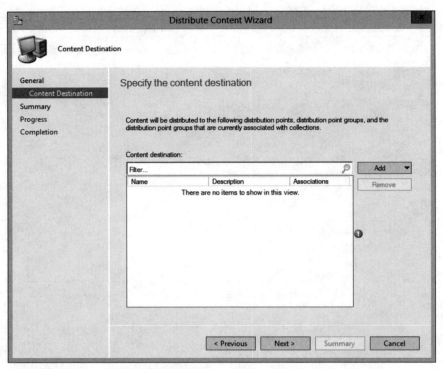

FIGURE 3-34 Distribute Content Wizard, Content Destination page

4. In the Add Distribution Points window, as shown in Figure 3-35, select the available distribution point you want to use and then click OK. If you do not see an available distribution point, check to ensure that the content is not already stored on the distribution point.

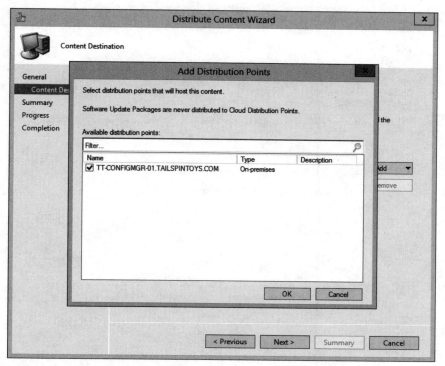

FIGURE 3-35 Distribute Content Wizard, Add Distribution Points dialog box

5. In the Summary window, as shown in Figure 3-36, validate the settings to ensure accuracy and then click Next.

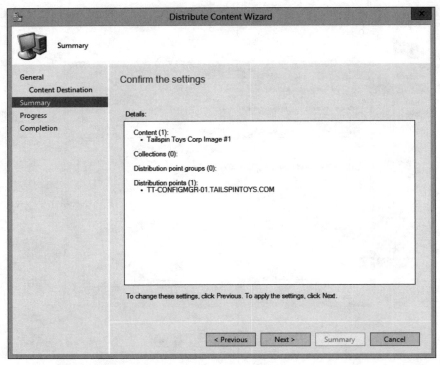

FIGURE 3-36 Distribute Content Wizard, Summary page

6. On the Completion page, as shown in Figure 3-37, you should see a message indicating that the distribution was successful. Click Close to complete the wizard.

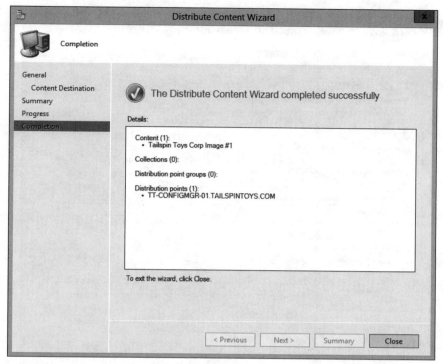

FIGURE 3-37 Distribute Content Wizard, Completion page

There are several configuration tabs for distribution points. The following section covers the remaining tabs while staying focused on OSD.

The General tab, as shown in Figure 3-38, contains a couple of settings related to OSD:

- **BranchCache** BranchCache is a Windows feature that enables more efficient use of a wide area network (WAN) by caching content locally when users or computers access content over the WAN. For deployments, it means that if you are imaging over a WAN, you can reduce the amount of network bandwidth used. After one client requests your image, the image is cached, and subsequent clients can retrieve that data on their local area network (LAN). You can take advantage of BranchCache by performing the following high-level steps:

  A. Add the BranchCache Windows feature on your distribution point. You can add the feature by using Server Manager.

  B. Enable the BranchCache feature on the clients. You can use Group Policy to enable and configure BranchCache on the clients.

  C. Enable BranchCache on the distribution point.

- **Prestaged content** You can enable a distribution point for prestaged content. When you have slow WAN links and remote distribution points, prestaging content can help you avoid long delays when you need to get content to the distribution point. Instead of copying large amounts of data over a slow WAN link, you can ship data on an external hard drive to have it copied and ready for use.

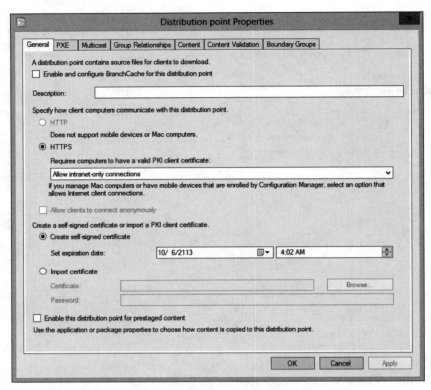

FIGURE 3-38 Distribution Point Properties window, General tab

MORE INFO **SETTING UP BRANCHCACHE**

To learn more about BranchCache deployment options and how to set up BranchCache, see the Windows Server 2012 BranchCache Deployment Guide at *http://www.microsoft.com /en-us/download/details.aspx?id=30418*. It contains additional details not covered in this book.

The Content tab, as shown below in Figure 3-39, shows you a listing of the content on the distribution point. It includes all the deployment package types, such as packages and operating system images. You can perform three tasks from the Content tab:

- **Validate content** To validate a package, click the package in the list and then click Validate. This starts a validation job that verifies the integrity of the files. You can view the status of the job in the Monitoring workspace. Note that, by default, a content validation job runs once a week.

- **Redistribute content** To redistribute the package to the distribution point, click the Redistribute button. This action copies the files from the site server to the distribution point. The existing files are overwritten by this action. You would redistribute content to repair corrupt content.

- **Remove content** If you no longer need a package on a distribution point, you can click it in the package list and then click Remove to remove the content from the distribution point.

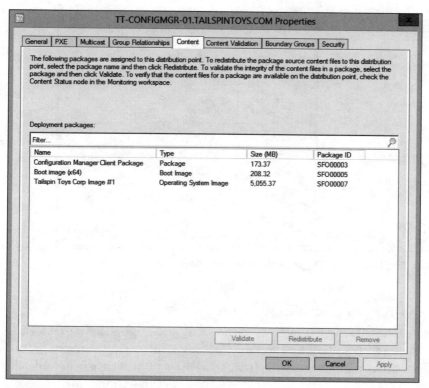

FIGURE 3-39 Distribution Point Properties window, Content tab

The Boundary Groups tab, as shown in Figure 3-40, shows the existing boundary groups. It also enables you to create new boundary groups and add existing boundary groups. A boundary group is a group of boundaries. A boundary can be a subnet, an IP address range or IPv6 prefix, or an Active Directory site. Every boundary must be assigned to a boundary group to use it. The majority of your clients will be associated with a boundary and boundary group. However, Internet clients do not use boundaries. You associate distribution points or state migration points with a boundary group. Boundary groups help internal Configuration Manager clients locate content and a site. Without the proper boundary setup, clients at a site with a distribution point might retrieve content from a remote distribution point instead of the local distribution point.

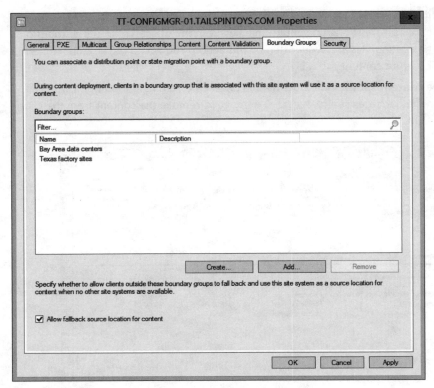

FIGURE 3-40 Distribution Point Properties window, Boundary Groups tab

> **MORE INFO   BOUNDARIES AND BOUNDARY GROUPS**
>
> If you haven't worked with boundaries and boundary groups, spend a few minutes reading the "Planning for Boundaries and Boundary Groups in Configuration Manager" content at *http://technet.microsoft.com/en-us/library/gg712679.aspx*. It contains additional details not covered in this book.

Create and configure distribution point groups

A distribution point group is a collection of distribution points and Configuration Manager collections. A distribution point group can be created without any distribution points or collections. Distribution point groups have the following benefits:

■ When you use a distribution point group for distribution, you can seamlessly add distribution points to the group later. When you add distribution points, they automatically receive all the content that was previously distributed to the distribution point group.

- When you add collections to a distribution point group, the associated distribution point members automatically receive the content whenever you distribute content to the collections.

- You can specify a single entity, in this case a distribution point group, to distribute content such as operating system images to multiple distribution points. This reduces administrative overhead in a couple of ways: you don't have to remember all the distribution points, and you don't have to specify multiple distribution points.

You can add a new distribution point group by using Windows PowerShell or by using the Configuration Manager console.

To add a new and empty distribution point group named "Sales offices" by using Windows PowerShell, run the following command:

```
New-CMDistributionPointGroup –Name "Sales offices"
```

To add a new distribution point group in the Configuration Manager console, perform the following steps:

1. Click the Administration workspace. In the left pane, expand Security, right-click Distribution Point Groups, and then click Create Group.

2. In the Create New Distribution Point Group window, shown in Figure 3-41, type a name and a description. On the Members tab, click Add. In the Add Distribution Points window, shown in Figure 3-42, select an available distribution point and then click OK.

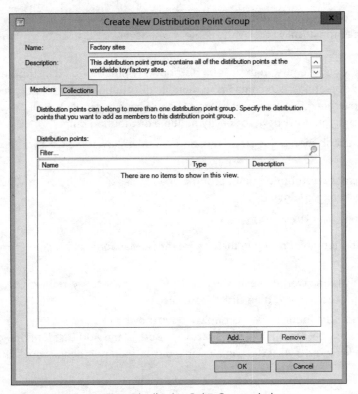

FIGURE 3-41 Create New Distribution Point Group window

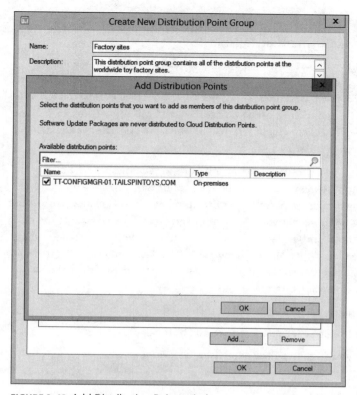

FIGURE 3-42 Add Distribution Points window

3. In the Create New Distribution Point Group window, click OK to complete the creation process. After the creation, you should see the distribution point group listed in the console.

You distribute content to distribution point groups just as you distribute content to distribution points; you use the same wizard. The only difference is that you choose a distribution group as the target.

Windows 8.1 deployment at Tailspin Toys

Tailspin Toys has five offices. The main office is in San Francisco, and the other offices are in Mexico City, Houston, Miami, and Toronto. The offices are connected by a Multiprotocol Label Switching (MPLS) network. The office in Houston has a 1.5 MB connection, and the rest of the offices have a 10 MB connection. Each office has approximately 300 client computers, half of which are portable. All client computers run Windows 7 Enterprise.

The company plans to upgrade all client computers to Windows 8.1. The plan is to use five operating system images based on the specific requirements of various departments. The management team wants to automate the installation process but minimize disruption to the network. To meet the project schedule, a minimum of 10 computers a day must be imaged. In addition, the security team has requested you to maximize the security of the deployments. You decide to use Configuration Manager with PXE to automate the deployments. To help you assess your knowledge, answer the following questions:

1. In which offices should you have distribution points?
2. What should you do to maximize the security of the deployments?
3. What should you do to minimize administrative overhead?

Objective summary

- When you enable multicast or PXE on a distribution point, WDS will be automatically installed.
- If you have two PXE servers on a network, you can add a PXE server response delay to direct PXE requests to a specific PXE server.
- Configuration Manager packages can contain drivers, applications, operating system images, boot images, and task sequences.
- Create distribution point groups to group distribution points and collections. This reduces administrative overhead by automating content distribution for future distribution point group members.
- Use BranchCache to reduce usage of your WAN by enabling clients to retrieve cached content from the LAN.
- Create boundaries and boundary groups to ensure that clients use their local or closest distribution point. This minimizes latency and improves overall performance.

Objective review

Answer the following questions to test your knowledge of the information in this objective. You can find the answers to these questions and explanations of why each answer choice is correct or incorrect in the "Answers" section at the end of this chapter.

1. You have two offices in San Francisco and two offices in New York. One office in San Francisco has a distribution point, and one office in New York has a distribution point. Which technology should you use to ensure that all clients use the closest distribution point?

   A. Boundary groups

   B. Distribution point groups

   C. BranchCache

   D. Management point

2. You are attempting to distribute an operating system image to a distribution point named DP1. When you get to the step to add the distribution point, it isn't available to select. What should you do?

   A. Run the Set-CMDistributionPointGroup -Force command and then try again.

   B. Redistribute all content on the distribution point and then try again.

   C. Remove the existing deployment package on the distribution point and then try again.

   D. Manually run a content validation job on all existing content and then try again.

3. You plan to use BranchCache for your client computer operating system deployments in Configuration Manager. What should you do? (Choose all that apply.)

   A. Create a GPO to enable and configure BranchCache on client computers.

   B. Create a GPO to enable and configure BranchCache on domain controllers.

   C. Add the BranchCache feature on distribution points.

   D. Enable BranchCache in the Configuration Manager console on the distribution points.

   E. Deploy a BranchCache certificate to all of the client computers.

4. You need to be able to image any computer by using your deployment infrastructure, which consists of Configuration Manager, WDS, and MDT. Which two methods should you use? (Choose two. Each correct answer provides part of a complete solution.)

   A. Enable unknown computer support.

   B. Enable user device affinity.

   C. Grant the Everyone group Read permissions on your images.

   D. Prestage computers in Active Directory.

Objective 3.3: Configure MDT and Configuration Manager integration

As discussed in Chapter 2, MDT enables you to prepare and customize various aspects of the deployment process. MDT can also be integrated with System Center Configuration Manager. This section further expands on MDT by introducing integration with Configuration Manager and discussing additional management tasks.

> **This objective covers how to:**
> - Use MDT-specific task sequences
> - Create MDT boot images
> - Create custom task sequences using MDT components

After it's integrated with MDT, Configuration Manager can use the task sequences and other information defined in MDT. To configure the integration between the two, use the Configure ConfigMgr Integration Wizard, as shown in Figure 3-43. As part of the MDT install, you have a Configure ConfigMgr Integration program on the MDT server. The Options menu of the wizard specifies the options to install or remove the integration as well as the site server name and site code of the ConfigMgr deployment.

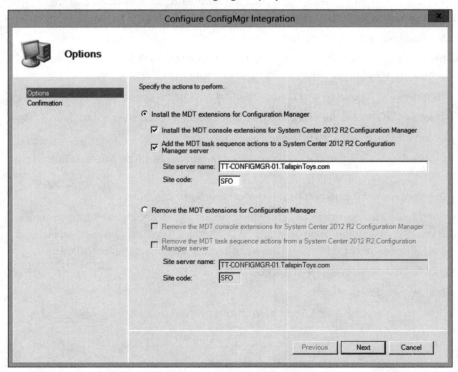

FIGURE 3-43 Configure ConfigMgr Integration, Options page

By default, if MDT is not integrated, the installation option will be selected. If MDT is already integrated, the removal option will be selected by default. Click Next to complete the wizard to integrate MDT with ConfigMgr. If successful, the success message appears in the Confirmation screen of the Configure ConfigMgr Integration Wizard.

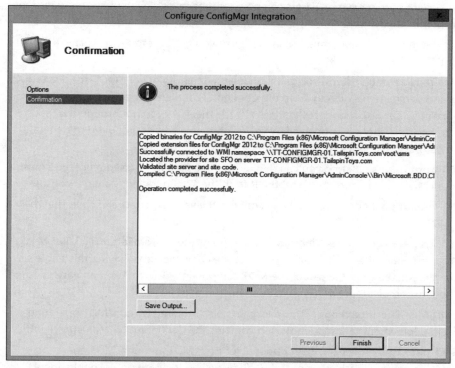

FIGURE 3-44 Configure ConfigMgr Integration, Confirmation page

> *MORE INFO* **INTEGRATE CONFIGURATION MANAGER WITH MDT 2013**
>
> For more information about integrating MDT with ConfigMgr, see *http://technet.microsoft .com/en-us/library/dn744295.aspx*.

Using MDT-specific task sequences

After integrating MDT with Configuration Manager, you can use the MDT-specific task sequences and components within Configuration Manager. Some of the features included in the integration are:

- **Dynamic Deployments** This feature enables you to use the CustomSettings.ini file for a broader range of imaging scenarios without the need for multiple task sequences.

- **Real-time Monitoring**   Real-time monitoring enables you to view current and recently completed image deployments. The monitoring provides percentage results of completion, errors, and time remaining until completion.

- **User-Driven Installation (UDI)**   UDI introduces a customizable wizard for images that require user interaction. Users can now respond to deployment-related questions during the deployment.

MDT integration with Configuration Manager gives you the best tools to achieve a ZTI deployment.

Following the integration steps, you can manage the majority of your MDT-specific task sequences and deployments directly from the Configuration Manager console. They all reside side by side with other task sequences that are already there. As you go through the task sequence architecture for MDT, notice a few key components that are required to generate and use an MDT task sequence. These include the following:

- **MDT boot image**   Before you can deploy an MDT-specific task sequence, you must add an MDT boot image and distribute it from the Configuration Manager console.

- **MDT toolkit package**   This package contains the various scripts and tools that make up MDT.

- **Settings package**   The settings package contains the CustomSettings.ini file. As you familiarize yourself with this package, notice the convenience of having this single settings file isolated from the rest of the MDT components. This makes it an easy package to update and distribute as things in your environment evolve.

- **ConfigMgr Client package**   This package is also required by non-MDT operating system deployment task sequences and contains the Configuration Manager client.

- **USMT package**   This package is optional for both MDT and non-MDT operating system deployment task sequences, but if you will be focusing on ZTI deployments, it will be a key component.

Each of these components makes up an MDT operating system deployment task sequence. One of the other nice aspects of the MDT integration is the simplicity of generating these packages, which is covered in more detail throughout this objective.

Creating MDT boot images

Chapter 2 covered an overview of boot images and how they are used. This section discusses how to create an MDTboot image for ConfigMgr. When integrated with ConfigMgr, a boot image can be created with Windows Preinstallation Environment (Windows PE) 5.0 that includes customized components and features. To proceed, make sure that you have already integrated MDT with Configuration Manager and then perform the following steps:

1.   In the Configuration Manager console, click the Software Library workspace, expand Operating Systems, right-click Boot Images, and then click Create Boot Image Using MDT.

The Create Boot Image Using MDT Wizard starts. If you do not see the menu option, you must integrate MDT with Configuration Manager as discussed earlier in this chapter. If you did the integration but still don't see this menu option, close the Configuration Manager console, reopen it, and try again.

2. On the Package Source page, shown in Figure 3-45, specify the UNC path of the source folder that will be used as the source directory for the new boot image.

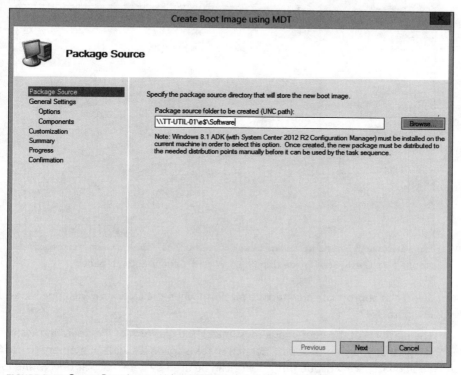

FIGURE 3-45 Create Boot Image Using MDT Wizard, Package Source page

3. The General Settings page, as shown in Figure 3-46, enables you to specify name, version, and comments for the customized Windows PE boot image. Enter the desired name and then click Next.

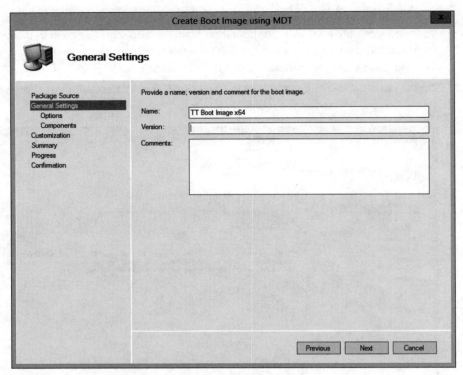

FIGURE 3-46 Create Boot Image Using MDT Wizard, General Settings page

4. Select the appropriate architecture platform when the Options page appears, as shown in Figure 3-47.

   The platform of the boot image must match the platform of the operating system image that you plan to deploy. Scratch space is space set aside in memory to use for additional space if needed. This space can be used by items such as drivers and log files. Historically, you needed to set the scratch space higher than the default to deal with large drivers or other issues. After you select the architecture, you can add components to the Windows PE image.

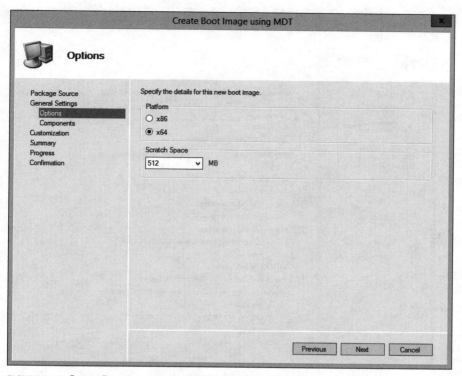

FIGURE 3-47 Create Boot Image Using MDT Wizard, Options page

5. On the Components page, as shown in Figure 3-48, select the desired components of the image and then continue with the wizard.

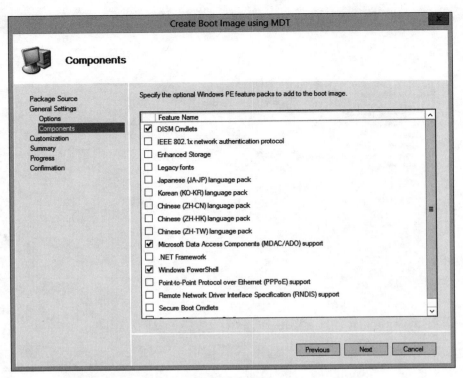

FIGURE 3-48 Create Boot Image Using MDT Wizard, Components page

6. On the Customization page, shown in Figure 3-49, run a command to clean the disk on the destination computer.

   Although you can also use an MDT task sequence to take care of partitioning, it is often necessary to clean the disk if you are reimaging computers that have BitLocker-encrypted volumes. The cleandisk.txt file is stored in the \\tt-util-01\e$\misc folder.

7. If desired, you can also set a custom background by specifying the UNC path of an image to use as the background. When you finish with your desired settings, click Next.

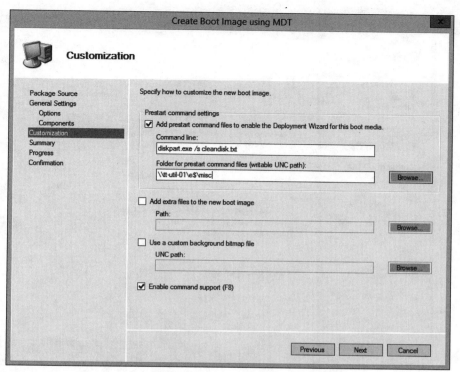

FIGURE 3-49 Create Boot Image Using MDT Wizard, Customization page

8. On the Summary page, shown in Figure 3-50, review the settings and then click Next.

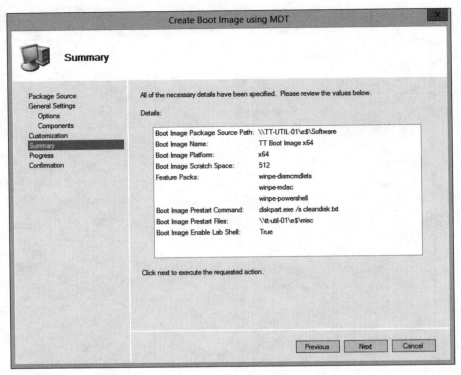

FIGURE 3-50 Create Boot Image Using MDT Wizard, Summary page

After you have configured all the wizard settings, the boot image will be generated and stored in the folder you specified on the Package Source page. The boot image can then be distributed to a distribution point for use when deploying operating systems.

> **MORE INFO   WINPE OPTIONAL COMPONENTS**
>
> For more information about WinPE optional components, see the optional components reference at *http://technet.microsoft.com/en-us/library/hh824926.aspx*.

Creating custom task sequences by using MDT components

Chapter 2 discussed how to create task sequences by using MDT as a stand-alone application. This section examines the MDT-specific task sequences and how to create them after integrating with Configuration Manager. Perform the following steps to get started:

1. In the Configuration Manager console, click the Software Library workspace.

2. In the left pane, expand Operating Systems.

3. Right-click Task Sequences and then click Create MDT Task Sequence.

4. On the Choose Template page of the Create MDT Task Sequence Wizard, click the drop-down menu to display the available task sequence templates. Because you integrated MDT and Configuration Manager, you can now take advantage of the following task sequence templates:

- **Client Task Sequence**   This task sequence covers the deployment of client operating systems for all scenarios with the exception of the MDT replacement scenario.
- **Client Replace Task Sequence**   This task sequence captures user state data for computer migrations through the Computer deployment scenario.
- **Microsoft Deployment Custom Task Sequence**   This task sequence provides a skeleton framework from which you build your desired configuration.
- **Server Task Sequence**   This task sequence covers the deployment of server operating systems for all scenarios.
- **User Driven Installation Replace Task Sequence**   This task sequence captures user state data for computer migrations through the computer deployment scenario by using UDI.

Based on the template you choose, the wizard automatically adjusts the information gathering to accommodate the necessary values for the task sequence. For this example, you use Client Task Sequence.

5. On the Choose Template page, select Client Task Sequence, as shown in Figure 3-51, from the drop-down menu and click Next.

6. On the General page, provide a name for the task sequence and any important administrative comments. Click Next.

7. On the Details page under Join Workgroup Or Domain, type a workgroup name or domain. If you provide a domain, use the Set button to enter credentials with permission to join computers to the domain. Under Windows Settings, enter a user name, organization name, and product key. Click Next.

8. On the Capture Settings page, you can optionally provide a share location and instruct the task sequence to capture a copy of the image to that destination. (This might be useful if you want to use this task sequence to build and capture a reference image.) Select This Task Sequence Will Never Be Used To Capture An Image. Click Next.

9. On the Boot Image page, specify the path to a preexisting MDT boot image or create one directly from the wizard. (Note that MDT-specific task sequences must use an MDT boot image.) Select Create A New Boot Image Package and then specify a UNC path for the package to be stored. Click Next.

10. On the General Settings page, provide a name, version, and administrative comments. Click Next.

11. On the Options page, specify the platform you are booting from (x86 or x64). Configuration Manager dynamically adjusts the scratch space, so leave it at the default setting. Click Next.

12. On the Components page, select any of the available components to have them available in Windows PE. Select Windows PowerShell. Click Next.

13. On the Customization page, you have a few options:

- **Prestart Command Settings** Select this box to add the MDT prestart command files. This is a helpful tool if you need to prompt for information before a task sequence is selected.

- **Add Extra Files To The New Boot Image** Select this box and specify a path to any additional files you need to include in your image. This is helpful if you need to have any files available within Windows PE, such as a BIOS configuration utility for enabling the Trusted Platform Module (TPM) chip for BitLocker.

- **Use A Custom Background Bitmap File** Select this box and specify a path to your organization's custom branding.

- **Enable Command Support (F8)** Select this box if you want to have quick access to command-line support. For security purposes, it is recommended that you leave this box cleared for production imaging. With it selected, you can press F8 anytime outside of a reboot to access a command prompt.

14. On the MDT Package page, specify the path to a preexisting MDT package or create one directly from the wizard.

    The MDT package is a required component for all MDT-specific task sequences and contains the various components that make the task sequence run.

15. Select Create A New Microsoft Deployment Toolkit Files Package and specify a path to save the files to. Click Next.

16. On the MDT Details page, provide a name, version, language, manufacturer, and any administrative comments for the MDT package. The name is the only required entry. Click Next.

17. On the OS Image page, you have a few options:

- **Specify An Existing OS Image** If you have already created and imported an image into Configuration Manager, you can select it here.

- **Create A New OS Image** If you have not imported an image into Configuration Manager, you can point to an image file—your reference image or the version from the installation media—and provide a source folder to create the corresponding package automatically.

- **Specify An Existing OS Install Package** If you have imported the Windows install package into Configuration Manager, you can select that for your operating system install.

- **Create A New OS Install Package** If you have not imported the Windows install package and would like to use it, you can point to the installation media and provide a source folder to create the corresponding package automatically.

18. On the OS Image Index page, if you are using an image file that includes multiple images, specify the appropriate index number for the image you wish to install. Click Next.

19. On the Deployment Method page, specify whether this image will be a Zero Touch Installation or User-Driven Installation. The user-driven installation will incorporate a custom wizard that enables the end user to customize the image at deployment time. Choose Zero Touch Installation. Click Next.

20. On the Client Package page, specify a preexisting ConfigMgr client package or have the wizard create a new one for you. Use the preexisting package for this example. Click Next.

21. On the USMT Package page, specify a preexisting USMT package or have the wizard create one for you. Create one using the wizard for this example. To do this, select Create A New USMT Package. The wizard automatically identifies the files, and you enter a source folder to create the package in Configuration Manager. Click Next.

22. On the USMT Details page, provide a name, version, language, manufacturer, and any administrative comments for the USMT package. The name is the only required field. Click Next.

23. On the Settings Package page, specify a preexisting MDT settings package or have the wizard create one for you. For this example, create one using the wizard. To do this, select Create A New Settings Package and specify a source folder to create the package in Configuration Manager. Click Next.

24. On the Settings Details page, provide a name, version, language, manufacturer, and any administrative comments for this settings package. Note the check box that tags this settings package for Server Core installations. Click Next.

25. On the Sysprep Package page, there is nothing to change or enter. Click Next.

26. On the Summary page, review the configuration and then click Next.

27. On the Confirmation page, ensure that there were no errors or warnings. Click Close.

After completing this process, you are left with a new task sequence and all the corresponding components required to use it. MDT integration simplifies many of the prerequisites by including the option to create them from directly within the wizard. However, as with all packages in Configuration Manager, you must distribute the content of those new packages before using the new task sequence.

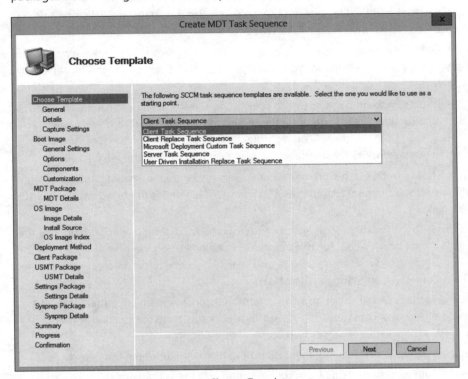

FIGURE 3-51 Create MDT Task Sequence, Choose Template page

MORE INFO **CREATE A TASK SEQUENCE WITH CONFIGURATION MANAGER AND MDT**

For more information about creating a task sequence with MDT, see the article at *http://technet.microsoft.com/en-us/library/dn744302.aspx*.

Thought experiment

New Windows 8.1 deployment with multiple languages

You are the desktop engineer at your company. Your company has two offices in the United States and two offices in France. You are planning to deploy 500 new client computers that run Windows 8.1. The following deployment requirements have been agreed on:

- There will be one keyboard layout for the United States and a different keyboard layout for France.

- A different product key will be used in each country/region.

- Installed languages must be customized based on the country/region.

- The new computers must have BitLocker enabled automatically.

You need to plan for the deployment based on these requirements.

1. How many custom task sequences would you need to create?

2. How would a custom Windows PE boot image assist in this deployment scenario?

3. How should you enable BitLocker?

Objective summary

- You can configure MDT to integrate with Configuration Manager.
- You can use MDT task sequences to customize an operating system deployment.
- You can use tasks with the LiteTouch.wsf file in the \DeploymentShare\Scripts \directory.
- You can create MDT boot images and customize them by using Configuration Manager.
- After you create a boot image, you can add it to a distribution point.
- You can customize task sequence templates by using MDT.

Objective review

Answer the following questions to test your knowledge of the information in this objective. You can find the answers to these questions and explanations of why each answer choice is correct or incorrect in the "Answers" section at the end of this chapter.

1. What information is needed to configure Configuration Manager Integration with MDT?

    A. Server name and site code

    B. Server name and user credentials

    C. Site code and user credentials

    D. User credentials

2. What is the default scratch space if a target system has at least 1 GB of RAM?

    A. 256 MB

    B. 512 MB

    C. 1 GB

    D. 2 GB

3. Where is a new boot image stored when creating a boot image by using the Create Boot Image Using MDT Wizard?

    A. Deployment share folder

    B. Specified UNC path

    C. C:\Program Files (x86)\Microsoft Configuration Manager

    D. C:\Windows\Boot

4. After being created with MDT, how can a boot image be used with Configuration Manager?

    A. Add the boot image to a Windows Deployment Services server.

    B. Distribute the boot image to a distribution point.

    C. Associate the boot image with a task sequence.

    D. Create a custom task sequence that uses the boot image.

Answers

This section contains the solutions to the thought experiments and answers to the objective review questions in this chapter.

Objective 3.1

Thought experiment

1. You should specify an uninstall command. This is a good practice to help you maintain applications in your environment.
2. You should use driver categories. Driver categories enable you to find drivers easily. In addition, you can filter the output for a specific category to simplify driver updates.
3. You should use a build and capture template. When capturing a computer, you need to have a capture action.

Objective review

1. **Correct answer:** B

    A. **Incorrect:** Scratch space is not relevant to simplifying the troubleshooting process; it is used as extra space for Windows PE for items such as drivers.

    B. **Correct:** Command support should be enabled. It enables you to press F8 and display a command prompt for troubleshooting purposes.

    C. **Incorrect:** Importing the WDS module isn't relevant to troubleshooting issues that arise during deployment, especially when the infrastructure is using Configuration Manager and MDT.

    D. **Incorrect:** A prestart command that launches cmd.exe wouldn't be helpful because it would run for every deployment, even deployments that aren't having trouble.

2. **Correct answer:** A

    A. **Correct:** A prestart command is a good way to repartition and clean disks prior to deploying the operating system image. This is a common tactic to use when you are reimaging computers that have BitLocker-encrypted volumes.

    B. **Incorrect:** Command support enables you to open a command prompt from Windows PE, but it is not useful for automating repartitioning.

    C. **Incorrect:** Manually repartitioning the disks isn't an activity that scales well, and this answer doesn't meet the requirement to repartition automatically.

    D. **Incorrect:** An operating system install package is not relevant to cleaning the disk.

3. **Correct answer:** C

   A. **Incorrect:** Validating the content doesn't update the content, which is what is needed after updating source files.

   B. **Incorrect:** The content validation job only runs once a week. Updating the priority doesn't change the schedule, so you could still have to wait a week before the updated source files are used.

   C. **Correct:** Redistributing the content is the best way to ensure that the updated source files are used because the redistribution ensures that the distribution point has the latest files.

   D. **Incorrect:** The Add-Content Windows PowerShell command adds text to the end of a text file and is not relevant to this question.

Objective 3.2

Thought experiment

1. You should have a distribution point at each office. Because you have multiple images and need to image 10 computers per day while minimizing network disruptions, your solution should minimize the amount of data that has to travel over the MPLS network. By placing a distribution point in each office, you can meet the goals. Other factors are the number of clients at each office and the available bandwidth. In this case, there are enough clients to warrant a distribution server.

2. You should require a PXE password, use multicast encryption, set permissions on the operating system images, and configure your environment so that only prestaged computers can be imaged. Security is enhanced with a multilayered strategy, so it is a good practice to use as many of the security options as you can without affecting needed functionality.

3. One way to minimize administrative overhead is to automate manual tasks that are performed routinely. Another way is to delegate tasks. Don't force the entire IT team to come to you or your team for every action needed. For operating system deployments, strive for a ZTI, automate as many of the preinstallation tasks (such as prestaging computer accounts) and post-installation tasks (such as importing the user state data) as possible, and take advantage of small and incremental improvements such as using distribution point groups and boundary groups.

Objective review

1. **Correct answer:** A

   A. **Correct:** Boundary groups should be used to ensure that clients use the closest distribution point.

   B. **Incorrect:** Distribution point groups are used to group multiple distribution points, not to control which distribution points clients use.

C.   Incorrect: BranchCache reduces bandwidth use over the WAN but does not control which distribution points clients use.

D.   Incorrect: A management point is used for managing your environment and isn't related to controlling client connectivity to distribution points.

2.   **Correct answer:** C

   A.   Incorrect: The Set-CMDistributionPointGroup -Force command won't actually do anything without additional parameters. Furthermore, the command isn't relevant to the problem.

   B.   Incorrect: Redistributing all content won't help because you can't add the image when it is already there.

   C.   Correct: By removing the existing package, you can add it again. When content is already stored on a distribution point, it cannot be added again until removed.

   D.   Incorrect: Content validation can fix corruption for existing content, but that will not fix the problem.

3.   **Correct answers:** A, C, and D

   A.   Correct: To take advantage of BranchCache, it must be enabled and configured on all clients. You can use Group Policy to enable and configure clients.

   B.   Incorrect: BranchCache is not needed on the domain controllers for operating system deployments to take advantage of BranchCache.

   C.   Correct: BranchCache must be added to distribution points that take part in your deployments.

   D.   Correct: To take advantage of BranchCache, you need to enable it on the distribution points.

   E.   Incorrect: Although a BranchCache certificate is plausible, it isn't needed.

4.   **Correct answers:** A and D

   A.   Correct: There are two ways to ensure that you can image any computer. One is by enabling unknown computer support, and the other is by prestaging computers.

   B.   Incorrect: User device affinity isn't relevant to the imaging task but instead is part of associating a user with a computer after imaging.

   C.   Incorrect: The default permissions for operating system images are sufficient to image computers. Additional permissions would not help in this situation.

   D.   Correct: There are two ways to ensure that you can image any computer. One is by enabling unknown computer support, and the other is by prestaging computers.

Objective 3.3

Thought experiment

1. You should create a custom task sequence for France and one for the United States. This would enable you to meet the deployment requirements, which dictated different settings for each country/region.

2. You could customize a Windows PE boot image for each country/region so that each country/region used its own language. In addition, you could customize the support information for each country/region as well as perform other customizations.

3. You should use the Pre-provision BitLocker task sequence step in Windows PE and then follow that by using the Enable BitLocker task sequence after Windows 8.1 is deployed.

Objective review

1. **Correct answer:** A
   - **A.** **Correct:** You need the server name and site code to perform the integration.
   - **B.** **Incorrect:** You need the server name and site code, not the server name and user credentials, to perform the integration.
   - **C.** **Incorrect:** You need the server name and site code, not the site code and user credentials, to perform the integration.
   - **D.** **Incorrect:** You need the server name and site code, not just the user credentials, to perform the integration.

2. **Correct answer:** B
   - **A.** **Incorrect:** The default scratch space for computers with at least 1 GB of memory is 512 MB, not 256 MB.
   - **B.** **Correct:** The default scratch space for computers with at least 1 GB of memory is 512 MB.
   - **C.** **Incorrect:** The default scratch space for computers with at least 1 GB of memory is 512 MB, not 1 GB.
   - **D.** **Incorrect:** The default scratch space for computers with at least 1 GB of memory is 512 MB, not 2 GB. The maximum size is also 512 MB.

3. **Correct answer:** B
   - **A.** **Incorrect:** As with most of the Configuration Manager storage locations, a UNC path is used, and it is requested during the wizard.
   - **B.** **Correct:** The UNC path specified during the wizard is the path that is used.
   - **C.** **Incorrect:** The default installation path for ConfigMgr is not used for the image.
   - **D.** **Incorrect:** C:\Windows\Boot is not used for the image.

4. Correct answer: B

A. Incorrect: WDS is not relevant here.

B. Correct: A distribution point stores all images as well as other content.

C. Incorrect: Associating the boot image with a task sequence won't work because the boot image must be added to the distribution point before it can be used.

D. Incorrect: Creating a custom task sequence that uses the boot image won't work because the boot image must be added to the distribution point before it can be used.

CHAPTER 4

Create and maintain desktop images

After you deploy your deployment infrastructure, you will spend much of your time creating and maintaining images for your client computers. As the administrator, you must understand your imaging options and project requirements so that you can create images to meet or exceed the requirements. To maximize the effectiveness of your images, you need to spend time planning your image strategy before you begin capturing, deploying, and updating images.

Objectives in this chapter:

- Objective 4.1: Plan images
- Objective 4.2: Capture images
- Objective 4.3: Maintain images

Objective 4.1: Plan images

Previous chapters covered the operating system deployment (OSD) infrastructure, the types of deployment, and many of the technologies you use during a deployment project. In this objective, the focus is on the planning aspects of OSD. The most successful deployment projects combine qualified people, the necessary technologies, good execution, time, and money. However, what is sometimes overlooked is the planning. In addition to overall project management, you need technical planning long before you begin installing or configuring anything.

> **This objective covers how to:**
> - Consider design implications of thin, thick, and hybrid images
> - Consider design implications of WDS image types
> - Consider design implications of image format (VHD or WIM)
> - Consider design implications of number of images based on operating system or hardware platform, drivers, and operating features

Considering design implications of thin, thick, and hybrid images

Now that you have a good understanding of implementing an OSD infrastructure, Lite-Touch installment deployments (LTI), and Zero-Touch installment (ZTI) deployments, you can start planning for your desktop images. There are three primary types of images that you should consider: thin, thick, and hybrid. Your choice of image will be based on the OSD components and types of hardware and software you have and the deployment requirements that usually come from the project.

Thin images

Thin images are the smallest of the available images because they usually do not contain anything except the Windows operating system. If you decide to use thin images, try to minimize the add-ons to the image such as software and customizations. The smaller, the better. There are several characteristics about thin images that you should be familiar with:

- Thin images deploy over the network faster than thick images or hybrid images. There are a few common situations when minimizing the network usage is critical:
  - Deployments run on the production network, and you need to image regularly during business hours. In this case, starting several image deployments at one time could have an impact on the network, depending on how robust the network is.
  - Your network is outdated or running close to maximum capacity. If your network is already struggling to keep up with demand, adding image deployments to it will probably create serious congestion problems and degrade the user experience.
  - Your OSD infrastructure requires you to deploy images over a wide-area network (WAN). Although deploying operating system images over a WAN is something to try to avoid, sometimes this is unavoidable in the real world. By using thin images, you can minimize the overall degradation of the WAN for those times when you need to deploy images over it.
- Thin images require the most postdeployment work. After a thin image is deployed, you've really only installed the base operating system. For users to be productive, they need much more than that. They need applications. Often, they need many applications. They also need security software such as antivirus software and antimalware software. If you use thin images, consider the ramifications of postdeployment tasks. Your goal should be to automate the postdeployment tasks to reduce the administrative overhead of deployment.
- Thin images might be vulnerable immediately after deployment because they don't have any added software and might not have the security protection they need. Until the security software is installed, they can be vulnerable to attack. When using thin images, take this vulnerability into account and consider pushing the security software as the first task after deployment. Technically, as you begin adding software, you are moving your thin image to a hybrid image, which is discussed later in this objective.

- Thin images can take up less disk space, but don't jump to any conclusions with that phrase. Although it is true that the image file types take up less room on a disk, there really isn't much, if any, disk space savings. You still have to store all the applications on disks, so what you've done is separate your disk storage into two parts—one part contains the image, and the other part contains everything else, including the applications. So be wary of claims about thin images using less disk space.

Thick images

Thick images are the largest of the three kinds of images. Think of thick images as the opposite of thin images. Thin images are small. Thick images are large. You build a thick image to contain everything that is needed in an image: the base operating system, the applications, and all customizations. Look at the characteristics of thick images:

- Thick images take longer to deploy over the network. In addition, each deployment requires more bandwidth than a thin image or a hybrid image deployment.

- Thick images require little or no postdeployment work. Although having no postdeployment work is a good thing, there are some trade-offs. For example, thick images often contain applications that some users or departments don't use. Some licensed software might have to be purchased for users who never even use the software just because it is automatically installed with the thick image.

- Thick images require more predeployment work. Because thick images have more customizations and all the applications, the predeployment image-testing process takes longer.

- Thick images are usually too large to fit on media. If you plan to perform media deployments by booting to a DVD or similar media, thick images likely won't work due to the size of the thick image.

Hybrid images

As you are probably thinking, hybrid images can be described as somewhere between thin images and thick images. They aren't small. They aren't large. A hybrid image is very popular because it often meets deployment requirements without the complexity of thin images or the rigidity of thick images. Hybrid images have the following characteristics:

- Hybrid images typically contain the operating system, drivers, a few customizations, and the core applications that all employees use. For example, you would install antivirus software, antimalware software, and Microsoft Office 2013. You might also add other applications that the entire company relies on such as Microsoft Lync. For specialty applications such as engineering applications, you would not add them to your hybrid image. Instead, you would deliver those by using Microsoft Application Virtualization (App-V), Group Policy, or another application distribution system.

- Organizations that have used thick images but want to move to thin images can use a hybrid image as a stepping-stone. Sometimes, switching from thick images to thin images is too big a leap in a single project. Hybrid images enable you to get a feel for thinner images and ultimately enable you to figure out whether your organization can take advantage of a thin image.

- Hybrid images represent a balanced approach to imaging. For many IT administrators, hybrid images are also the most attainable image, often due to limitations in the OSD infrastructure or time constraints.

The Venn diagram shown in Figure 4-1 represents a visual picture of how the different image types relate to each other. On the left are thick images, which often have all your applications. On the right are thin images, which usually do not have any applications. In the middle, the hybrid image has characteristics of thick and thin images.

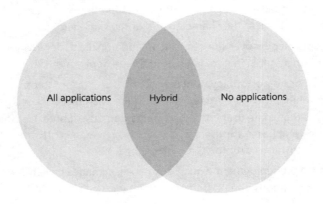

FIGURE 4-1 Venn diagram of image types

Now that you have a good idea of the characteristics of the image types, you can figure out which image is best suited for your environment. Although you should strive for a single image type and a single image, it isn't easily achieved. Exceptions, politics, outdated hardware, and other factors always play into your design, so don't be surprised if you end up with a few different images with each image being used for a particular use case. The diagram in Figure 4-2 shows a simple decision tree to help you quickly see the type of image that best suits your organization.

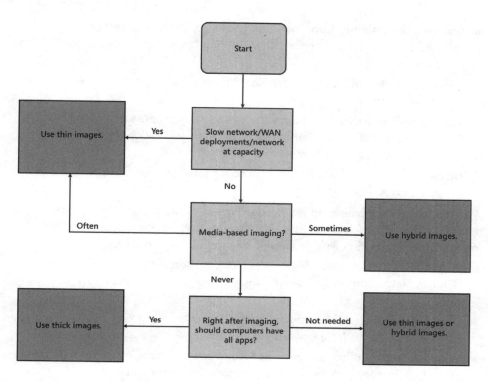

FIGURE 4-2 Image type flowchart

Considering design implications of WDS image types

Chapter 2, "Implement a Lite-Touch deployment," defined the four image types you can use in Windows Deployment Services (WDS): boot images, install images, capture images, and discover images. This section focuses more on the design implications and some of the factors that you need to consider before you move forward with a deployment project.

Design implications of boot images

When you think about boot images, it will often be about the operational aspects of boot images that were discussed in previous chapters: creating boot images and using boot images. Although there aren't many design implications specific to boot images, there are a few design questions to answer concerning boot images:

- How many boot images do you need? First, you must determine whether you intend to deploy x86-based computers and x64-based computers. If you do, you must determine whether either of them will require special drivers. If not, you can use a single boot image. If so, you might need more than one boot image.

- Do you need any custom boot images? A custom boot image is the boot.wim file from the Windows media plus one or more of the following:

- **Optional components** Optional components are included as part of the Windows Assessment and Deployment Kit (ADK). You can add the components by using the Dism.exe command.

- **Language packs** You can add specific language support to Windows PE by using the Dism.exe command.

- **Applications or scripts** You can add applications or scripts such as startup scripts to your Windows PE image. You can even have your applications launch as part of the Windows PE startup sequence.

- **Drivers** You can add drivers needed at boot-up such as mass storage drivers or network card drivers.

- Which optional components do you need to have in the boot images? There are a number of optional components that you can add based on your specific requirements. The following list contains a few of the most used components:

  - **WinPE-HTA** This component provides HTML support for WinPE. You can use HTML to build a custom application such as a deployment graphical user interface (GUI).

  - **WinPE-PowerShell** This component provides limited Windows PowerShell support inside of WinPE. Note that remote Windows PowerShell is not functional.

  - **WinPE-MDAC** This component is needed to establish connectivity to a database. This is helpful when building automation into your deployment process.

> *MORE INFO* **OPTIONAL COMPONENTS REFERENCE**
>
> To see a complete list of optional components and understand how to work with them in detail, see the Optional Components Reference page at *http://technet.microsoft.com /en-us/library/hh824926.aspx*.

Design implications of install images

Install images are the most complex image type. This topic focuses on the design implications of WDS install images and discusses related topics, such as the number of images you should have, in an upcoming section of this chapter. Design implications of install images are limited to the following areas:

- **Organizing your install images** If you manage a high-security environment or a large enterprise environment, you might have a large number of images. Often, you'll have images for multiple versions of a client operating system, images for multiple versions of a server-based operating system, and images for specific departments. Managing all those images is cumbersome. By using image groups in WDS, you can bring some organization to the images, as shown in Figure 4-3. Image groups organize your images and make it easy for you to grant permissions to multiple images at one time by applying permissions to the image group. In addition, image groups reduce storage usage because they use shared file resources across the image group, which gives you storage performance similar to Single Instance Store (SIS).

- **Securing your install images**   For this information, see the "Restricting who can receive images" section in Chapter 2. That section discusses prestaging computers, permissions, and other security enhancements.

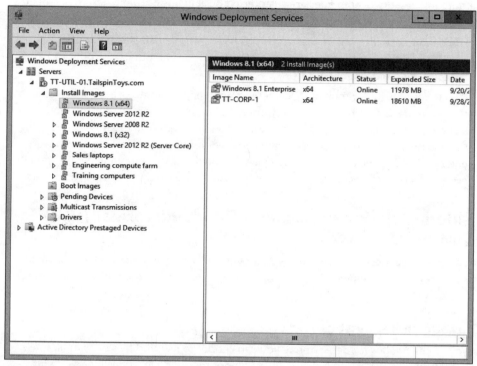

FIGURE 4-3 WDS console

Design implications of capture images

You don't need to think about too much when considering capture images. The concept is very straightforward. Even so, you should be familiar with a couple of factors:

- You must determine which capture images you need. If you plan to capture 32-bit computers, you need a 32-bit boot image and a 32-bit capture image. If you plan to capture 64-bit computers, you can use a 32-bit or a 64-bit boot image and a 32-bit or a 64-bit capture image. Often, you can even use just the 32-bit images unless each platform has unique requirements such as custom drivers. Thus, when designing your OSD solution, you should perform a discovery of the existing environment so that you can factor it into your design.

- You need to come up with a standard naming convention for your images. This especially applies to boot images and capture images. When you boot to PXE, you are presented with a list of all boot and capture images that are available to you. To avoid confusion, capture images need to be easily distinguishable from standard boot images so that you can select the correct image when you boot to PXE.

Design implications of discover images

Like capture images, discover images are customized boot images. From a design perspective, familiarize yourself with the following concepts:

- You need to use discover images when you have computers that can't boot to PXE. As part of your discovery process, find out whether all the computers can boot to PXE. If not, plan for discover images.
- If your design calls for multiple WDS servers, you might want to use a discover image to ensure that a specific WDS server is used. For example, imagine that you work for a company that has an engineering team and a sales team. You use a WDS server for the engineering team and a separate WDS server for the sales team. You can use an engineering-specific discover image when you deploy images to engineering comput-ers and a sales-specific discover image when you deploy images to sales computers.

Considering design implications of image format (VHD or WIM)

As part of your initial design, determine whether you will use .wim files, .vhd files, or both. This section discusses the characteristics of both image formats and the typical use cases for each one.

VHD image characteristics

When you create images for deployment, you can choose to use .vhd files or .wim files. Microsoft introduced the ability for computers to boot to a .vhd file with Windows 7 and Windows Server 2008 R2. Alongside that, WDS was updated to support using .vhd files for images. Although not in widespread use, there are some valid use cases and characteristics that you should be familiar with:

- Using .vhd images enables you to set up a computer easily for booting into different operating systems. You could have one .vhd image that runs Windows 8.1 and another that runs Windows Server 2012 R2. Without .vhd images, you would have to partition your hard drive for dual booting.
- Deploying a .vhd image to a computer involves just a single file: the .vhd file. This sim-plifies the deployment and backups.
- A .vhd file is portable. It can be used on multiple hardware platforms for testing or recoverability.
- In Windows Server 2012, a new virtual hard disk format was released. It uses .vhdx files, which are compatible with Windows 8, Windows 8.1, Windows Server 2012, and Windows Server 2012 R2.

WIM image characteristics

The Microsoft Windows Imaging (WIM) file format was introduced with Windows Vista. Since then, it has been used as the default image file format for Windows operating system media. A .wim file is also the default file format used when you capture an image in WDS. From a design consideration standpoint, the only consideration is whether your requirements can be met using .wim files. For most use cases, .wim files will meet all your needs. However, .vhd or .vhdx files might be worthy of consideration if you have specific requirements such as dual booting, portability, or reusing a single image on multiple physical computers.

Considering design implications of creating and maintaining multiple images based on operating system or hardware platform, drivers, and operating features

The number of images that will be used in an environment depends strongly on the environment. There will typically be a minimum of two images: one for 32-bit computers and one for 64-bit computers. Additional images might be necessary for additional support for applications. One primary use case for having multiple images is that you need at least one image for the operating system you are deploying. In many organizations, there are multiple versions of client computer and server-based operating systems. It is not uncommon to find organizations that still run some computers on Windows XP while they are migrating to Windows 8.1. On the server side, the move to the latest operating system is usually slower than on the client computing side. It is common to find organizations that have some servers running Windows Server 2003 R2, Windows Server 2008, Windows Server 2008 R2, Windows Server 2012, and Windows Server 2012 R2. On the server side, you might not need an installation image for every operating system, especially if only a couple of servers are running one of the operating systems.

EXAM TIP

The system architectures are critical in creating and deploying images. Remember that a 32-bit image can be deployed to a 64-bit computer. However, a 64-bit image cannot be deployed to a 32-bit computer.

Another consideration that could affect the number of images depends on whether Microsoft BitLocker will be used during the deployment. To use BitLocker during the deployment process, the computer hardware must have a Trusted Platform Module (TPM). A TPM is a hardware feature, and all your computers might not have it.

Depending on the image type you select, device drivers could affect the number of images that are needed too. Some drivers might interfere with each other and must be thoroughly tested together. When using thick images, drivers that can cause conflicts might need to be installed in separate images or on demand.

Furthermore, the use case of the deployment might require the use of a specific image strategy. As discussed earlier in this chapter, there are three image types: thick, thin, and hybrid. A smaller deployment environment might favor thick images, where the administrative time necessary to configure applications after the deployment would not be needed. In a large environment, however, thin images can speed up the deployment process. Users can then select or specify which applications they need to install for their workload. With that in mind, if a thick image is used in a large organization, you would need to install all applications in the image. The IT department would receive the applications that the Sales department uses, and Sales department users would receive the IT applications. This might not be desirable, especially with certain application licensing models that require a license for each installed computer. However, when using a hybrid image, you can install the core applications that all users need, and the individual department applications can be installed after the operating system deployment. This also avoids conflicts that can arise if two applications are not compatible on the same computer.

As a good practice, try to minimize the total number of images. The more images are in use, the more maintenance and upkeep is required. This also increases the margin for an administrative error maintaining the images. However, a downside of using a single image for each architecture type is that if a problem arises in the image, it could affect all computers in the environment. For example, if a driver update is corrupt, or incompatible with other drivers, not only does it affect the current deployment, it would affect any refresh that would be needed. Therefore, another recommendation is to keep previous versions of image files. This is especially true if a new image file is created for a new hardware platform.

> **MORE INFO**   **CHOOSING A DEPLOYMENT STRATEGY**
>
> For more information about choosing a deployment strategy, see the article at *http://technet.microsoft.com/en-us/library/dd919185%28v=ws.10%29.aspx.*

Thought experiment

Windows 8.1 deployment at Tailspin Toys

Tailspin Toys has one office. The company has approximately 800 client computers, half of which are portable computers. The company has a large development group that develops applications for toy stores. The group uses 11 development tools, and all the developers have multiple computers to support their development efforts.

The company plans to upgrade all client computers to Windows 8.1. In addition, the company is planning to reduce the total number of computers by limiting each employee to a single computer. You plan to use the existing Configuration Manager, WDS, and Microsoft Deployment Toolkit (MDT) technologies to assist the company in meeting the requirements. To help you assess your knowledge, answer the following questions:

1. Should you try to use a single install image across the company?

2. To allow the developers to test their applications across multiple operating systems on a single computer, what should you do?

3. Should the development computers be imaged with a thin, thick, or hybrid image?

Objective summary

- A thin image is the smallest image type. It often doesn't contain anything except the operating system.

- A thick image is the largest image type. It often contains all the applications in an environment. It takes longer to deploy over the network but often requires less post-deployment work than other image types.

- A hybrid image is a cross between a thin image and a thick image. It often contains the operating system and a core set of applications such as Microsoft Office and security software.

- You can use a single 32-bit boot image for 32-bit and 64-bit computers. However, a 64-bit boot image is only valid for 64-bit computers.

- You can use WDS image groups to organize your install images. By doing so, you can reduce your image storage space requirements while organizing images based on platform, operating system, or security requirements.

- You can use the .vhd format or the .wim format for your install images. The .wim format is the most widely used and the default image file format.

- A number of considerations factor into your image strategy. Using 32-bit and 64-bit computers, BitLocker, and multiple versions of an operating system can increase the total number of images you need to create, maintain, and deploy.

Objective review

Answer the following questions to test your knowledge of the information in this objective. You can find the answers to these questions and explanations of why each answer choice is correct or incorrect in the "Answers" section at the end of this chapter.

1. You are planning an image strategy for client computers. You must ensure that users have basic operating system functionality immediately following the imaging process. You also need to minimize the image file size. What should you do? (Choose two. Each correct answer represents part of a complete solution.)

   A. Use a thin image.

   B. Use a thick image.

   C. Use a hybrid image.

   D. Use a VHD-based thin image.

2. You are planning to deploy 100 training computers that run Windows 8.1. A default installation of Windows 8.1 must be deployed to them. What should you do in WDS?

   A. Use the install.wim file from the Windows 8.1 media as an install image.

   B. Use the boot.wim file from the Windows 8.1 media as an install image.

   C. Use the install.wim file from the Windows 8.1 media as a boot image.

   D. Use the boot.wim file from the Windows 8.1 media as a boot image.

3. You are planning a new deployment project with Configuration Manager. The project calls for a deployment of Windows 8.1 (32-bit) and Windows Server 2012 R2. You have portable computers and desktop computers for Windows 8.1 and a single server model for Windows Server 2012 R2. You need to minimize the total number of install images. How many install images should you use?

   A. 1

   B. 2

   C. 3

   D. 4

4. You are planning a new deployment project with Configuration Manager. The project calls for a deployment of Windows 8.1 (64-bit). You must also deploy a licensed application to about half of the employees. You must ensure that licensing costs are minimized, and you want to minimize the total number of images. What should you do? (Choose two. Each answer represents a complete solution.)

   A. Use a thick image and package the application for postdeployment.

   B. Use a thin image and package the application for postdeployment.

   C. Use a hybrid image and package the application for postdeployment.

   D. Use a thick image and create a filter for the employees who need the licensed application.

5. You are planning a new deployment project with WDS. The project calls for a deployment of Windows 8.1 and Windows Server 2012 R2. You must perform the following deployment tasks as part of the project:

- Deploy Windows Server 2012 R2 based on the installation media.

- Customize Windows 8.1, which is currently installed on a reference computer, and then create an install image from the reference computer.

- Deploy Windows 8.1 to some kiosk computers that are not capable of booting to PXE.

Which of the following WDS image types will you need on your WDS server? (Choose all that apply.)

A. Boot

B. Capture

C. Discover

D. Install

Objective 4.2: Create images

You can create images by using WDS, MDT, or Configuration Manager. The method you use to capture an image is a preference that often depends on the tools you have available.

> **This objective covers how to:**
> - Prepare the operating system for capture
> - Create capture images by using WDS
> - Capture an image to an existing or new WIM file
> - Capture an operating system image by using Configuration Manager

Preparing the operating system for capture

Chapter 2 discussed some preparation for capturing an image in WDS. This section expands on that information by adding Configuration Manager to the mix. In Configuration Manager, there are two primary methods of preparing an operating system for capture:

- Automated configuration
- Manual configuration

An automated configuration provides the ability to configure a reference operating system without any manual steps by an administrator. When using an automated configuration method, you create task sequences that deploy software applications, drivers, packages, and any other aspect that must be part of the image. These task sequences can then be reused and customized to create additional images, without the need to re-create a task sequence or configure a new reference computer. However, automated configurations can initially take a long time to create and test. Changes in the requirements for an image can also increase the administrative effort and time required to re-create or reconfigure the task sequences for a new image. Another method of automated configuration could use answer files.

> **MORE INFO** **USING ANSWER FILES**
>
> For more information about using answer files, see the "Create and manage answer files" section in Chapter 2.

A manual configuration does not require the additional time to create or test task sequences and enables administrators to set up one computer as a reference computer, just as they would for a user in the organization. This is a faster method of initially creating the first reference computer, but it's a more error-prone approach because of the manual configuration process. In a manual configuration, an administrator configures settings and installs applications manually. Configuring a reference computer manually requires verification and testing, so not much time is saved over an automated configuration. One major drawback to the manual configuration is that you have to configure settings and install applications on each reference computer. If you have many reference computers, the manual configuration option will cost you extra time.

After you choose a configuration method and perform the desired configuration, prepare the reference computer for capture by using the System Preparation Tool (Sysprep). Chapter 2 discussed the different configuration passes of an answer file that Sysprep uses. The passes of an answer file are:

- windowsPE
- offlineServicing
- generalize
- specialize
- auditSystem
- auditUser
- oobeSystem

The generalize pass is specifically used to prepare a computer to be captured as a reference image. As the name implies, the generalize pass of the answer file, and of Sysprep, removes machine-specific information from an operating system, such as the security identifier and some drivers, and enables the image to be used on different computers.

To generalize a computer, Sysprep must be run. Sysprep has both a command line and graphical user interface (GUI). (The command-line interface [CLI] method was discussed in Chapter 2.) To use the GUI, run Sysprep.exe. In Windows Server 2012 R2, sysprep.exe is in the %SYSTEMDRIVE%\Windows\System32\Sysprep folder. To use Sysprep on a different computer, copy the Sysprep folder contents to the desired computer.

After running Sysprep.exe, the System Preparation Tool 3.14 window appears, as shown in Figure 4-4.

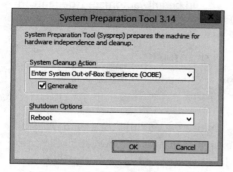

FIGURE 4-4 System Preparation Tool 3.14

Figure 4-4 shows Sysprep configured to enter the System Out-Of-Box Experience (OOBE), generalize the system, and then reboot. Alternatively, Sysprep can also be configured in audit mode or to shut down the computer instead of restarting, as shown in Figure 4-5.

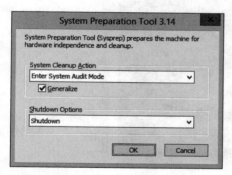

FIGURE 4-5 System Preparation Tool 3.14

After the Sysprep process has completed, the reference computer is ready to be captured by using the desired method.

> **MORE INFO** **SYSPREP (SYSTEM PREPARATION) OVERVIEW**
>
> For more information about Sysprep, see the article at *http://technet.microsoft.com/en-us /library/hh825209.aspx*.

Creating capture images by using WDS

Chapter 2 discussed capture images and how to add them to a WDS server by using the GUI. After a capture image has been added to the server, reference computers can boot that image, and then a capture of the reference computer can begin. If the reference computer has been through Sysprep with the generalize pass, any computer that is deployed with the captured image will have an identical operating system configuration but will still perform Windows Setup each time. The Windows Setup process could be fully automated, depending on the deployment method.

MORE INFO **CREATE AN INSTALL, CAPTURE, OR DISCOVER IMAGE**

For more information about creating a capture image, see the article at *http://technet .microsoft.com/en-us/library/cc730837%28v=ws.10%29.aspx.*

An alternate method of creating a capture image is to use the WDSutil command. WDSutil is a utility you can use to manage a WDS server. For example, to create a new capture image, run the following command, as shown in Figure 4-6, from an elevated command prompt:

```
WDSUtil /new-captureimage /image:"Boot" /architecture:x64 /destinationimage
/filepath:E:\Shares\Capture.wim /Name:"New Capture Image"
```

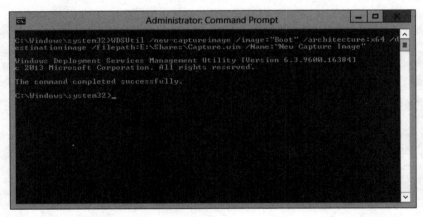

FIGURE 4-6 WDSutil example

In the WDSutil command and in Figure 4-6, "Boot" is the name of the existing boot image from which the capture image is being created. The architecture is set to 64-bit (x64), and the destination file path of the new capture image is E:\Shares\Capture.wim. The name of the new image is "New Capture Image." The WDSutil utility requires all the parameters in the example.

Capturing an image to an existing or new WIM file

Before you capture an image from a reference computer, make sure that Dynamic Host Configuration Protocol (DHCP) is already running, PXE is running, and a valid boot and capture image is available in WDS.

To capture an image to WDS, perform the following high-level steps:

1. Prepare a computer with an operating system, applications, and customizations. This computer will be known as the reference computer.

2. Use Sysprep to generalize the operating system of the reference computer by running the Sysprep /generalize /oobe command, as shown in Figure 4-7.

   This step is required to capture the image with a WDS capture image. After the command completes, the computer will automatically shut down. If desired, you can use the /reboot switch in the command to reboot automatically after completion.

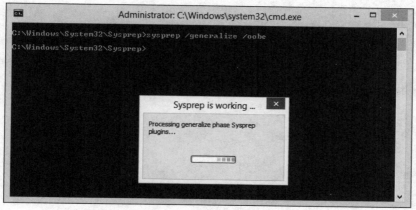

FIGURE 4-7 Sysprep command running

3. Start the reference computer and press F12 while the computer is starting up. Pressing F12 during startup is required with a default installation of WDS, but you can update the settings so that it isn't required. By pressing F12 during the startup, the computer boots to PXE. You can configure the computer's boot order to use the network first, and then you can press Enter to boot to PXE, as shown in Figure 4-8.

FIGURE 4-8 Initial network boot of a VM

4. When you boot to PXE, you are presented with a list of operating systems. The list comes from the available images in WDS. Select the capture image, as shown in Figure 4-9, and then press Enter.

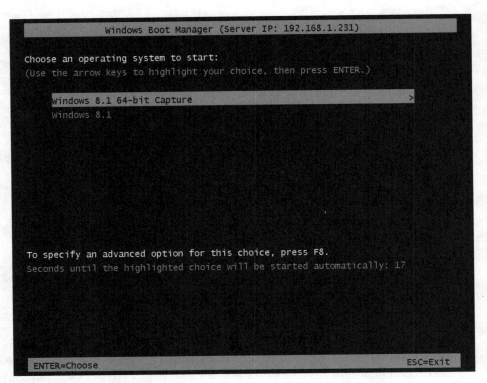

FIGURE 4-9 Windows Boot Manager

5. After booting to a capture image, the WDS Image Capture Wizard launches to begin
    the capture process, as shown in Figure 4-10. Click Next to continue.

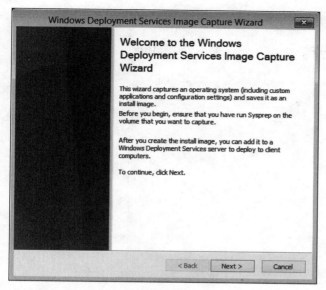

FIGURE 4-10 WDS Image Capture Wizard

6. On the Directory To Capture page, select the volume you want to capture in the drop-down menu, as shown in Figure 4-11. Enter a name and a description before clicking Next. In some cases, you might not see a volume to capture. The most common reason for not seeing it is that the Sysprep /generalize command was not run on it. You can troubleshoot the issue to find out the problem. From the Directory To Capture page, press Shift+F10 to open a Windows PE command prompt. From there, you can check whether the volume you want to capture is available. To do that, run the diskpart command. From the DISKPART prompt, run the list vol command to view the available volumes. In some cases, a storage driver might be needed.

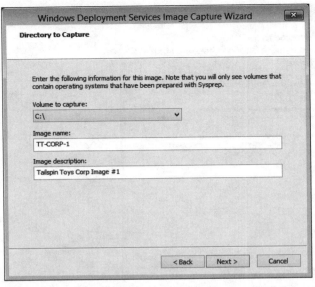

FIGURE 4-11 WDS Image Capture Wizard, selecting the directory to capture

7. On the New Image Location page, select the location to store the image. This can be your local hard drive if it has enough room. It can also be a portable hard drive or a shared folder on the network. To automate the upload of the captured image to WDS, select Upload Image To A Windows Deployment Services Server (Optional). Type the WDS server name, click Connect, and then select the desired image group name. A completed New Image Location page is shown in Figure 4-12. Click Next to continue.

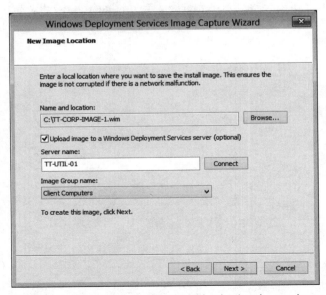

FIGURE 4-12 WDS Image Capture Wizard, selecting the new image location

The capture process can take a long time, depending on the reference computer's performance and network characteristics such as the latency and bandwidth. During the process, the capture task progress bar appears. When it's complete, you see a message notifying you that the image was created successfully, as shown in Figure 4-13. Click Finish to complete the process.

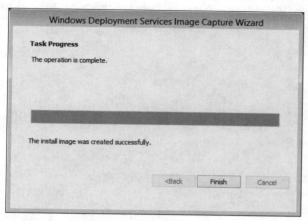

FIGURE 4-13 WDS Image Capture Wizard, finishing the process

After the operation completes, check the Install Images folder in WDS to ensure that the image appears, as shown in Figure 4-14.

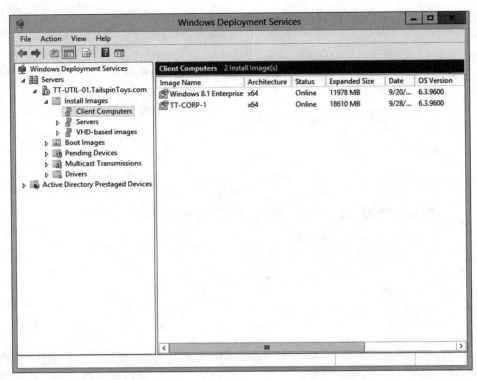

FIGURE 4-14 WDS console

Capturing an operating system image by using Configuration Manager

If your environment has System Center Configuration Manager, you can also use it to capture reference computers. Configuration Manager uses task sequences to capture images. To build a computer and then capture it in Configuration Manager, perform the following steps.

1. Create a new task sequence from the Operating System folder of the software library. For this example, the Build And Capture A Reference Operating System Image template is used, as shown in Figure 4-15. This performs an automated build of the reference computer with a few applications and then captures it. After selecting the Build And Capture A Reference Operating System Image template, click Next.

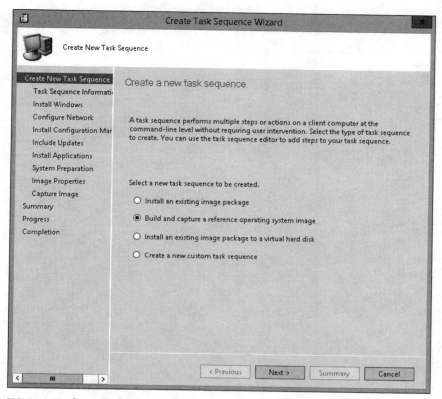

FIGURE 4-15 Create Task Sequence Wizard, Create New Task Sequence page

2. On the Task Sequence Information page, shown in Figure 4-16, type a name for the task sequence, such as CaptureSequence. Specify the boot image that will be used as part of the sequence. The boot image must already exist in Configuration Manager for it to appear in the wizard. Click Next.

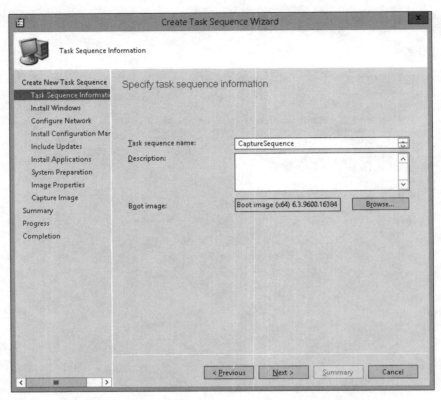

FIGURE 4-16 Create Task Sequence Wizard, Task Sequence Information page

3. On the Install Windows page, shown in Figure 4-17, choose the install image to use. You can use a custom image that has already been configured or the base install image that can be customized further in the task sequence. The image file must already exist in Configuration Manager for it to appear in the list. Specify any other desired information and then click Next.

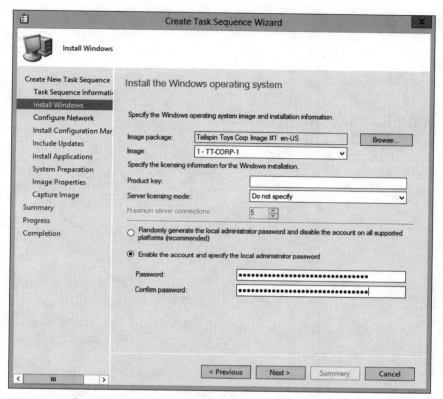

FIGURE 4-17 Create Task Sequence Wizard, Install Windows page

4. Specify the workgroup or domain to join, as shown in Figure 4-18. If you specify a domain, you must also specify the organizational unit (OU) and domain account to use.

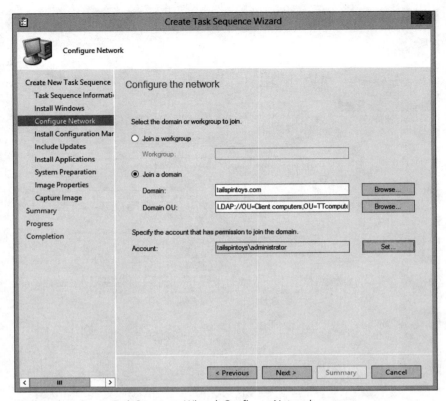

FIGURE 4-18 Create Task Sequence Wizard, Configure Network page

5. Select the default package to install the Configuration Manager client on the target computer and image, as shown in Figure 4-19. By default, the Configuration Manager Client Package is selected. You can select another package that has been added in ConfigMgr instead.

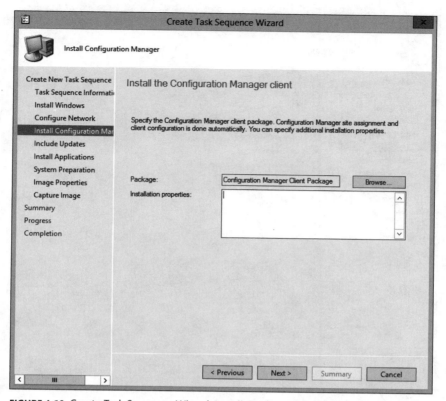

FIGURE 4-19 Create Task Sequence Wizard, Install Configuration Manager page

6. Choose which action to take for updates that have been assigned to the computer, as shown in Figure 4-20. The available options are:

- Install Mandatory Software Updates.

- Install All Software Updates.

- Do Not Install Any Software Updates.

Select the desired action and then click Next.

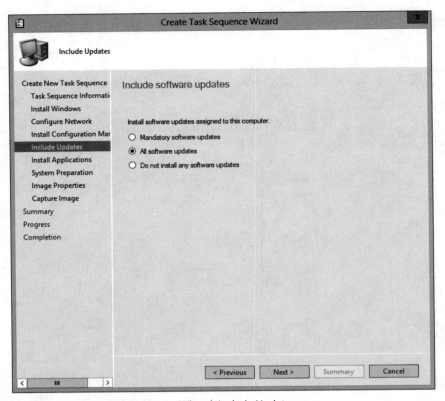

FIGURE 4-20 Create Task Sequence Wizard, Include Updates page

7. By using a task sequence, you can also install software that has been added in Configuration Manager, as shown in Figure 4-21. Adding software by using the task sequence can increase the time to configure the reference computer initially. However, by doing so, you can save much time later, when an upgrade or modification is necessary. Add the desired software and then click Next.

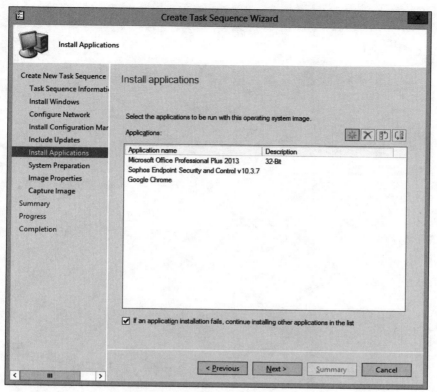

FIGURE 4-21 Create Task Sequence Wizard, Install Applications page

8. The System Preparation page appears, as shown in Figure 4-22. System preparation is not necessary for this example, so click Next to continue.

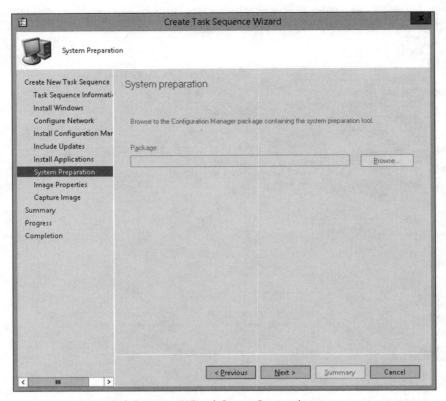

FIGURE 4-22 Create Task Sequence Wizard, System Preparation page

EXAM TIP

System preparation is only necessary when deploying operating systems prior to Windows Vista. Beginning with Windows Vista, the necessary version of Sysprep is included with the operating system files. Therefore, this screen is used only when deploying Windows XP or Windows Server 2003.

9. The Image Properties page, shown in Figure 4-23, contains metadata for use and reference by the administrator who is managing the images. Define the desired values for the Created By, Version, and Description fields and then click Next.

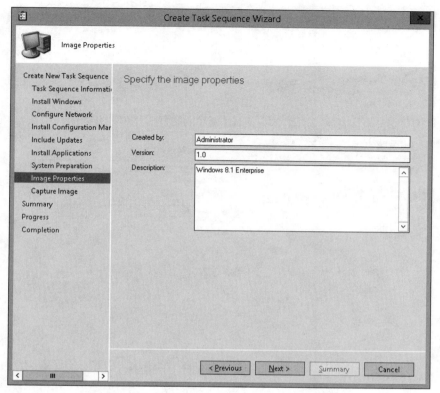

FIGURE 4-23 Create Task Sequence Wizard, Image Properties page

10. On the Capture Image page, shown in Figure 4-24, specify the path to save the image and the user account to use for access to the path.

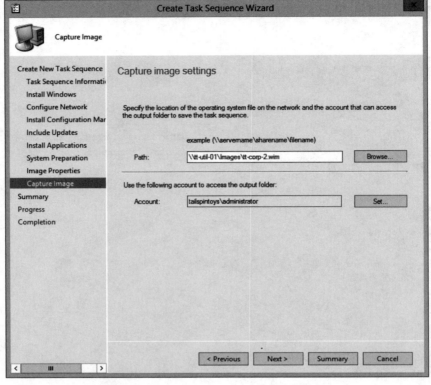

FIGURE 4-24 Create Task Sequence Wizard, Capture Image page

11. The Summary page displays all the configured settings, as shown in Figure 4-25. If all the settings look correct, click Next to create the task sequence.

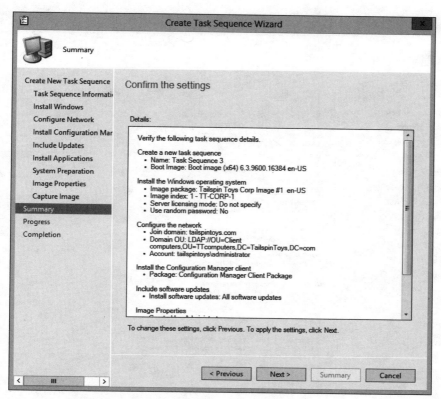

FIGURE 4-25 Create Task Sequence Wizard, Summary page

After you click Next, the task sequence will be created, as shown in Figure 4-26. It will then be available to run on target computers to install the defined image, customize any settings, and capture it.

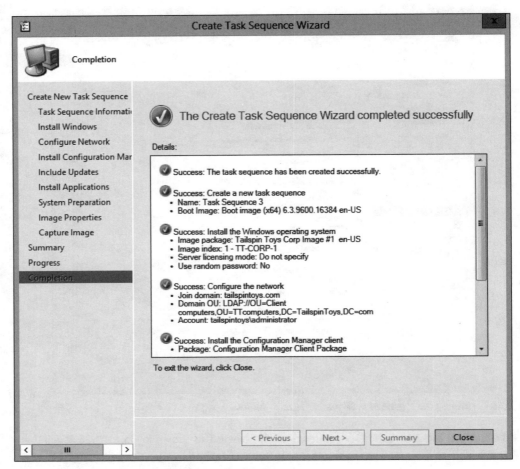

FIGURE 4-26 Create Task Sequence Wizard, Completion page

After the task sequence has been created, it can be deployed to collections.

MICROSOFT VIRTUAL ACADEMY **SYSTEM CENTER CONFIGURATION MANAGER**

The Microsoft Virtual Academy offers free training, which is delivered by industry experts. For this exam, System Center Configuration Manager plays a big role. If you haven't had a chance to use it, take a look at the overview of the System Center 2012 Configuration Manager course on Microsoft Virtual Academy. It covers a number of relevant features for the exam and lasts a little bit longer than an hour. It is available at *http://www.microsoft virtualacademy.com/training-courses/overview-and-infrastructure-changes-in-sccm-2012.*

Thought experiment

Windows build and capture project at Tailspin Toys

You are a client systems engineer for Tailspin Toys. The company uses Configuration Manager and WDS to automate its client computer deployments. You are working on a new deployment project that has the following requirements:

- Deploy a new reference computer with several applications and then capture the reference computer to an install image.

- Automate as many of the tasks as possible.

To help you assess your knowledge, answer the following questions:

1. Should you use Configuration Manager or WDS to deploy the new reference computer? Why?

2. You are about to capture a reference computer, but you run into an error. How can you troubleshoot from Windows PE?

3. Upon booting to PXE, you see several images. Only one of them is listed as a capture image. How do you explain this?

Objective summary

- A reference computer can be prepared manually or automated. An automated build often includes applications and other customizations that you would perform manually in a manual preparation scenario.

- Manually configuring reference computers can be error prone and isn't scalable.

- Automated configurations can take a long time to develop initially but are customizable and upgradable.

- Sysprep can be used from the command line or the GUI to prepare a reference computer. The command line is the most common usage.

- Generalizing a reference computer enables the image to be deployed to other computers. If you don't generalize a reference computer, most of the deployment tools will not capture the computer.

- WDS capture images are used to create an install image from a reference computer.

- ConfigMgr task sequences can be used to deploy an image and capture an image. You can do the tasks separately or as part of one task sequence.

Objective review

Answer the following questions to test your knowledge of the information in this objective. You can find the answers to these questions and explanations of why each answer choice is correct or incorrect in the "Answers" section at the end of this chapter.

1. Which operating system component is removed during the generalize pass of Sysprep?

   A. Default user profile

   B. Security identifier

   C. User applications

   D. Application metadata

2. You want to ensure that Office 2013 is part of a new build and capture task sequence. What should you do before creating the task sequence?

   A. Add Office 2013 to the boot image in the task sequence.

   B. Create a new package for Office 2013.

   C. Create a new application for Office 2013.

   D. Create a Windows Sideloading key.

3. Which of the following must you preconfigure in ConfigMgr to create a task sequence for deployment? (Choose two. Each correct answer provides part of a complete solution.)

   A. Windows install image

   B. Windows capture image

   C. Windows boot image

   D. Windows VHD-based capture image

4. Which operating system began bundling system preparation files with the operating system?

   A. Windows XP

   B. Windows Server 2003

   C. Windows Vista

   D. Windows 7

5. When using ConfigMgr, where is the captured image stored?

   A. Network path

   B. Local path

   C. ConfigMgr repository

   D. WDS repository

Objective 4.3: Maintain images

Managing a successful deployment architecture over an extended period of time requires regular maintenance to ensure its effectiveness. The first image you put into production will be relative at that moment, but over time things need to be added, removed, and updated. So far, this book has reviewed technologies such as WDS, MDT, and Configuration Manager.

These applications provide ways of simplifying regular maintenance tasks. Objective 4.3 explores the Deployment Image Servicing and Management (DISM) tool.

> **This objective covers how to:**
> - Update images by using DISM
> - Apply updates, drivers, settings, and files to online and offline images
> - Apply service packs to images
> - Manage embedded applications

Updating images by using DISM

DISM is a command-line tool that was designed to service Windows images. You can use this tool to manage Windows Imaging files (.wim) or virtual hard disks (.vhd or .vhdx). DISM provides management capabilities for both online and offline images. There are two methods for servicing an image by using DISM.

- **Servicing online images**   This task involves the manipulation of a running operating system by using the DISM tool. Some available actions include:
  - Adding language packs
  - Enabling or disabling Windows features
  - Retrieving installed drivers and packages
- **Servicing offline images**   This task involves the manipulation of a Windows image file or virtual hard disk. In most scenarios, offline servicing involves mounting the image by using DISM. From there, you manipulate the image and commit your changes. Some available actions include:
  - Adding and removing drivers
  - Adding and removing Windows features
  - Adding and removing language packs
  - Applying Windows updates
  - Applying configuration settings by using unattend.xml

The DISM tool provides a number of benefits:

- DISM is compatible with Windows 7, Windows 8, and Windows 8.1. Previous tools, such as ImageX, were deprecated with the introduction of Windows 8.
- DISM comes preinstalled with Windows 8.1 and Windows Server 2012 R2. This makes it easily accessible.
- DISM is a command-line tool. This gives you the flexibility to automate simple maintenance tasks such as applying Windows updates.

Before using DISM, you must meet a few prerequisites. First, become familiar with the list of compatible operating systems. The DISM tool is supported across the following operating systems:

- Windows PE 3.0, Windows PE 4.0, and Windows PE 5.0
- Windows 7, Windows 8, and Windows 8.1
- Windows Server 2008 SP2 and Windows Server 2008 R2
- Windows Server 2012 and Windows Server 2012 R2

You need a reliable build environment for creating and managing your images by using DISM. This should include the reference computer that you plan to use for capturing images and a stable administrative system for servicing your images. DISM has been around since Windows Vista and now comes preinstalled with Windows 8 and Windows 8.1, but the latest release is also available through the Windows Assessment and Deployment Kit (Windows ADK). Keep in mind that older versions of the DISM tool are not compatible with newer Windows versions. For example, the version of DISM that was released to service Windows 7 images will not work with Windows 8 images. Alternatively, you can download and install the Windows ADK, which includes the latest DISM binary and associated files.

You must also know how to run DISM. This command-line tool requires elevated privileges to run commands successfully, so start by opening an elevated command prompt. Running the tool is as simple as running Dism.exe */option*. Many of the DISM tasks can be performed with Windows PowerShell. These can be run using an elevated Windows PowerShell prompt.

In the following example, you take the install.wim file from the Sources folder of the Windows 8.1 installation media and retrieve the image file details, as shown in Figure 4-27.

From an elevated command prompt, run the following command:

```
Dism.exe /Get-ImageInfo /ImageFile:C:\test\images\install.wim
```

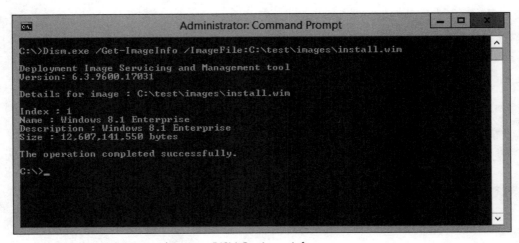

FIGURE 4-27 Elevated command prompt, DISM Get-ImageInfo

The output of this command provides the following details:

- **DISM version**   The version number for the DISM tool. If you need to work with an older operating system, you might need to reference this version number to know whether the operating system and DISM are compatible.

- **Index number**   The index number for the corresponding Windows image. DISM enables you to embed multiple images in a single file.

- **Name**   The name associated with the Windows image.

- **Description**   The description that was given to the image.

- **Size**   The actual file size of the Windows image in an uncompressed state.

From an elevated Windows PowerShell prompt, you can get the same results using the Get-WindowsImage -ImagePath C:\test\images\install.wim command, as shown in Figure 4-28.

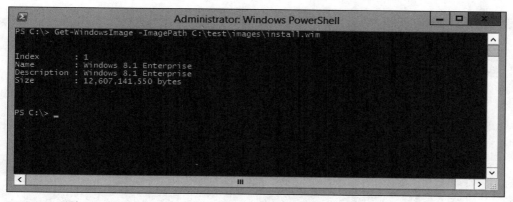

FIGURE 4-28   Elevated Windows PowerShell prompt showing image info

MORE INFO   **WHAT IS DISM?**

For more information about the basics of DISM and compatibility, see *http://technet .microsoft.com/en-us/library/hh825236.aspx*.

Applying updates, drivers, settings, and files to online and offline images

Previous chapters covered the various methods for capturing a reference image. This objective focuses on servicing existing Windows images. The actions taken to service an image do not depend on how or when the image was created. DISM can be used with any supported .wim, .vhd, or .vhdx file.

Applying updates

Applying the latest Windows updates to an image is a relatively easy action. There are numerous ways to achieve the result, some easier than others. DISM handles the update task in four fundamental steps. As you progress through this objective, notice that these steps share a common framework for handling the majority of the servicing needs. The steps include:

- Mounting the image
- Applying the desired Windows updates
- Committing the changes
- Unmounting the image

Before proceeding, become familiar with the following prerequisites:

- The Windows image file (.wim) must be saved to a local directory.
- You need an empty folder with enough free space to mount the image.
- You need a folder with the software updates that need to be applied.

In the following example, a series of updates is applied to an offline Windows 8.1 image, using the steps previously outlined. Before making any changes, first retrieve a list of the installed packages.

1. From an elevated command prompt, run the following command to mount the Windows image file, as shown in Figure 4-29:

```
Dism.exe /Mount-Image /ImageFile:C:\test\images\install.wim /Index:1
/MountDir:C:\test\offline
```

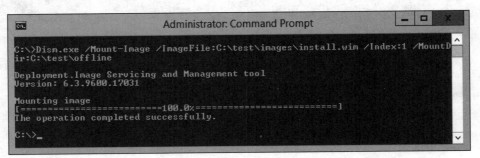

FIGURE 4-29 Elevated command prompt, DISM Mount-Image command

The same action can be accomplished through Windows PowerShell by using the Mount-WindowsImage cmdlet:

```
Mount-WindowsImage –ImagePath C:\test\images\install.wim –Index 1 –Path C:\test
\offline
```

2. Run the following command to see all the packages currently installed in the image.

   The list will be in chronological order, starting with the oldest package first, as shown in Figure 4-30. The applied update is at the bottom of the list.

```
Dism.exe /Image:C:\test\offline /Get-Packages /Format:Table
```

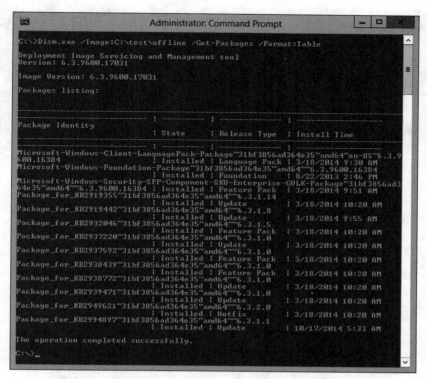

FIGURE 4-30 Elevated command prompt, DISM Get-Packages command

The same action can be accomplished through Windows PowerShell, using the Get-WindowsPackage cmdlet:

```
Get-WindowsPackage -Path C:\test\offline
```

Both of these commands can also be used with online images to review current package inventory.

The preceding output indicates which updates have already been applied and the associated time stamp. Now you apply the update.

3. Run the following command to apply the desired Windows update, as shown in Figure 4-31:

```
Dism.exe /image:C:\test\offline /Add-Package /PackagePath:C:\test\updates
\Windows8.1-KB2994897-x64.msu
```

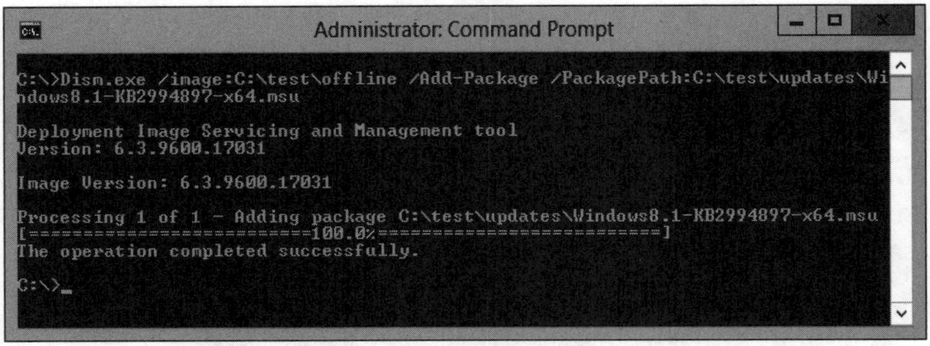

FIGURE 4-31 Elevated command prompt, DISM Add Package command

The same action can be accomplished by using the Add-WindowsPackage cmdlet in Windows PowerShell:

```
Add-WindowsPackage –Path C:\test\offline –PackagePath C:\test\updates
\Windows8.1-KB2994897-x64.msu
```

4. Run the following command to commit the changes to the image, as shown in Figure 4-32:

```
Dism.exe /Commit-Image /MountDir:C:\test\offline
```

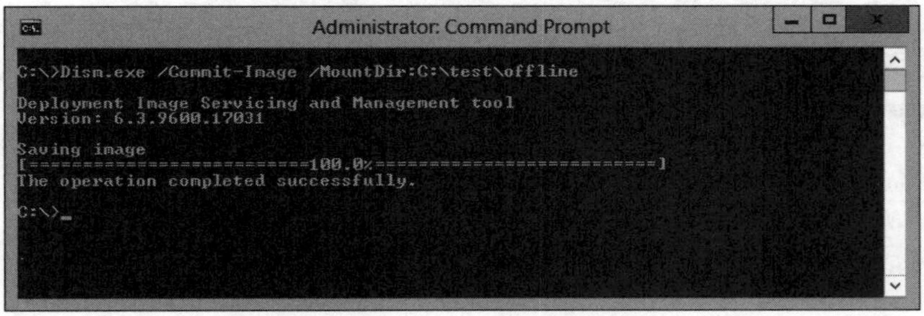

FIGURE 4-32 Elevated command prompt, DISM Commit-Image command

The same action can be accomplished by using the Save-WindowsImage cmdlet in Windows PowerShell:

```
Save-WindowsImage –Path C:\test\offline
```

5. Run the Get-Packages command again (as in Step 2) to confirm that the installed update is listed in the table with a matching time stamp.

6. Run the following command to dismount the updated image, as shown in Figure 4-33. Note that /Unmount-Image requires you to include the commit action or discard any changes that weren't previously committed.

```
Dism.exe /Unmount-Image /MountDir:C:\test\offline /Commit
```

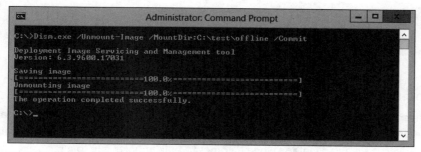

FIGURE 4-33 Elevated command prompt, DISM Unmount-Image command

7. The same action can be accomplished through Windows PowerShell by using the Dismount-WindowsImage cmdlet:

```
Dismount-WindowsImage –Path C:\test\offline –Save
```

The preceding steps outlined the procedure for applying a single update or, possibly, a handful of updates if you don't mind rerunning the same command a few times. For bulk changes, you should create a Windows PowerShell script to automate repetitive steps.

> **MORE INFO   APPLYING WINDOWS UPDATES BY USING A WINDOWS POWERSHELL SCRIPT**
>
> For more information about applying Windows updates in bulk, along with a sample script, see *http://blogs.technet.com/b/configmgrdogs/archive/2012/02/15/applying-windows-updates-to-a-base-wim-using-dism-and-powershell.aspx*.

You can remove packages from images by using Remove-Package DISM, as shown in Figure 4-34. Alternatively, you can use the Remove-WindowsPackage Windows PowerShell cmdlet.

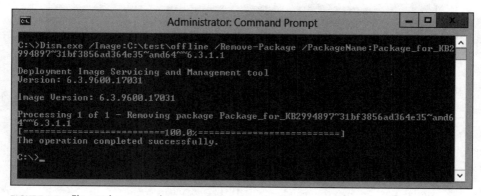

FIGURE 4-34 Elevated command prompt, DISM /Remove-Package command

Applying drivers

Device drivers are another fundamental piece when managing images. The process for applying device drivers uses the same framework as described when applying Windows updates. However, drivers gain an advantage when it comes to bulk imports due to a recursive switch.

The prerequisites for this procedure are that:

- The Windows image file (.wim) must be saved to a local directory.
- An empty directory must be available to mount the image.
- You need a folder with the device drivers that need to be applied.
- An adequate amount of free disk space must be available on the system that you will be mounting the image on.

In the following example, you add a series of network drivers to the same offline image. Before making any changes, first retrieve a list of the installed drivers.

1. From an elevated command prompt, mount the Windows image file:

```
Dism.exe /Mount-Image /ImageFile:C:\test\images\install.wim /Index:1
/MountDir:C:\test\offline
```

2. Run the following command to retrieve a list of currently installed device drivers, as shown in Figure 4-35:

```
Dism.exe /Image:C:\test\offline /Get-Drivers
```

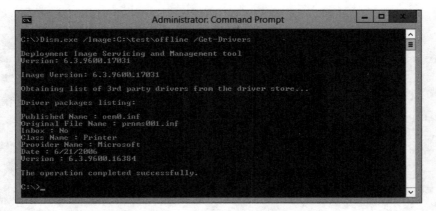

FIGURE 4-35 Elevated command prompt, DISM Get-Drivers command

The same action can be accomplished through Windows PowerShell by using the Get-WindowsDriver cmdlet:

```
Get-WindowsDriver -Path C:\test\offline
```

Both commands can also be used with online images to review current device driver inventory.

The output indicates what device drivers have already been applied with their associated time stamp. Now you apply the drivers.

Run the following command to add the desired device drivers, as shown in Figure 4-36. Note that you are using the /ForceUnsigned switch to ensure that any unsigned drivers are also added. This switch is not necessary if you are adding signed drivers.

```
Dism.exe /Image:C:\test\offline /Add-Driver /Driver:C:\test\drivers\ /recurse
/ForceUnsigned
```

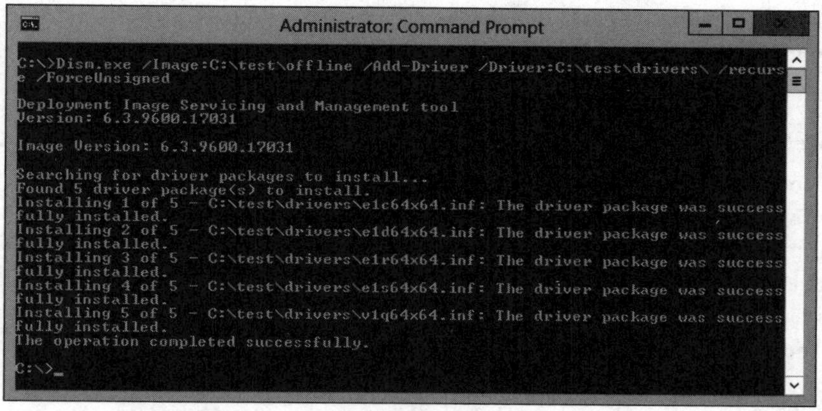

FIGURE 4-36 Elevated command prompt, DISM Add-Driver command

The same action can be accomplished by using the Add-WindowsDriver cmdlet in Windows PowerShell:

```
Add-WindowsDriver -Path C:\test\offline -Driver C:\test\drivers\ -Recurse
```

This is a good opportunity to rerun the DISM command with Get-Drivers to confirm that the device drivers are listed and have a matching time stamp.

1. Run the following command to commit the changes:

```
Dism.exe /Commit-Image /MountDir:C:\test\offline
```

2. Run the following command to unmount the image, as shown in Figure 4-37:

```
Dism.exe /Unmount-Image /MountDir:C:\test\offline /Commit
```

Similar to working with packages, you can also remove a device driver, if necessary, by using DISM Remove-Driver or the Remove-WindowsDriver Windows PowerShell cmdlet.

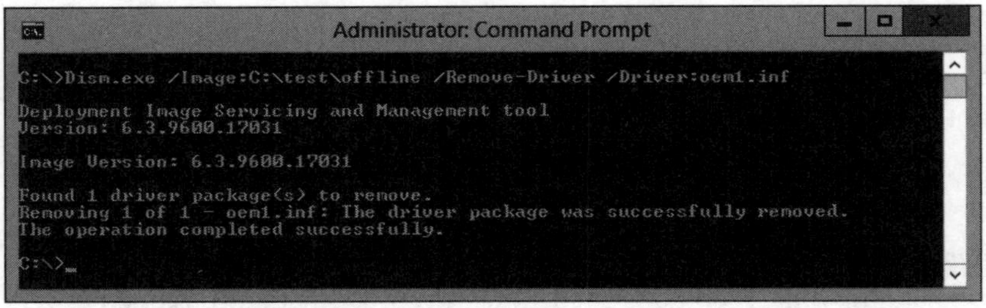

FIGURE 4-37 Elevated command prompt, DISM Remove-Driver command

> **MORE INFO** **ADDITIONAL DRIVER SERVICING COMMANDS**
>
> For more information about servicing drivers, see *http://technet.microsoft.com/en-us /library/hh825070.aspx*.

Applying settings

Up to this point, you have explored the processes for mounting an image, applying packages and drivers, saving those changes, and dismounting the image. You can run each of the commands manually or add it to a script to help automate routine maintenance. Another option is to implement an answer file that provides options for an unattended installation. An answer file is an XML-based file that contains setting definitions and values to use during Windows Setup. In the case of DISM, you would use the offlineServicing pass, which runs during Windows Setup. During this pass, any settings defined in the answer file will be triggered automatically. This can include tasks such as installing packages, software updates, and device drivers.

Applying an answer file to your image can reduce the overhead incurred with manually applying changes. Using this solution offers a few key benefits:

- **Simplicity** With this configuration, drivers can be added on the fly, without the need to update the image and reseed it to your deployment architecture.

- **Speed** Uploading new drivers to their source location makes them immediately available to any new image deployments.

- **Consistency** Using the same answer file in all your images ensures that all deployments are consistent with the desired configuration.

You can create an answer file by using the Windows System Image Manager (Windows SIM), which is included as part of the Windows ADK. This tool ensures that the answer file is formatted properly based on the operating system, and it includes a built-in error checker. In the following example, you see two sections of a sample answer file, demonstrating the solution for package and driver management.

REAL WORLD **MANAGING DEVICE DRIVERS WITH AN ANSWER FILE**

I worked in an environment that used DISM and local USB media for regular image deployments. The USB drives were limited on storage, so image size was an important factor for the deployments. In this environment, the customer had to support a variety of computer models from multiple vendors. At one point, we had driver support for 16 hardware models. It was apparent that using the DISM Add-Driver command to inject all 16 models would not work. This was when a properly formatted answer file came in handy. I set up a centralized network share with each hardware model and then pointed the answer file to the share. This approach prevented unnecessary image bloat and gave the customer the flexibility to update the drivers in an easy way.

Managing packages in an answer file is straightforward. First, create a distribution share.

1. Open Windows System Image Manager.
2. In the Distribution Share pane, right-click an empty area and then click Create Distribution Share.
3. Type the path to the share and then click Open. Three folders are created in the distribution share as part of this process.
4. Next, populate the Packages folder with the packages (.cab files) you want to include in the image.
5. In the Windows SIM console, right-click the Packages folder and then click Add To Answer File.

   The package details and share location will be imported into the answer file.

The XML code for package servicing looks similar to the example shown in Figure 4-38.

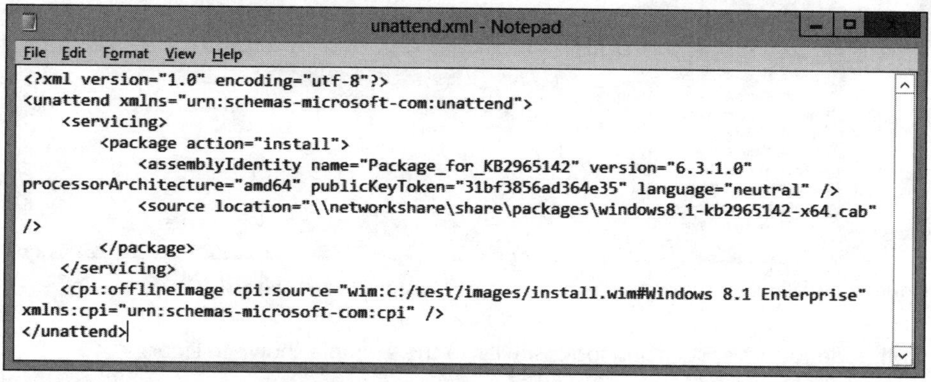
unattend.xml - Notepad
File Edit Format View Help

```
<?xml version="1.0" encoding="utf-8"?>
<unattend xmlns="urn:schemas-microsoft-com:unattend">
    <servicing>
        <package action="install">
            <assemblyIdentity name="Package_for_KB2965142" version="6.3.1.0"
processorArchitecture="amd64" publicKeyToken="31bf3856ad364e35" language="neutral" />
            <source location="\\networkshare\share\packages\windows8.1-kb2965142-x64.cab"
/>
        </package>
    </servicing>
    <cpi:offlineImage cpi:source="wim:c:/test/images/install.wim#Windows 8.1 Enterprise"
xmlns:cpi="urn:schemas-microsoft-com:cpi" />
</unattend>
```

FIGURE 4-38 Unattend.xml, servicing pass, packages

Adding a driver source location to the answer file is another quick addition. Follow these steps:

1. Open Windows System Image Manager.

2. In the Windows Image pane, expand Components and then add the following component to pass 2 – offline servicing:

`amd64_Microsoft-Windows-PnpCustomizationsNonWinPE_6.3.9600.16384_neutral`

3. In the main window, as shown in Figure 4-39, right-click the new component and then click Insert New PathAndCredentials. Fill in the appropriate fields.

FIGURE 4-39 Windows System Image Manager, PnP Customization, Drivers

The XML code for driver servicing looks similar to the example shown in Figure 4-40.

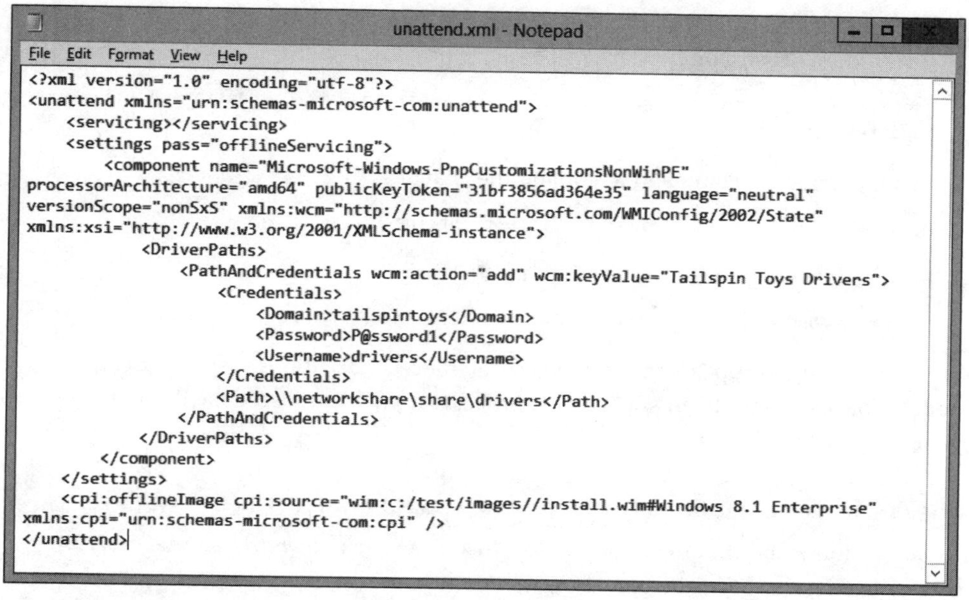


```xml
<?xml version="1.0" encoding="utf-8"?>
<unattend xmlns="urn:schemas-microsoft-com:unattend">
    <servicing></servicing>
    <settings pass="offlineServicing">
        <component name="Microsoft-Windows-PnpCustomizationsNonWinPE"
processorArchitecture="amd64" publicKeyToken="31bf3856ad364e35" language="neutral"
versionScope="nonSxS" xmlns:wcm="http://schemas.microsoft.com/WMIConfig/2002/State"
xmlns:xsi="http://www.w3.org/2001/XMLSchema-instance">
            <DriverPaths>
                <PathAndCredentials wcm:action="add" wcm:keyValue="Tailspin Toys Drivers">
                    <Credentials>
                        <Domain>tailspintoys</Domain>
                        <Password>P@ssword1</Password>
                        <Username>drivers</Username>
                    </Credentials>
                    <Path>\\networkshare\share\drivers</Path>
                </PathAndCredentials>
            </DriverPaths>
        </component>
    </settings>
    <cpi:offlineImage cpi:source="wim:c:/test/images//install.wim#Windows 8.1 Enterprise"
xmlns:cpi="urn:schemas-microsoft-com:cpi" />
</unattend>
```

FIGURE 4-40 Unattend.xml, servicing pass, drivers

After creating a working answer file, you can use DISM to apply the settings to the image. Applying an answer file in this way will only apply the offlineServicing configuration pass and any included packages.

The following example applies the newly created unattend.xml to the Windows 8.1 image. The same fundamentals about mounting the image, committing the changes, and then dismounting apply in this scenario.

1. From an elevated command prompt, mount the Windows image file:

   ```
   Dism.exe /Mount-Image /ImageFile:C:\test\images\install.wim /Index:1 /MountDir:C
   :\test\offline
   ```

2. Run the following command to apply the unattend.xml answer file to the image, as shown in Figure 4-41:

   ```
   Dism.exe /Image:C:\test\offline /Apply-Unattend:C:\test\answerfile\unattend.xml
   ```

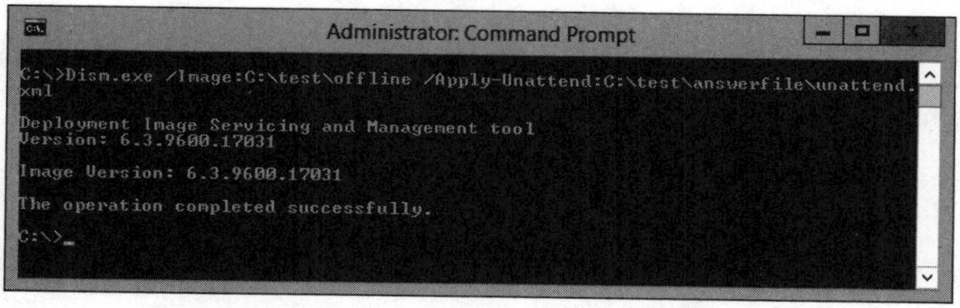


```
C:\>Dism.exe /Image:C:\test\offline /Apply-Unattend:C:\test\answerfile\unattend.
xml

Deployment Image Servicing and Management tool
Version: 6.3.9600.17031

Image Version: 6.3.9600.17031

The operation completed successfully.

C:\>_
```

FIGURE 4-41 Elevated command prompt, DISM /Apply-Unattend command

The same action can be accomplished through Windows PowerShell, using the Use-WindowsUnattend cmdlet:

```
Use-WindowsUnattend –Image C:\test\offline –UnattendPath C:\test\answerfile
\unattend.xml
```

3. Run the following command to commit the changes:

```
Dism.exe /Commit-Image /MountDir:C:\test\offline
```

4. Run the following command to unmount the image:

```
Dism.exe /Unmount-Image /MountDir:C:\test\offline /Commit
```

With the answer file applied, the image now references the settings that have been defined. To make changes to an applied answer file, reapply the updated file through another mount/unmount session.

> **MORE INFO**   **LEARN MORE ABOUT WINDOWS SIM AND ANSWER FILES**
>
> For more information about Windows System Image Manager, see *http://technet.microsoft .com/en-us/library/cc766347(v=ws.10).aspx.*

Applying files

Earlier in this section, you explored mounting a WIM file by using DISM. The mount action requires you to define an empty mount folder. After the image is mounted to that folder, the file system is accessible for additional servicing. At this point, manipulating files and folders is a very simple task. In various scenarios, servicing files and folders can be useful. Some examples include:

- **Creating a task-specific directory structure**   This could include something as simple as a folder at the root path, called XYZ Setup. Files necessary for your image deployment could then be saved to this directory, ensuring their availability during the image sequence. You can then use an answer file to call those files.

- **Embedding an answer file**   This enables you to use the other sections of an answer file to simplify your deployment further. Items such as partitioning a disk drive or configuring a time zone could be set with the answer file.

In the following example, a Windows 8.1 image is mounted and then a custom answer file is applied along with a script to clean up the unattend.xml after the image completes. The cleanup routine is captured using the SetupComplete.cmd file. After Windows is installed, but before the logon screen appears, Windows Setup searches for the SetupComplete.cmd file in the %WINDIR%\Setup\Scripts directory. If the file is found, it will run automatically, using local system privileges. The actions are recorded in the Setupact.log file.

1. From an elevated command prompt, mount the Windows image file:

   ```
   Dism.exe /Mount-Image /ImageFile:C:\test\images\install.wim /Index:1
   /MountDir:C:\test\offline
   ```

2. Open File Explorer and navigate to the mounted image directory structure. Proceed to the Sysprep folder (C:\test\offline\Windows\System32\Sysprep).

3. Copy a working copy of the unattend.xml into the Sysprep folder.

4. Navigate to the Setup folder (C:\test\offline\Windows\Setup).

5. Create a folder named **Scripts**.

6. Create a text file named **SetupComplete.cmd** within the Scripts folder.

7. Open the text file, type the following two lines, as shown in Figure 4-42, and then save the changes:

   ```
   del /q /f c:\windows\system32\sysprep\unattend.xml

   del /q /f c:\windows\panther\unattend.xml
   ```

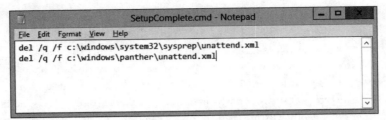

FIGURE 4-42 SetupComplete.cmd, unattend.xml file cleanup

8. Run the following command to commit the changes:

   ```
   Dism.exe /Commit-Image /MountDir:C:\test\offline
   ```

9. Run the following command to unmount your image:

   ```
   Dism.exe /Unmount-Image /MountDir:C:\test\offline /Commit
   ```

With these changes applied, this image now references the embedded answer file during deployment. After the image deployment completes, the SetupComplete script runs and removes the answer file. Most content within an answer file is viewable in plaintext, so removing the file is a good security practice.

Applying service packs to images

Major content updates such as service packs and update rollups can put a snag in your image deployment process. When it is time to include these updates in your image, you can take a few directions. DISM offers a solution for servicing existing images, enabling you to install these major content updates without rebuilding from scratch.

First, understand the files incorporated with the update that you need to apply. The following example uses Windows 8.1 Update 1 (also known as KB 2919355), which incorporates a rollup of all the updates released between Windows 8.1 RTM and Windows 8.1 Update 1. This update is also required to receive future updates from Microsoft. The Knowledge Base article for this update indicates that Update 1 consists of a series of Microsoft update files (.msu) that must be installed in a particular order.

Retrieve the associated update files and prepare a workspace for updating the existing image. These updates are installed in sequence and then reviewed using the Get-Packages command.

1. Download the necessary update files and store them in a directory titled Update1.

2. From an elevated command prompt, mount the Windows image file:

   ```
   Dism.exe /Mount-Image /ImageFile:C:\test\images\install.wim
   ```

3. Use the DISM Add-Package command to add the updates in the C:\test\updates folder:

   ```
   Dism.exe /image:C:\test\offline /Add-Package /PackagePath:C:\test\updatesReview
   the list of install packages and validate:
   ```

```
Dism.exe /Image:C:\test\offline /Get-Packages /Format:Table
```

4. Run the following command to commit the changes:

```
Dism.exe /Commit-Image /MountDir:C:\test\offline
```

5. Run the following command to unmount the image:

```
Dism.exe /Unmount-Image /MountDir:C:\test\offline /Commit
```

With the image updated, a few additional steps need to be completed. The image needs to be installed on a reference computer and booted to complete the first-boot initialization pass associated with Update 1. Going through this process helps you in the following areas:

- **Complete initial patch startup**   Without booting the image, you see that subsequent deployments have delays at startup while the system initializes.

- **Cleanup files**   Update content can quickly become outdated or replaced by future rollups. Cleaning these files up after installation can save hard-drive space and reduce the image footprint.

- **Validating and testing**   Booting the image gives you an opportunity to verify that the updates were installed successfully and that Windows is reporting the proper version.

After applying the image, boot your reference computer into audit mode by pressing Ctrl+Shift+F3 at the OOBE screen during the initial boot process.

In audit mode, allow Windows to finish initializing and then confirm that the updates are installed properly.

1. Run the following command to report current installed packages:

```
Dism.exe /Online /Get-Packages
```

After the updates are confirmed, clean up the image.

2. Run the following command to clean up any remaining components:

```
Dism.exe /Cleanup-Image /Online /StartComponentCleanup /ResetBase
```

- **/StartComponentCleanup**   Cleans up component stores and reclaims space.

- **/ResetBase**   Removes all superseded versions of every component in the component store.

At this stage, you are ready to recapture the image. To do this, run Sysprep first and then boot into Windows PE to begin the capture process.

1. Prepare the system by using the following command:

```
C:\Windows\System32\Sysprep\sysprep.exe /generalize /oobe /shutdown
```

2. Boot the computer by using a Windows PE boot image. This is necessary to capture the image.

3. Run the following command to capture the image:

```
Dism.exe /Capture-Image /ImageFile:"\\networkshare\share\images\updated_install
.wim" /CaptureDir:C: /Name:"Windows 8.1 Enterprise Update 1"
```

The same action can be accomplished by using the New-WindowsImage cmdlet in Windows PowerShell:

```
New-WindowsImage -ImagePath "\\networkshare\share\images\updated_install
.wim" -CapturePath C:\ -Name "Windows 8.1 Enterprise Update 1"
```

The updated image is saved to the network path you provided. From there, you can reapply any answer files, packages, or drivers. Note that this updating scenario is only one example, but generally, any large-scale changes should be validated on a reference computer and recaptured to ensure a working baseline.

> **MORE INFO** **LEARN MORE ABOUT CAPTURING IMAGES BY USING DISM**
>
> For more information about capturing images with DISM, see *http://technet.microsoft .com/en-us/library/hh825072.aspx*.

Managing embedded applications

Application management is a suitable topic to address now that you are more familiar with the capabilities of DISM. A variety of techniques for servicing a Windows image have been covered, most of which can be used to manage embedded applications. These are some of the available options that have been reviewed:

- Mount an image and use the DISM Add-Package command to apply updates to embedded Windows applications. This requires a compatible .cab or .msu package and is limited to Windows applications.

- Mount an image and apply an answer file that installs or updates applications. The answer file can be used to run commands or execute a script that updates the target applications.

- Mount an image and modify the application through file and folder access. This is more ideal for configuration-based files such as .ini files.

- Mount an image and incorporate the SetupComplete script, which can be used to install or update applications after an image deployment.

A topic not yet addressed in detail is Windows features. DISM is tightly integrated with the Windows Feature component, enabling you to service feature changes in online and offline images. DISM provides options for displaying all available Windows features, displaying status (enabled or disabled), and allowing you to enable or disable them.

The following example reviews the available servicing options related to Windows features. The focus is on retrieving a list of available features and enabling the Telnet client in

Windows 8.1, using online servicing options. You can use these same steps for an offline image by using the corresponding options.

1. Run the following command to retrieve a list of all available Windows features, as shown in Figure 4-43. The output provides Feature Name and State (enabled or disabled).

    ```
    Dism.exe /Online /Get-Features
    ```

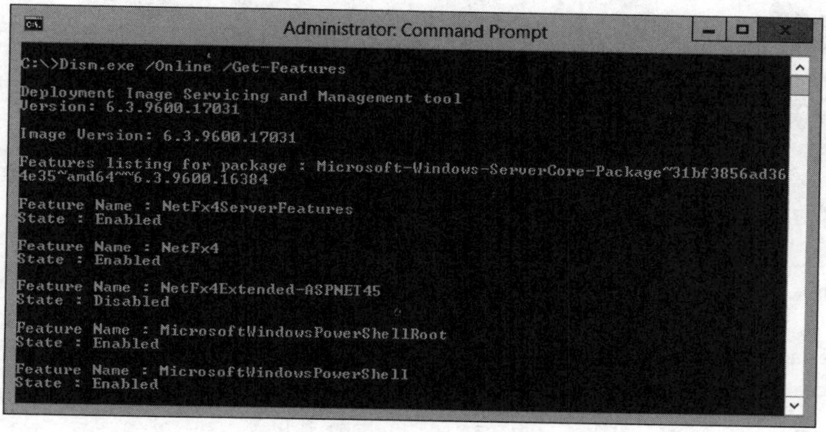

FIGURE 4-43 Elevated command prompt, DISM Get-Features command

    The same action can be accomplished by using the Get-WindowsOptionalFeature cmdlet in Windows PowerShell:

    ```
    Get-WindowsOptionalFeature -Online
    ```

2. Run the following command to retrieve more information about the Telnet client, as shown in Figure 4-44:

    ```
    Dism.exe /Online /Get-FeatureInfo /FeatureName:TelnetClient
    ```

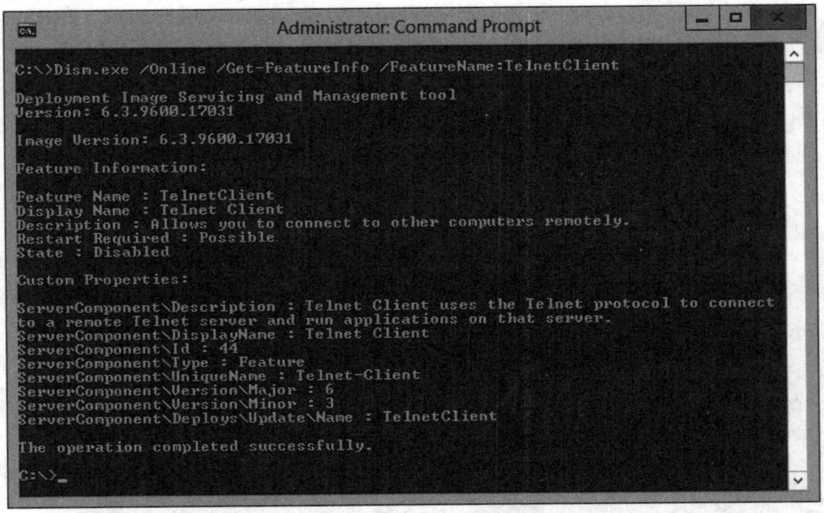

FIGURE 4-44 Elevated command prompt, DISM Get-FeatureInfo command

The same action can be accomplished by using the Get-WindowsOptionalFeature cmdlet in Windows PowerShell:

```
Get-WindowsOptionalFeature –Online –FeatureName TelnetClient
```

3. Run the following command to enable the Telnet client, where /All enables all parent features, as shown in Figure 4-45:

```
Dism.exe /Online /Enable-Feature /FeatureName:TelentClient /All
```

FIGURE 4-45 Elevated command prompt, DISM Enable-Feature command

The same action can be accomplished by using the Enable-WindowsOptionalFeature cmdlet in Windows PowerShell:

```
Enable-WindowsOptionalFeature –Online –FeatureName TelnetClient –All
```

You can service an offline image to enable or disable specific features by mounting the image and applying the desired changes. Alternatively, you can incorporate these changes by using an answer file.

1. Open Windows System Image Manager.

2. Under Windows Image in the left pane, expand Packages > Foundation.

3. Right-click Microsoft-Windows-Foundation-Package and then click Add To Answer File.

4. Select the new component in the main window, as shown in Figure 4-46. Toggle the appropriate features for your deployment to their proper state and save your changes.

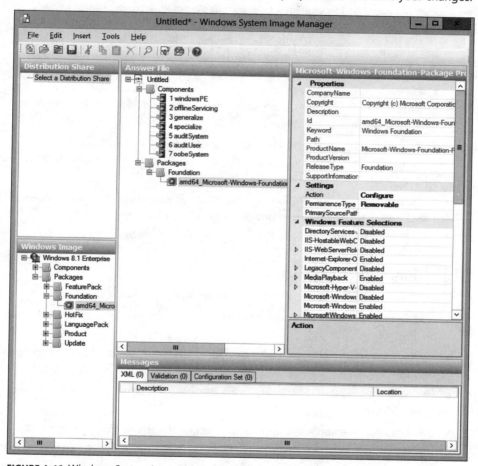

FIGURE 4-46 Windows System Image Manager, Foundation, Windows Features

---

MORE INFO **ENABLE OR DISABLE WINDOWS FEATURES BY USING DISM**

For more information about enabling or disabling features, see *http://technet.microsoft .com/en-us/library/hh824822.aspx*.

Thought experiment

Maintaining and updating images at Tailspin Toys

Tailspin Toys has hired you to help update a series of Windows images. This is a small organization of 150 employees in a single office. Tailspin Toys has a mixed environment and supports both a Windows 7 image and a Windows 8.1 image. The team has asked you to implement a maintenance solution to assist with monthly image updates.

You need to prepare an updated image that can be serviced more easily. To help you plan better for the project, answer the following questions:

1. The system administrator at Tailspin Toys has manually injected dozens of drivers into the Windows images, many of which are now outdated. Which method can you use to uninstall the drivers?

2. The Windows 7 image is lacking Service Pack 1, but the image has very little customization. How would you go about providing an updated Windows 7 image that includes Service Pack 1?

3. Tailspin Toys needs a solution that allows it to update drivers and packages without regularly updating its Windows image. What addition can you make to the images to alleviate the need to update the image regularly?

Objective summary

- DISM supports adding and removing Windows features.
- Adding and removing Windows features can be performed with online and offline images.
- Unattended answer files can be implemented to enable and disable the appropriate Windows features.
- Windows updates and device drivers are serviceable products that can be applied to offline images by using DISM.
- DISM can retrieve applied updates and drivers from offline and online images.
- An unattended answer file can be applied to an offline image to simplify package and driver updates.
- Windows images mounted with DISM can be manipulated at a file and folder level.
- Major content updates and patch rollups can be implemented using DISM.
- Audit mode is a preproduction environment that enables an administrator to customize an image and validate changes.
- DISM can be used to capture a reference computer and save the image to a local or remote location by using the Capture-Image command.

- DISM requires elevated permissions to run.
- Many of the DISM commands have a Windows PowerShell alternative.

Objective review

Answer the following questions to test your knowledge of the information in this objective. You can find the answers to these questions and explanations of why each answer choice is correct or incorrect in the "Answers" section at the end of this chapter.

1. Which of the following file types does DISM support for online and offline servicing? (Choose all that apply.)

   A. WIM

   B. VHD

   C. VHDX

   D. ISO

2. You need to apply the latest Windows updates to an existing install image. Which of the following sequences of tasks should you use?

   A. Mount the image, apply the updates, unmount the image, and commit the changes.

   B. Mount the image, apply the updates, commit the changes, and unmount the image.

   C. Apply the updates, mount the image, commit the changes, and unmount the image.

   D. Apply the updates, mount the image, unmount the image, and commit the changes.

3. Which pass of Windows Setup does DISM use to install device drivers to an image?

   A. specialize

   B. offlineServicing

   C. windowsPE

   D. generalize

Answers

This section contains the solutions to the thought experiments and answers to the lesson review questions in this chapter.

Objective 4.1

Thought experiment

1. You should always try to minimize the total number of images when requirements allow. Often, moving to a single image for client computers and a single image for servers is an optimal scenario for administrators. Based on the scenario of just having to deploy Windows 8.1, you should try to use a single install image. You can deploy the development tools after the install image.

2. You can use VHD-based install images for the developers. This would enable them to boot to multiple versions of Windows as part of their testing. A VHD-based install image enables simplified booting of different operating systems on the same hardware.

3. Thick images are definitely out because you wouldn't want your development apps on all the client computers. If you just used a dedicated developer image, a thick image would be good, as long as you were okay with having multiple Windows 8.1 images for different situations. However, a hybrid image might be the best approach. The scenario didn't call out any need to minimize the image size and didn't mention any existing issues with the WAN or storage space. A hybrid image enables users to attain core functionality immediately following the image process. Office 2013 is often included in a hybrid image along with the core security software. A thin image would also meet the requirements, but users would have to wait longer to attain functionality after the deployment process completes.

Objective review

1. **Correct answers:** A and D

   A. **Correct:** The users need basic operating system functionality only. A thin image will give them the functionality they need while minimizing the image file size.

   B. **Incorrect:** A thick image will give users the basic operating system functionality they need, but the image size will not be minimized, which is a requirement.

   C. **Incorrect:** A hybrid image will give users the basic operating system functionality they need, but the image size, although smaller than a thick image, will not be minimized.

   D. **Correct:** A VHD-based thin image will meet the requirements of giving users basic operating system functionality and minimizing the image file size.

2. **Correct answer:** A

   A. Correct: To deploy a default installation of Windows 8.1, you should use the install.
   wim file from the Windows 8.1 media as an install image.

   B. Incorrect: The boot.wim file is a boot image and cannot be used to install
   Windows 8.1.

   C. Incorrect: The install.wim file is an install image and cannot be used for booting.

   D. Incorrect: The boot.wim file is a boot image and cannot be used to install
   Windows 8.1.

3. **Correct answer:** B

   A. Incorrect: You need an install image for Windows 8.1 and an install image for
   Windows Server 2012 R2. Thus, you need a minimum of two images. You do not
   need to have more than one install image for Windows 8.1 for different models or
   drivers because you can handle those without requiring another image.

   B. Correct: At least two images are required. Because the question calls for minimizing the total number of images, you should use two images. You need one image
   to install Windows 8.1 and another to install Windows Server 2012 R2.

   C. Incorrect: Three images are more than you need. You need an install image for
   Windows 8.1 and an install image for Windows Server 2012 R2. Thus, you need a
   minimum of two images. You do not need to have more than one install image for
   Windows 8.1 for different models or drivers because you can handle those without
   requiring another image.

   D. Incorrect: Four images are more than you need. You need an install image for
   Windows 8.1 and an install image for Windows Server 2012 R2. Thus, you need a
   minimum of two images. You do not need to have more than one install image for
   Windows 8.1 for different models or drivers because you can handle those without
   requiring another image.

4. **Correct answers:** B and C

   A. Incorrect: If you are using a thick image, you don't need to package the application after deployment. The question calls for minimizing license costs; using a thick
   image doesn't meet that requirement.

   B. Correct: A thin image meets the requirements as long as the application is packaged after deployment.

   C. Correct: A hybrid image meets the requirements as long as the application is
   packaged after deployment. You should add the common applications the entire
   company uses to the hybrid image and package the other applications for deployment outside of the image.

   D. Incorrect: A thick image goes against the requirement to minimize license costs. A
   filter won't help in this situation.

5. **Correct answers:** A, B, C, and D

   A. **Correct:** To perform a capture or an installation, you need a boot image.

   B. **Correct:** To meet the requirement of using the reference computer's operating system, you need a capture image so that you can capture the reference computer and use it as an install image.

   C. **Correct:** The kiosk computers can't boot to PXE, so you need a discover image to deploy install images to them.

   D. **Correct:** You need an install image to deploy Windows. The requirements call for a Windows Server 2012 R2 deployment and a Windows 8.1 deployment to kiosk computers.

Objective 4.2

Thought experiment

1. You should use Configuration Manager because it will meet the requirement to automate as many of the tasks as possible. By using the Build And Capture A Reference Operating System Image template, you can automate the deployment of the reference computer and the capture in a single task sequence.

2. From WindowsPE, you can press Shift+F10 to open a command prompt. From there, you will have access to several troubleshooting tools, including tools such as DiskPart.

3. When you boot to PXE, you see all the boot images available to you on the server. This includes standard boot images and capture images. The only way to differentiate between boot images and capture images is by the name that you give each image when you create it. It is important to give your images descriptive names to ensure that you are using the appropriate image type and image in a given situation.

Objective review

1. **Correct answer:** B

   A. **Incorrect:** The default user profile remains after Sysprep.

   B. **Correct:** Sysprep removes the computer's security identifier (SID).

   C. **Incorrect:** User applications remain after Sysprep.

   D. **Incorrect:** Application metadata remain after Sysprep.

2. **Correct answer:** C

   A. **Incorrect:** A boot image is not used for installing an operating system, so Office 2013, if it will be put into an image, should go in an install image.

   B. **Incorrect:** The task sequence requires an application, not a package.

C. **Correct:** The task sequence enables you to add any preconfigured application as part of your build.

D. **Incorrect:** A Windows Sideloading key is not used for adding applications to an automated build. It is used for sideloading apps.

3. **Correct answers:** A and C

A. **Correct:** To deploy an operating system in Configuration Manager, you need a boot image (to boot from) and an install image.

B. **Incorrect:** A capture image is used for capturing an image, not for deploying an image.

C. **Correct:** To deploy an operating system in Configuration Manager, you need a boot image (to boot from) and an install image.

D. **Incorrect:** A capture image is used for capturing an image, not for deploying an image.

4. **Correct answer:** C

A. **Incorrect:** Windows XP did not include the bundled system preparation files.

B. **Incorrect:** Windows Server 2003 did not include the bundled system preparation files.

C. **Correct:** Windows Vista is the first operating system to have the bundled system preparation files.

D. **Incorrect:** Although Windows 7 bundled system preparation files, it wasn't the first Windows operating system to do so. That was Vista.

5. **Correct answer:** A

A. **Correct:** You must use a network path for the captured image.

B. **Incorrect:** A local path isn't valid for storing a captured image.

C. **Incorrect:** A ConfigMgr repository isn't valid for storing a captured image.

D. **Incorrect:** A WDS repository isn't valid for storing a captured image from ConfigMgr.

Objective 4.3

Thought experiment

1. You should retrieve a list of the currently applied drivers by using the DISM /Get-Drivers command. Identify the outdated drivers and then use the DISM /Remove-Drivers command to uninstall them. Then, add new drivers by using the DISM /Add-Driver command.

2. Because the image has very little customization, you could use the updated installation media to create a new image. Alternatively, you could deploy the image to a reference

computer, install Service Pack 1, and then capture the reference computer to update the image.

3. To avoid updating the image regularly, you can create an answer file and add it to the image. By assigning a distribution share and driver share and using the offline servicing pass, you can update drivers and packages without updating the image.

Objective review

1. **Correct answers:** A, B, C, and D

   A. **Correct:** DISM supports .wim files.

   B. **Correct:** DISM supports .vhd files.

   C. **Correct:** DISM supports .vhdx files.

   D. **Correct:** DISM supports .iso files.

2. **Correct answer:** B

   A. **Incorrect:** You have to commit the changes to the image before you unmount it; otherwise, your changes will be lost.

   B. **Correct:** This is the correct order: mount, apply, commit, and then unmount. If you don't follow the correct order, your changes will be lost.

   C. **Incorrect:** You can't apply updates if the image isn't mounted. You must mount the image before applying the updates.

   D. **Incorrect:** You can't apply updates if the image isn't mounted. You must mount the image before applying the updates. In addition, you have to commit the changes before you unmount the image.

3. **Correct answer:** B

   A. **Incorrect:** The specialize pass is when machine-specific information is added to an image, but it isn't used for installing device drivers.

   B. **Correct:** The offlineServicing pass is used for offline servicing of an image, including the installation of drivers.

   C. **Incorrect:** The windowsPE pass is used to configure Windows PE settings and isn't part of installing device drivers into the image.

   D. **Incorrect:** The generalize pass is used to remove machine-specific information from a reference computer before capturing it for use as an install image.

CHAPTER 5

Prepare and deploy the VDIapplication environment

You should perform several initial steps when preparing to deploy applications in your environment. First, perform a discovery of the current environment to understand the existing application landscape. This information will play a key role in preparing for application compatibility and remediation as well as prepare you to deploy applications such as Office 2013. Second, have a firm understanding of the installation options when deploying Office 2013 by using the Windows Installer (MSI) to customize a deployment, manage activation, and provide ongoing support and maintenance effectively. Finally, know the intricacies of deploying Office 2013 by using Click-to-Run so that you can manage licensing, perform the deployment, deploy updates, and provide ongoing usage monitoring.

Objectives in this chapter:

- Objective 5.1: Plan for and implement application compatibility and remediation
- Objective 5.2: Deploy Office 2013 by using MSI
- Objective 5.3: Deploy Office 2013 by using Click-to-Run

Objective 5.1: Plan for and implement application compatibility and remediation

Understanding the existing application landscape is the vital first task in an app deployment project. Know which apps are already deployed in the environment, the different versions of deployed applications, and compatibility of the deployed apps based on your existing and future operating systems. After you've gathered this information, you are ready to deploy tools and compatibility fixes to reach the desired state.

Planning for Remote Desktop Services (RDS)

Many organizations rely on multiple methods of delivering applications and desktops to users. RDS is one such method, used to deliver virtual applications and virtual desktops. It has other functionality that isn't applicable to the 70-695 exam and is not covered here. For the exam, this chapter focuses specifically on planning for an RDS deployment to support application compatibility and remediation.

Licensing

Planning for RDS licensing is one of the most important steps you take when embarking on an RDS project. Licensing is so important because it factors into your project budget, the decision whether RDS is the appropriate solution, and whether your organization is licensed for your specific use case. In some cases, not having the right licensing could mean that users cannot use the RDS environment. Every user who uses RDS must be covered by a Windows Server 2012 RDS Client Access License (CAL). In addition, there are two RDS CAL types for internal users:

- **RDS User CAL** An RDS User CAL is tied to a single user and allows that user to use RDS services on any of your RDS servers from any supported device. When you have users that use your RDS infrastructure from several of their devices, a User CAL is the best license choice to minimize license costs.

- **RDS Device CAL** An RDS Device CAL is tied to a single device and allows any users using that device to use RDS services on any of your RDS servers.

A single license is required for external users, such as those who access your RDS infrastructure from the Internet. The RDS External Connector allows Internet users to access a single server in your RDS environment. Each RDS server in your environment that serves Internet users must have an RDS External Connector.

A dedicated server role service, named Remote Desktop Licensing, is responsible for managing the RDS licenses needed in your RDS environment. It issues licenses to users and devices, it tracks existing license usage such as if you are running low on available licenses, and it allows you to install recently purchased licenses. Before it can perform any of those tasks, however, the licensing server must be activated with Microsoft. You can activate the licensing server online, through a web browser, or over the telephone. To activate a newly installed license server by using the automatic connection method, perform the following steps:

1. From Server Manager, click Tools and then click Terminal Services. In the context menu, click Remote Desktop Licensing Manager.

   In the RD Licensing Manager window, as shown in Figure 5-1, you see your license server and an activation status of Not Activated.

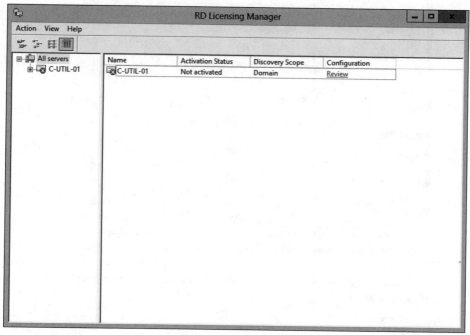

FIGURE 5-1 RD Licensing Manager console

2. Right-click your licensing server and then click Activate Server.

3. In the Activate Server Wizard window, on the Welcome To The Activate Server Wizard page, click Next.

4. On the Connection Method page, shown in Figure 5-2, ensure that the connection method is set to Automation Connection (Recommended) and then click Next.

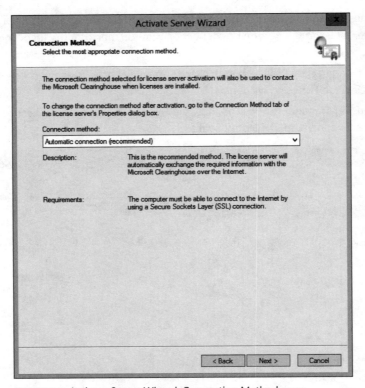

FIGURE 5-2 Activate Server Wizard, Connection Method page

5. On the Company Information page, shown in Figure 5-3, enter the information and then click Next.

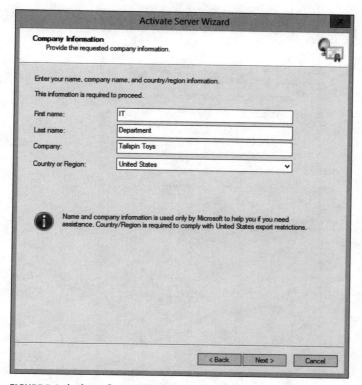

FIGURE 5-3 Activate Server Wizard, Company Information page

6. On the second Company Information page, shown in Figure 5-4, enter the optional information, or leave the fields blank, and then click Next.

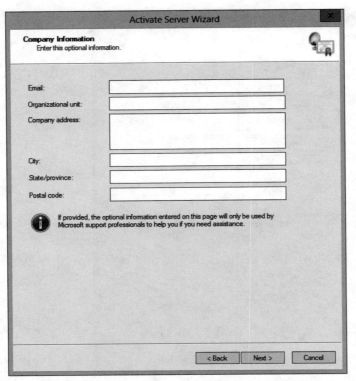

FIGURE 5-4 Activate Server Wizard, Company Information page (optional)

7. On the Completing The Activate Server Wizard page, shown in Figure 5-5, clear the Start Install Licenses Wizard Now check box and then click Finish.

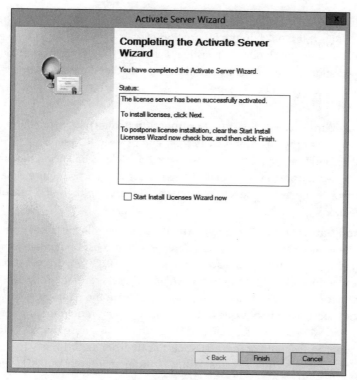

FIGURE 5-5 Activate Server Wizard, Completing The Activate Server Wizard page

After the license server is activated, you must add licenses based on your requirements. After you deploy RDS, you get a 120-day licensing grace period during which RDS is fully functional without RDS CALs. After the grace period expires, RDS services will not be available to users. Do not put off acquiring RDS CALs because of the grace period. It is not uncommon for organizations to face an RDS outage when the grace period expires before it purchases RDS CALs.

EXAM TIP

Watch for exam questions about RDS licensing when an environment has a large number of shared computing devices such as a call center, training rooms, or business locations with multiple shifts. In such scenarios, opt for RDS Device CALs because multiple users on the shared computing device can use RDS services under a single device license. This reduces the overall cost of your RDS licensing while still providing RDS services to all your users.

RDS roles

When planning for RDS, RDS roles make up the foundation of your planning. After you've gathered your business requirements, you can investigate which of the RDS roles should be part of your proposed solution. It is important to understand the roles, how they work together, and the prerequisites. The following are all the available RDS roles in Windows Server 2012 R2:

- **Remote Desktop Connection Broker (RD Connection Broker)**   A connection broker is a technology that provides connectivity from end users to RDS services such as virtual desktops or published applications. It also provides a load balancing mechanism to ensure that connections are evenly balanced across the RDS infrastructure. Finally, it provides a service that enables users to reconnect seamlessly to their RDS resources after a disconnection.

- **Remote Desktop Gateway (RD Gateway)**   The RD Gateway role facilitates connectivity from the Internet to an internal RDS deployment. It must be domain joined, which has a big impact on where you place it in your network. Often, organizations deploy the gateway on the local area network (LAN) and use a reverse proxy server in the perimeter network. However, it can also be deployed in the perimeter network, although that can complicate things due to the domain-joining requirement. A key prerequisite is having a Secure Sockets Layer (SSL) certificate. Because the RD Gateway services the Internet, you should obtain an SSL certificate from a third-party trusted certificate vendor. Although you can use a certificate from an internal public key infrastructure (PKI), your Internet-based users might not trust it.

- **Remote Desktop Licensing (RD Licensing)**   A licensing server manages all the RDS licensing for your organization. Although a license server is not required during the initial 120-day license grace period, a license server is required thereafter. The RD Licensing role can be collocated with another RDS role, but you should opt for a dedicated license server in larger organizations to maximize performance and security.

- **Remote Desktop Session Host (RD Session Host)**   The RD Session Host role provides session-based virtual desktop and published applications.

- **Remote Desktop Virtualization Host (RD Virtualization Host)**   The RD Virtualization Host role is a foundational role for a VDI. It provides the VDI management functionality, such as starting up virtual machines (VMs) on demand, as users request access to a VM. This role must be run on a Hyper-V server and thus requires hardware-assisted virtualization.

- **Remote Desktop Web Access (RD Web Access)**   RD Web Access is a web-based portal that users can use to run published applications or connect to virtualized desktops. Figure 5-6 shows the RD Web Access portal.

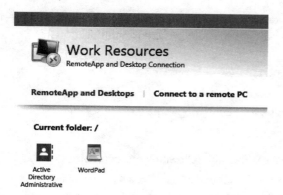

FIGURE 5-6 RD Web Access portal with published applications

Infrastructure and capacity planning

Planning for RDS also involves thinking about related infrastructure components and capacity. Before beginning, find the answers to the following questions:

- How many people will use RDS?
- Where do the users reside?
- Which RDS services will be offered?
- What activity level will the users generate?

Starting with the infrastructure, pay special attention to the following components:

- **Network**   On the network side, one important factor is response time (often referred to as round-trip time). For RDS services, 200ms has been established as the slowest response time that allows an acceptable user experience. When you design your RDS environment, look closely at response times from all the locations users will access RDS services. If response times are over 200ms, you should strongly consider placing RDS infrastructure closer to the access locations. Another important factor is bandwidth. For example, if you have 15 branch offices that currently access services at their respective branch office, moving those services to RDS at the corporate headquarters will have an impact on bandwidth, wide area network (WAN) performance, and user experience.

- **Security**   On the security side, plan for securing the communication to your RDS environment, especially for Internet-based connections. Although an internal PKI can provide SSL certificates to secure communications, you must evaluate whether all the RDS clients trust your PKI. If not, use a third-party SSL vendor. You must also plan for firewall changes. Although RDS mostly operates over Transmission Control Protocol (TCP) port 443, there are exceptions. For example, if you deploy the RD Gateway role to a perimeter network and join it to the internal domain, or if you deploy the

RD Gateway role to a perimeter network with Active Directory Domain Services (AD DS) that has a trust with the internal AD DS, you must open additional ports.

MORE INFO **RDS GATEWAY FIREWALL PORTS**

For more information about deploying RDS Gateway servers in a perimeter network, see *http://blogs.msdn.com/b/rds/archive/2009/07/31/rd-gateway-deployment-in-a-perimeter -network-firewall-rules.aspx*.

With regard to capacity planning for RDS, evaluate the following considerations:

- **Hardware**   You must acquire hardware so that you can service all the users with all the services, without performance degradation. Strive to right-size the hardware: acquire hardware that isn't undersized or oversized for the business requirements. To plan for hardware, understand the impact each connection has on the services. Microsoft has published some capacity-planning guides that walk through an actual capacity-planning test environment to help you plan your capacity needs.

- **Database**   A database is required for the RD Connection Broker server. It can be a SQL Server Express instance installed on the connection broker server. For large-capacity environments or environments that require high availability (HA), use a dedicated SQL server.

- **Proof of concept**   Although looking at the official capacity planning guides is extremely helpful, it is a good idea also to validate your design in your network. You must validate that the rest of the infrastructure is performing acceptably while the overall user experience is satisfactory. There are two primary tools to simulate RDS connections:

  - **TSGSServer.exe**   This tool simulates an RD Session Host server and is used from an RD Session Host server.

  - **TSGSClient.exe**   This tool simulates a Remote Desktop Connection client while also running from a Remote Desktop Connection client computer.

MORE INFO **RDS CAPACITY PLANNING GUIDES**

For more information about capacity planning for the RD Gateway role, see RD Gateway Capacity Planning in Windows Server 2012 at *http://www.microsoft.com/en-ie/download /details.aspx?id=38798*.

Published applications

Published applications, also known as RemoteApp programs, are applications installed on the RD Session Host servers and configured to be available to RDS users through their Start screen or through the RDS web portal. There are many use cases for published applications; the following use cases are popular:

- Provide users with older versions of software that are not compatible with their current client operating systems. In this use case, you might have migrated from Windows XP to Windows 8.1 but still require an older application for one of your departments. You can publish that application as a RemoteApp program and make it available to the department instead.

- Enable users to run multiple versions of the same application on their computers. In this use case, you can publish Internet Explorer 8 on one RD Session Host server, Internet Explorer 9 on another RD Session Host server, and Internet Explorer 10 on a third RD Session Host server. Users who have Internet Explorer 11 on their client computer can then use four versions of IE, even simultaneously. This is especially helpful for developers or IT staff that develop or troubleshoot end-user web incidents.

- Enable users to run corporate applications from any computing device. When you publish applications to the Internet (usually with the use of a gateway and reverse proxy), you can allow authenticated users to run corporate applications from their personal computing devices. This is a great benefit to organizations embarking on a bring-your-own-device (BYOD) initiative.

Publishing applications has some notable characteristics:

- By publishing an application, you drastically reduce the administrative overhead of deploying security and software updates because the application is only installed on RD Session Host servers.

- Published applications can appear to be locally installed applications to end users. When they launch the application, however, it actually connects to the published application automatically.

- Accessing published applications works the same way as accessing virtual desktops does, which is by using RDP. Thus, to provide a good user experience, the round-trip time over the network should be 200ms or less.

Plan for VDI

Two primary RDS solutions are in scope for the 70-695 exam. It is important to understand both of these services, including the specific use cases that each service is best suited for. The two primary solutions are virtual desktops and session-based desktops.

- **Virtual desktops**   Virtual desktops are virtualized client computers that you provide to your users. There are two methods of delivering virtual desktops.

- **Session-based desktops**   Session-based desktops are accessed through Remote Desktop Protocol (RDP). Session-based desktops are, at their foundation, an RDP session to an RD Session Host server. To end users, though, session-based desktops appear like many other virtualized desktops such as those delivered by a VDI, especially when users access them using the full-screen display. However, session-based desktops rely on the underlying operating system. Thus, the operating system for session-based desktops is actually a server-based operating system such as

Windows Server 2012 R2. This is an important distinction between session-based desktops and desktops delivered by a VDI, which is a client-based operating system such as Windows 8.1.

- **Virtual desktop infrastructure (VDI)**   VDI deployment first became available on Windows with the release of Windows Server 2008 R2. VDI provides virtualized Windows client computer desktops to end users. Thus, the operating system for the user is a desktop-based operating system such as Windows 8.1. Access to the VDI is by an RDP connection. There are two VM deployment methods for VDI:

  - **Pooled**   A pooled virtual machine collection is made up of identical VMs that can be used by any VDI user. All the VMs share a single master image of the operating system. A pooled collection reduces administrative overhead and storage costs. However, for power users that require more control, such as access to install applications, a pooled collection might not suffice.

  - **Personal**   A personal virtual machine collection gives every VDI user his or her own personal VM. With this option, VDI users can be local administrators on their VMs, install applications, and fully manage their VMs. Providing each VDI user with a personal VM results in additional administrative overhead to manage multiple images, manage storage space, troubleshoot, and support a wide variety of application compatibility scenarios. Although this is the most expensive option, it is also the most flexible and customizable.

> *MORE INFO*   **RDS CAPACITY PLANNING GUIDES**
>
> For more information about capacity planning for VDI, see the Windows Server 2012 Capacity Planning for VDI whitepaper at *http://download.microsoft.com/download/2/4 /B/24B5EC7D-1D03-49A2-B792-C7EDF24549EE/Windows_Server_2012_Capacity _Planning_for_VDI_White_Paper.pdf*.

Planning for Client Hyper-V

First introduced with Windows 8, Client Hyper-V is a client version of the Hyper-V role that runs on Windows Server. You can enable it by choosing Program and Features in Control Panel, as shown in Figure 5-7.

FIGURE 5-7 Enabling Hyper-V on Windows 8

Client Hyper-V is a virtualization technology that enables you to run virtualized instances of computers on Windows 8 and Windows 8.1. Client Hyper-V has the following requirements:

- A 64-bit process with second level address translation (SLAT)
- A 64-bit version of Windows 8 or later (Pro or Enterprise only)
- 4 GB of RAM

The primary use cases for Client Hyper-V are for:

- IT administrator testing such as when updating or making configuration changes.
- IT developers developing to different operating systems and needing to understand quickly the different application experience in those operating systems.

Although some organizations have large nonproduction environments in which IT administrators and developers can perform tests, often the environments are shared and do not provide all the necessary services.

Be aware of these characteristics of Hyper-V on Windows 8:

- You must have a Windows license for each Windows VM you run in Hyper-V on Windows 8. This is unlike Windows Server, which gives you virtualization rights, depending on the server license.
- The following features that are available when using Hyper-V on Windows Server are not available with Hyper-V on Windows 8:
  - Virtual Fibre Channel
  - Shared .VHDX, 32-bit single root I/O virtualization (SR-IOV) networking
  - Hyper-V Replica
  - Live migration
  - RemoteFX

- Connected Standby, which Windows tablets such as the Surface use, does not work after Hyper-V is enabled on Windows 8.

Planning for 32-bit versus 64-bit

Many operating systems, including Windows 8, offer a 32-bit version and a 64-bit version. Many applications, including Microsoft Office 2013, offer a 32-bit version and a 64-bit version. As an IT administrator, your understanding of the key differences between 32-bit and 64-bit implementations enables you to propose appropriate solutions for your organization. The following characteristics represent interoperability of 32-bit and 64-bit applications on Windows:

- Most 32-bit applications run without issue on 64-bit installations of Windows. Some common exceptions are antivirus applications. Drivers, although not thought of as applications, are also exceptions.
- 64-bit applications do not run on 32-bit installations of Windows.

Beyond interoperability, there are other 32-bit and 64-bit factors to consider when planning to deploy Windows or applications:

- Client Hyper-V requires the 64-bit version of Windows 8.
- The 64-bit version of Office 2013, although capable of higher performance than the 32-bit version, might not support all the plug-ins. For example, if you have third-party plug-ins for Microsoft Outlook, they might only be supported with the 32-bit version of Outlook. It is important to test the 64-bit version of Office 2013 in your environment to check compatibility with the existing applications.
- The 64-bit version of Windows generally provides higher performance than the 32-bit version of Windows. The performance difference is most noticeable, however, when you have 4 GB or more of RAM.
- The 64-bit version of Office generally provides higher performance than the 32-bit version of Windows. This is most noticeable with large Microsoft Excel and Project files. On 32-bit versions of Excel and Project, the maximum amount of virtual address space is 2 GB. This space must be shared with the Office application, the data being worked with, and the add-ons that are loaded. The 64-bit version of Office is only limited by the available memory, which is often much higher than 2 GB with a modern computer.

Planning for application version coexistence

Occasionally, you might need to run two versions of the same application on the same computer. Understand the available methods for application version coexistence as well as the limitations so that you can plan properly. There are two primary methods to deploy applications in coexistence:

- **Microsoft Application Virtualization (App-V)**   App-V is one of the tools in the Microsoft Desktop Optimization Pack (MDOP) for Microsoft Software Assurance customers. App-V is a tool to virtualize applications and then stream the applications to App-V clients. App-V clients download only a small portion of the overall application to start the application. Then, a local App-V cache is built up so that subsequent application launches use the cache to launch the application quickly. App-V can enable offline use of streamed applications, which is a major difference between App-V apps and RemoteApp programs because RemoteApp programs require a network connection.

- **RemoteApp**   Earlier in this chapter, the details of RemoteApp were discussed. For coexistence scenarios, the most common use of RemoteApp is to publish one version of the application through RemoteApp while installing the other version of the application locally on client computers. Although this is functional, it isn't as flexible as App-V, especially when you use more than two versions of an application.

> **MORE INFO   LEARN MORE ABOUT APP-V**
>
> For more information about virtualizing applications with App-V, see the video on the App-V Sequencer at *http://technet.microsoft.com/en-us/windows/jj835810.aspx*.

Using the Application Compatibility Toolkit

The Application Compatibility Toolkit (ACT) is a free suite of tools from Microsoft to manage application compatibility in your environment. ACT helps you assess and mitigate application compatibility with different versions of Windows. To demonstrate the typical use of ACT, suppose that you want to migrate an existing Windows 7 environment to Windows 8.1. The following high-level steps describe the core uses of ACT for your migration:

- **Inventory your existing Windows 7 environment**   You must create and deploy inventory-collector packages to perform an inventory of your existing computers. The inventory package installs compatibility evaluators, and the evaluators collect detailed hardware and software information about your client computers.

- **Test application compatibility on Windows 8.1**   In a migration or upgrade scenario, you must test application compatibility on the new operating system. This testing should occur before any migrations take place to avoid unexpected compatibility issues.

- **Analyze the compatibility data**   To move forward with your migration to Windows 8, you must analyze the data collected about your existing Windows 7 environment. Based on that analysis, you might be able to proceed with the migration without any changes, or you will begin to plan how to fix compatibility issues.

- **Remediate compatibility issues**   Sometimes, you can remedy compatibility issues by updating the application to the latest version or rewriting application code. Other times, you might need to use a workaround. A workaround is most often used when you are already running the latest version of the application or when you can't rewrite application code. The next section in this chapter discusses deploying application com-patibility fixes in more detail.

Before you can use ACT, you must install it and then walk through the initial configuration. The steps to configure ACT initially are as follows:

1. Run Application Compatibility Manager.

2. In the Application Compatibility Toolkit (ACT) Configuration Wizard window, click Next, as shown in Figure 5-8.

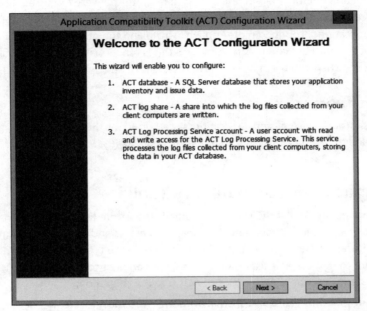

FIGURE 5-8 Application Compatibility Toolkit (ACT) Configuration Wizard, Welcome page

3. On the ACT Log Processing Service page, shown in Figure 5-9, leave the default selec-tion of Yes, which specifies the computer to run the log processing service, and then click Next.

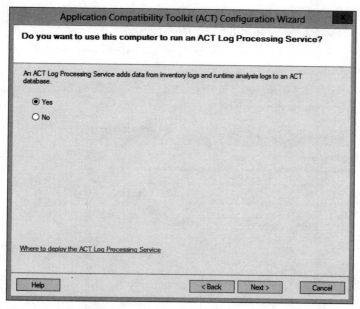

FIGURE 5-9 Application Compatibility Toolkit (ACT) Configuration Wizard, ACT Log Processing Service page

4. On the second Configure Your ACT Database Settings page, shown in Figure 5-10, specify the SQL Server name and database name and then click Next.

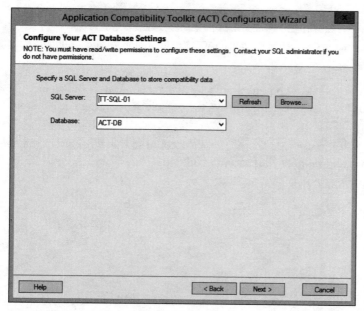

FIGURE 5-10 Application Compatibility Toolkit (ACT) Configuration Wizard, Configure Your ACT Database Settings page

5. On the second Configure Your ACT Database Settings page, review the necessary database permissions and then click Next.

6. On the Configure Your Log File Location page, type the path or existing share you want to use and then click Next.

   Note that an existing share is specified in Figure 5-11. The Domain Computers group must be able to write to the directory.

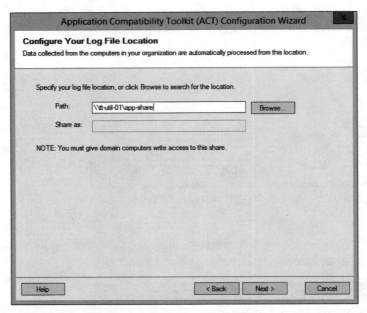

FIGURE 5-11 Application Compatibility Toolkit (ACT) Configuration Wizard, Configure Your Log File Location page

7. On the Configure Your ACT Log Processing Service Account page, shown in Figure 5-12, specify a user account or leave the default of using the Local System account.

   It is a good practice to use a dedicated service account so that you can set the necessary permissions and simplify your security auditing.

8. When you are finished, click Next.

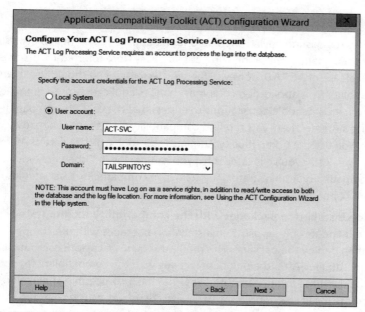

FIGURE 5-12 Application Compatibility Toolkit (ACT) Configuration Wizard, Configure Your Log Processing Service Account page

9. On the Congratulations page, shown in Figure 5-13, review and adjust any changes required for the usage data, update checks, and then click Finish.

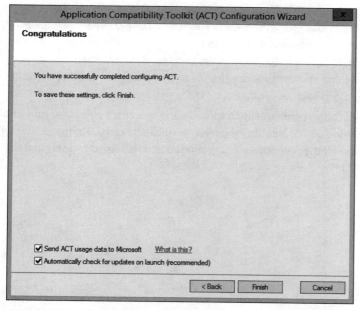

FIGURE 5-13 Application Compatibility Toolkit (ACT) Configuration Wizard, Congratulations page

Deploying compatibility fixes

After you've examined your existing environment and found application compatibility issues, decide how you want to fix them. Application compatibility fixes were referred to as *shims* for a long time. With the release of ACT 6.0, however, the new term that you should use is *compatibility fix*. A compatibility fix is application code that changes application programming interface (API) calls from incompatible applications to ensure that the calls are compatible with the new operating system. Often, you can find compatibility fixes that are already written and ready for use. You use the Compatibility Administrator tool, which is part of ACT, to search for existing fixes. After you've located a fix, you can deploy it. Otherwise, you can create a new fix in Compatibility Administrator. The following compatibility fix strategies represent the two available options:

- **Use application installation packages with the compatibility fix integrated**   In this scenario, you update your application installation packages with the compatibility fix and then deploy the package. This method requires a custom compatibility fix database (an .sdb file). After the database is ready with the compatibility fix, you must deploy the database to the computers that run the incompatible application and install the database locally by using the Sdbinst.exe command. Most organizations package the database and command in an .msi file and rely on their existing application deployment methods such as Group Policy or ConfigMgr to deploy the database. However, if you need to fix a large number of applications, consider the other strategy, which uses a centralized compatibility fix database. Otherwise, you will end up with many database deployments, which can be unwieldy to manage.

- **Use a centralized compatibility fix database**   In this scenario, you use a single compatibility fix database for all the applications that have compatibility issues. You deploy the database to computers that run the incompatible applications and install the database locally by using the Sdbinst.exe command. Most organizations package the database and command in an .msi file and rely on their existing application deployment methods such as Group Policy or ConfigMgr to deploy the database.

Because testing application compatibility happens early in a client computer migration project, you can usually include compatibility fixes in your client computer image. This greatly simplifies things because all the computers being imaged and delivered to users already have the application compatibility fixes.

Thought experiment

Configuring RDS at Contoso

You work as a systems administrator for Contoso, Ltd., a consulting company that provides infrastructure and cloud solutions to customers worldwide. About half the customers collocate their infrastructure in Contoso's private cloud.

Contoso has a call center for level 1 support. In the call center, 30 administrative computers are running Windows 7, which have several support applications the support team uses to manage and troubleshoot customers' hardware and software issues. There is an Active Directory Domain Services forest with a single domain named contoso.com. Call center employees are issued a laptop for home use.

The company has decided to offer call center employees an option to work from home for two days a week. You plan to update the infrastructure to ensure that call center employees can work effectively from home.

1. You are working with one of the call center managers. He reports that the call center employees often perform large file copy operations between their computers and customers' servers. He is concerned that copy operations might not perform adequately when call center employees are working at home. What should you propose to avoid affecting copy operations when employees are working from home?

2. Some of the support applications are licensed per device. The management team has expressed a desire to minimize licensing costs, especially in light of the laptops being issued for home use. What should you do to minimize licensing costs?

3. The laptops will be running Windows 8.1. Because some of the support applications will run on the laptops, you must validate application compatibility for Windows 8.1. What should you do before you issue the laptops?

Objective summary

- Remote Desktop Services requires a licensed server to function after the initial 120-day license grace period. You must activate your licensing server with Microsoft before you can add any licenses to it.

- An RDS User CAL is the appropriate license choice when users access RDS services from multiple devices.

- An RDS Device CAL is the appropriate license choice when users share computing devices, such as in a call center or factory with three shifts of workers.

- Be familiar with the functionality each RDS role provides: RD Connection Broker (load balancer and seamless reconnection services), RD Gateway (facilitates communication from the Internet to the RDS environment on the LAN), RD Licensing (manages all aspects of RDS licensing), RD Session Host (session-based desktops and published applications), and RD Virtualization Host (VDI).

- Publishing applications by using RemoteApp is a good solution for web developers or other IT staff who need to run multiple versions of an application from a single computer, even if the application versions are incompatible.
- The Application Compatibility Toolkit (ACT) is a suite of tools you use to assess application compatibility in your environment, especially before a migration to a new client operating system.
- You can use Compatibility Administrator to look for existing application compatibility fixes, create new application compatibility fixes, and deploy fixes to your computers.

Objective review

Answer the following questions to test your knowledge of the information in this objective. You can find the answers to these questions and explanations of why each answer choice is correct or incorrect in the "Answers" section at the end of this chapter.

1. You are preparing to deploy RDS in your environment. The management team has requested a proof of concept to be deployed and tested before purchasing RDS CALs. How many days can you use RDS before you must add RDS CALs to the environment?

   A. 60
   B. 90
   C. 120
   D. 180

2. You have an existing LAN environment with a single AD DS domain. You also have a perimeter network. Not all computers in the perimeter network are joined to a domain. You are preparing to deploy an RDS Gateway server and a reverse proxy server. To maximize security, to which environments should you deploy each server?

   A. Deploy the RDS Gateway server and the reverse proxy server in the perimeter network.
   B. Deploy the RDS Gateway server in the LAN environment and the reverse proxy server in the perimeter network.
   C. Deploy the RDS Gateway server in the perimeter network and reverse proxy server in the LAN environment.
   D. Deploy the RDS Gateway server and the reverse proxy server in the LAN environment.

3. You are planning to virtualize a software development application for your developers. The developers have requested the ability to use the application even if they are not connected to your corporate network. Which technology should you use?

   A. App-V
   B. System Center App Controller
   C. Client Hyper-V
   D. VDI

Objective 5.2: Deploy Office 2013 by using MSI

Office 2013 has many supported deployment methods, such as deploying by using MSI or deploying by using Click-to-Run. This section discusses using the Windows Installer (MSI).

This objective covers how to:

- Customize deployments
- Manage Office 2013 activation
- Manage Office 2013 settings
- Integrate Lite-Touch deployment
- Rearm Office 2013
- Provide slipstream updates

Capabilities of MSI deployments

Deploying Office by using an MSI provides many options for managing and customizing the deployment process. MSI deployments use a volume license key, which can be activated by using either a Key Management Service (KMS) or a multiple activation key (MAK). When using MSI deployments, the product activations are device-based.

To update an MSI installation, the updates and service packs must be downloaded separately before they can be applied. A benefit of using this model is that different levels of updates can be applied for each product within Office. For example, Microsoft Word could have all available updates applied, but Excel could only apply critical updates.

Office MSI deployments are also highly customizable by using either the Office Customization Tool (OCT) or by customizing the Config.xml file.

Supported deployment methods

You can deploy an Office MSI by using a variety of methods. The supported installation methods when using MSI include:

- Local installation.
- Network installation.
- Group Policy script.
- System Center Configuration Manager (ConfigMgr).
- Microsoft Intune.
- Remote Desktop Services (RDS).
- Microsoft Application Virtualization (App-V).
- Microsoft Deployment Toolkit (MDT).

For local installations, the Office product and language files can be copied to the local computer, and then the setup files can be run from the local source. To complete this installation, the user account running the setup files must be of a local administrator on the client computer to run and install the Office setup.

To use a network installation, copy the Office product and language files to a network share that is accessible from the client computers. The user accounts need only the Read permission on the network share. Users can access the network share and run the Office setup normally. In addition, you can use a script or batch file to automate the installation from the network share. The user completing the installation is still required to have a local administrator account on the client computer.

One method of deploying Office to client computers is by using a Group Policy object (GPO). By using a computer startup script in a GPO, the Office setup will be completed before a user logs on. GPO scripts run by using the Local System account, so user accounts do not require any additional permissions to complete the installation.

EXAM TIP

The only supported method of using a GPO to deploy Office 2013 is by using a startup script. Using Group Policy software installation is not a supported deployment method.

A common method of deploying Office 2013 is by using a software distribution product. This could be either ConfigMgr or Intune. A software distribution product is a valuable method of deploying software because of the additional capabilities that provide updating and reporting of the deployed software. Another benefit of using a software distribution product is that the users are not required to be local administrators of the client computer.

You can also deploy Office 2013 by using virtualization technologies such as RDS and App-V. By using RDS, users can log on to an RD Session Host server to access an Office 2013 installation from their computing device. This is especially useful if the device does not meet the requirements for Office. App-V offers a similar deployment method, by which the Office installation is located on a centrally located server. Instead of accessing the installation remotely, however, App-V streams the application directly to the client device.

MORE INFO   **OFFICE 2013 PREREQUISITES**

For more detailed information about the system requirements for Office 2013, see *http://technet.microsoft.com/en-us/library/ee624351(v=office.15).aspx.*

Finally, the Office product can also be preinstalled in your corporate images so that client computers receive a preconfigured version of Office with their operating system. This can be accomplished by using MDT or ConfigMgr. These tools enable either a Lite-Touch or Zero-Touch deployment method.

MORE INFO   **DEPLOYMENT METHODS FOR OFFICE 2013**

For more detailed information about the supported deployment methods for Office 2013, see *http://technet.microsoft.com/en-us/library/ee656739%28v=office.15%29.aspx*.

Customizing deployments

As mentioned earlier in the chapter, Office deployments can be customized by using either the Office Customization Tool (OCT) or by modifying the Config.xml file.

Using the Office Customization Tool

You can use the OCT to perform many deployment tasks for Office, including

- Specifying installation options.
- Selecting Office applications and features.
- Setting default user settings.
- Customizing additional files, registry entries, and shortcuts.
- Specifying server settings, profiles, and email accounts in Outlook.

NOTE   **VOLUME LICENSES ONLY**

OCT is only available with a volume license version of Office. To verify that the media you are using is a volume license version, check for a folder named Admin in the root of the installation media. The admin folder is only available on volume license media.

Start OCT by running the setup.exe /admin command from the Office 2013 installation files location. When you run the OCT, you are asked whether to create a new customization file or open an existing configur ation. When creating a new customization file, the OCT displays a welcome screen, as shown in Figure 5-14.

Microsoft Office Customization Tool

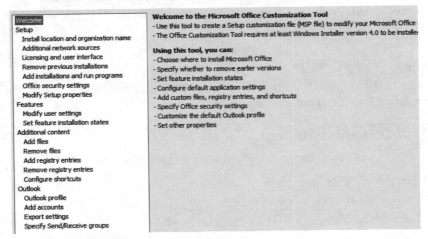

FIGURE 5-14 Microsoft Office Customization Tool

In the following section, you use the OCT to customize an Office 2013 deployment. Although the OCT can customize a multitude of Office settings, step through a sample of often-customized settings. As you prepare for the exam, spend some time working with the OCT and looking through the various settings. In an upcoming section, Table 5-1 displays the available settings along with some supporting information. To customize an Office 2013 deployment with the OCT, perform the following steps:

1. Run the OCT.

2. In the Select Product window, shown in Figure 5-15, click OK to create a new custom-ization file.

   If you had created a customization file, you could choose to open an existing file instead.

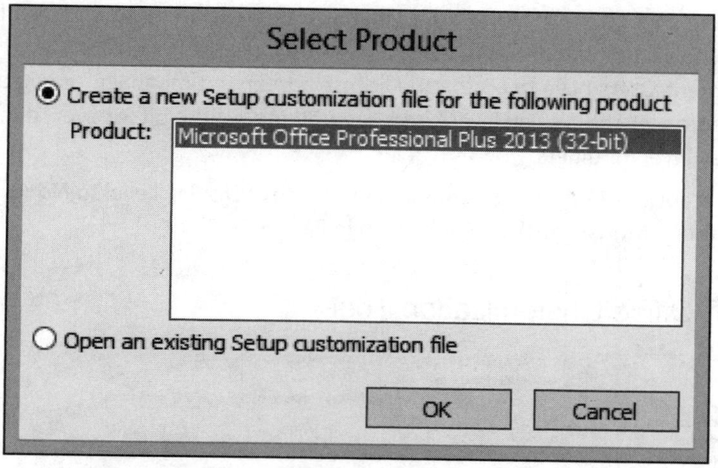

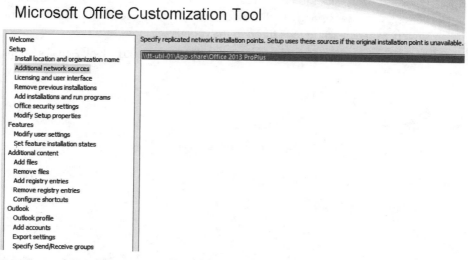

FIGURE 5-15 OCT Select Product window

3. In the left pane, click Additional network sources. In the right pane, click Add, specify the UNC path to the Office 2013 installation files, and then click OK.

Figure 5-16 shows an additional network source. After installation of Office 2013, each computer has a local installation source, which is useful for repairing an installation or adding additional applications to the local installation. If the local installation source is deleted or becomes corrupt, Office 2013 attempts to contact the original network installation source for the needed files. If that source is no longer available, it will use additional specified network sources. This setting is useful in large enterprise environments.

FIGURE 5-16 OCT, additional network sources settings

One of the most important customizations you make is to the licensing and user interface section. This section handles the product key (KMS or MAK), the acceptance of the license agreement (users have to accept the license agreement manually, or you automate the acceptance), the display level (users see nothing, a little bit, or everything), and the display level modifiers.

4. Select The I Accept The License Agreement check box, set Display Level to None, and select the Suppress Modal check box, as shown in Figure 5-17.

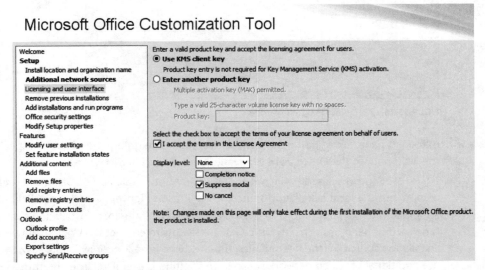

FIGURE 5-17 OCT, licensing and user interface settings

5. In the left pane, click Modify user settings, after which you can customize a large number of Office user settings. In the middle pane, each Office 2013 application is represented. Expand each to look through the various settings.

In the example shown cropped in Figure 5-18, Outlook 2013 Junk E-mail settings are adjusted.

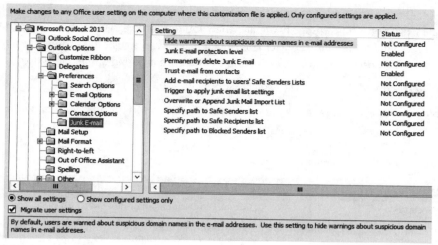

FIGURE 5-18 OCT, modifying user settings

6. In the left pane, click Set Feature Installation States.

This is another heavily used customization area. From here, you can dictate which Office applications and features are installed and available for later installation. In the example shown in Figure 5-19, Microsoft Access, Microsoft Publisher, and Microsoft InfoPath are removed.

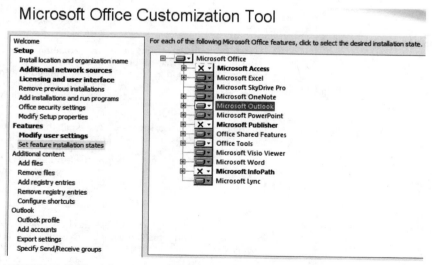

FIGURE 5-19 OCT, set feature installation states

7. After customizing the Office deployment with the OCT, save the customization file and place it in the Updates folder of the installation media.

OCT files can also be used to update an installation after it has been deployed. For a manual installation, you can specify the file when you run setup.exe from the command line with the /adminfile parameter. For example, if you have saved a customization file to a file server, you could use the following command to reference it during a manual setup:

```
setup.exe /adminfile "\\tt-util-02\software\Office 2013\office2013.msp"
```

Table 5-1 discusses some of the additional customization settings that you can use in the OCT.

Table 5-1 OCT optional customization settings

OCT Options	Description	Real-World Example
Setup Section	Customize installation options for Office 2013.	
Install Location And Organization Name	Specify the organization name and default installation path.	This option enables you to set your organization name and adjust the default installation path. In most cases, the default installation path remains unchanged ([ProgramFilesFolder]\Microsoft Office).
Additional Network Sources	Specify additional network locations for the installation source.	This option is helpful in environments that are distributing Office 2013 from various file shares. Providing multiple network sources provides load balancing during the file copy process.
Licensing And User Interface	Specify product key details, accept the license terms, and adjust the user interface display settings during setup.	In an enterprise environment, common options include KMS licensing, accepting the license agreement, and using a display level of None for a silent deployment.
Remove Previous Installations	In an upgrade scenario, specify the Office applications that you want to remove.	By default, the installation removes any previous Office applications. Depending on the features you choose to install, you may configure this option to uninstall only Word, Excel, Microsoft PowerPoint, and Outlook.
Add Installations And Run Programs	Specify additional programs to install before or after the Office installation.	Many environments use add-ins with their Office installation. For example, you can configure a network source to host the WebEx productivity tools and have the installer execute as a postinstall step.

OCT Options	Description	Real-World Example
Office Security Settings	Specify application-specific security settings. Options include adding digital certificates for trusted publishers, adding trusted paths, and setting default security settings for each application.	Use this option to preapprove a trusted publisher or assign a trusted path for a macro-enabled application. Common adjustments include altering macro warning behavior.
Modify Setup Properties	Specify additional setup properties and their assigned values during the installation.	Several properties are available. For example, for a silent deployment, use SETUP_REBOOT = NEVER. For automatic activation, use AUTO_ACTIVATE = 1.
Features Section	Configure which features are installed and customize the user experience for each Office application.	
Modify User Settings	Specify user-specific settings for each of the features being installed.	This option applies to every application and feature. Some common adjustments include disabling the First Run dialog under the Microsoft Office 2013 category or adjusting the Outlook 2013 Cached Exchange Mode to All. It is important to note that the user can change these settings later. For permanent adjustments, use Group Policy.
Set Feature Installation State	Specify the features and applications that will be installed and their installation state.	A full installation is set by default, but you might need to exclude applications, such as Publisher, if they aren't widely used in your organization or you have licensing limitations.
Additional Content Section	Customize the postinstallation setup of Office 2013.	
Add Files	Specify additional files to be added to the target computer during installation.	One example of adding files is to include a basic script to rearrange the shortcuts on the user's taskbar. Another example is to include the MSI for an Outlook add-in that you will call by using Add Installations And Run Programs.
Remove Files	Specify files to remove from the target computer during installation.	This option provides an easy solution for cleaning up scripts or additional files that you added using Add Files. Specifying their location removes them after the installation completes.

OCT Options	Description	Real-World Example
Add Registry Entries	Specify registry key entries to be added to the target computer during installation.	One example of adding a registry key might include a run-once entry that launches an internal website with Office 2013 training material at next logon.
Remove Registry Entries	Specify registry key entries to be removed from the target computer during installation.	One example of removing a registry key includes clearing entries related to the previous version of Office. Another example is dealing with a third-party add-in that needs to be reset as part of the upgrade.
Configure Shortcuts	Specify the included shortcut names and locations.	By default, each application generates its own set of shortcuts in its default folder. You can adjust these options if you want to generate shortcuts in multiple locations rather than in the default ProgramMenuFolder.
Outlook Section	Customize the Outlook 2013 user experience and configuration.	
Outlook Profile	Specify the user's default Outlook profile settings. Options include Use Existing Profile, Modify Profile, New Profile, and Apply PRF.	In upgrade scenarios, you might want to leave the user's Outlook profile unmodified. Other options include modifying a current profile, generating a new profile, or providing a preconfigured .prf file. Generating a new profile can be useful to avoid any upgrade issues with a preexisting offline storage file (OST) file.
Add Accounts	Specify additional accounts to be added to an existing Outlook profile.	This option requires the Outlook profile option to be set to Modify Profile. Adding additional accounts can be useful for adding shared mailboxes for departmental deployments.
Export Settings	Export a working PRF file by using the Outlook configuration options defined in the Outlook section.	The OCT helps you generate a working PRF file for use in this deployment or other projects. Selecting this option enables you to export the Outlook settings defined previously.

OCT Options	Description	Real-World Example
Specify Send/Receive Groups	Specify extensive options for customizing the send and receive behavior within Outlook.	This option requires you to modify an existing profile or create a new one. Settings that are often used include the ability to change the send/receive interval and adjusting the folders that are synced during a send /receive action.

MORE INFO   **OFFICE CUSTOMIZATION TOOL REFERENCE FOR OFFICE 2013**

For more information about how to customize Office, see *http://technet.microsoft.com /en-us/library/cc179097%28v=office.15%29.aspx.*

IMPORTANT   **OFFICE 2013 SECURITY SETTINGS**

Although the OCT is the primary tool for customizing an Office 2013 deployment, you should be aware of one important caveat. Some settings that you specify in the OCT, such as security-related Office settings, can be changed by users after the installation. To enforce such settings, use Group Policy. For more information about using Group Policy for securing Office 2013, see *http://technet.microsoft.com/en-us/library/ff400327(v=office.15) .aspx.*

Using the Config.xml file

You can use the Config.xml file in addition to or separately from the OCT. The Config.xml file can customize the same settings that you can customize with the OCT. Often, administrators choose one or the other but prefer the OCT tool. If you use Config.xml and the OCT to customize a deployment, the Config.xml file overrides OCT settings if there is a conflict. By default, the Config.xml file is stored in the core product folder. For example, for Office 2013 ProPlus, the core product folder is ProPlus.WW. The Config.xml file customizes many installation options, including:

- The path of the network installation point.
- The product(s) to install.
- User, company name, and other logging options.
- Additional languages.

You can also use the Config.xml file to modify the settings of existing installations by running Setup again. After you customize a Config.xml file, you can reference it when launching the Office setup program, as follows:

```
\\tt-util-03\share\Office\setup.exe /config \\tt-util-03\share\Office\ProPlus.WW\Config.xml
```

A Config.xml file might look similar to the following:

```
<Configuration Product="ProPlus">

<Display Level="full" CompletionNotice="yes" SuppressModal="no" AcceptEula="yes" />

<USERNAME Value="User01" />

<COMPANYNAME Value="Tailspin Toys" />

<INSTALLLOCATION Value="%programfiles%\Microsoft Office" />

<LIS CACHEACTION="CacheOnly" />

<LIS SOURCELIST="\\tt-util-03\share\Office" />

<DistributionPoint Location="\\tt-util-03\share\Office" />

<OptionState Id="OptionID" State="absent" Children="force" />

<Setting Id="SETUP_REBOOT" Value="IfNeeded" />

<Command Path="%windir%\system32\msiexec.exe" Args="/i \\tt-util-03\share\office.msi"
QuietArg="/q" ChainPosition="after" Execute="install" />

</Configuration>
```

Managing Office 2013 activation

When using the MSI method of deploying Office, Office is usually activated by using volume
licenses. As mentioned earlier in this chapter, volume licenses can be activated by using either
a KMS or a MAK. When using KMS, you don't need to specify the product key as part of the
installation. The product key is entered on the KMS host instead. However, if you're using
MAK, the customization method, either OCT or Config.xml, you must define the MAK
product key.

If the customization method's product key isn't defined, the installation will still proceed. In such a case, you can configure the MAK after Office installation by using either the Volume Activation Management Tool (VAMT) or the Office Software Protection Platform script (ospp.vbs).

Volume Activation Management Tool

The VAMT is a free license management tool from Microsoft. It comes prepackaged with the Windows Assessment and Deployment Kit. After it's installed, you can use it to manage license keys and activations centrally for Windows operating systems, Microsoft Office 2010, and Microsoft Office 2013. It can work as a stand-alone solution or with KMS and Active Directory–based activation. You can use the VAMT to perform the following tasks.

- Remotely install license keys on computers. For example, you can add a license key remotely to a computer that just had Office 2013 installed.

- Remotely activate computers. You can activate Windows or Office remotely from the VAMT management console.

- Centrally manage your product keys for Windows and Office.

- Run built-in licensing reports to view a variety of licensing and activation-related information such as which products are unlicensed, which products are not activated, and current usage of MAKs.

Upon first starting the VAMT, connect the VAMT to an existing SQL server, as shown in Figure 5-20; or you can install Microsoft SQL Server Express on the VAMT server. For best performance, use a dedicated SQL server. Specify the database name. If it doesn't exist, VAMT creates a new database. The VAMT prompts you to create the database if it doesn't find an existing database based on the specified name.

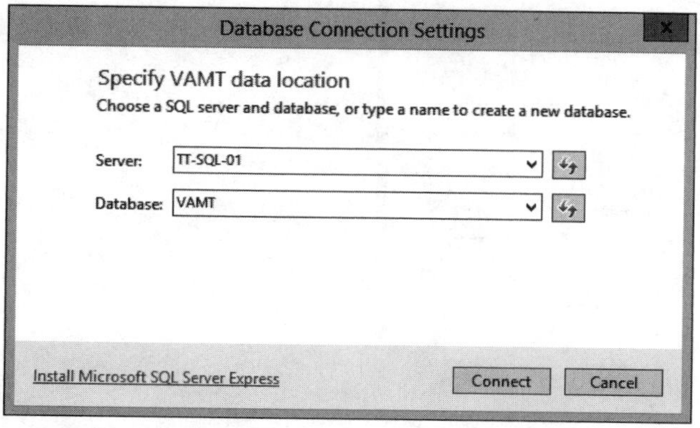

FIGURE 5-20 VAMT database connection

After connecting the VAMT to a database, the management console populates the tool with management areas. Initially, you won't see any products or keys, as shown in Figure 5-21.

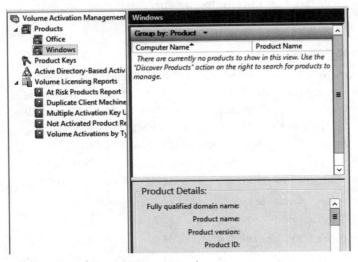

FIGURE 5-21 VAMT management console

Populate the VAMT with computers. To do this, right-click Products in the left pane and then click Discover Products. In the Discover Products dialog box, shown in Figure 5-22, leave the default option of Search For Computers In The Active Directory and then click Search.

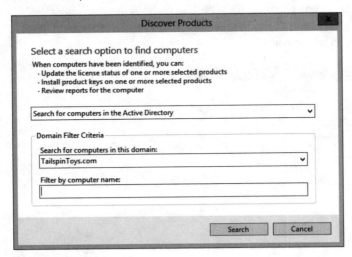

FIGURE 5-22 VAMT discovery

If successful, a pop-up window appears that indicates how many computers were discovered, as shown in Figure 5-23.

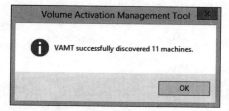

FIGURE 5-23 VAMT successful discovery

Add your product keys to VAMT. Although the exam focuses strictly on activating Office, be aware that you can add Windows product keys and Office product keys to VAMT. In Figure 5-24, the Add Product Keys dialog box shows example keys being added to VAMT.

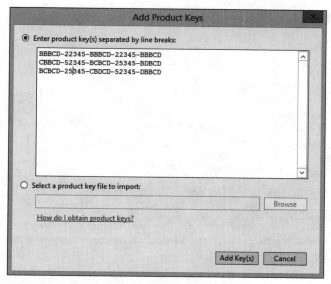

FIGURE 5-24 VAMT Add Product Keys dialog box

If the keys are added successfully, a notification window appears, indicating how many of the keys were successfully added, as shown in Figure 5-25.

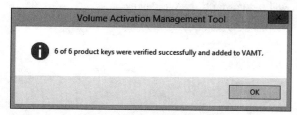

FIGURE 5-25 VAMT successful addition of product keys

At this point, you've added some computers and some product keys to VAMT. You can now install product keys and activate products remotely. In the following procedure, an Office 2013 product key is installed on a computer named TT-W7CLIENT-01, and Office is activated remotely.

1. In the VAMT console, shown in Figure 5-26, right-click the computer in the list of computers and then click Install Product Key.

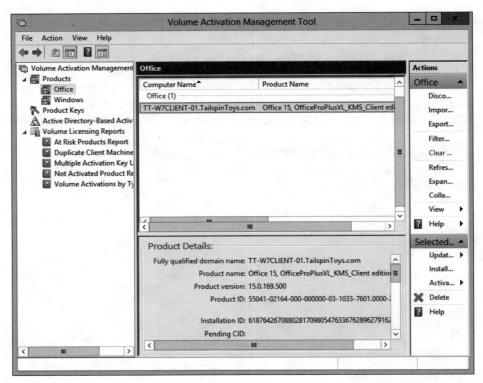

FIGURE 5-26 VAMT console

In the Install Product Key dialog box, shown in Figure 5-27, a list of the available product keys appears. The VAMT usually displays a recommended key. The recommended key is the product key that corresponds to the product. For example, if you add multiple Windows keys and one Office key to VAMT and you decide to install an Office product key on a computer, VAMT will recommend the Office key.

2. Click to select the desired key and then click Install Key.

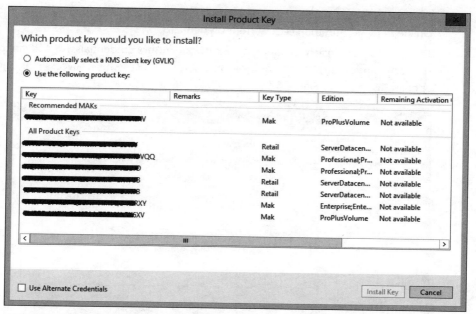

FIGURE 5-27 VAMT Install Product Key dialog box

VAMT installs the product key on the selected computer and reports the status when complete. If successful, you see a success message, as shown in Figure 5-28.

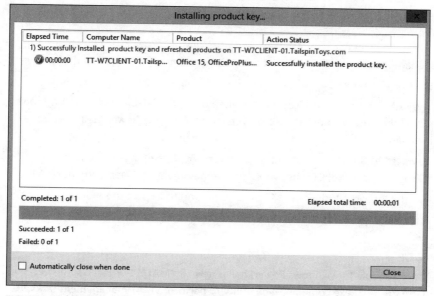

FIGURE 5-28 VAMT Installing Product Key window

3. Activate the product. Right-click the computer in the right pane, click Activate, click Online Activate, and then click Current Credential.

   This attempts an online activation by using your current credentials. An Activating Products window displays the progress and status. If successful, a success message appears, as shown in Figure 5-29.

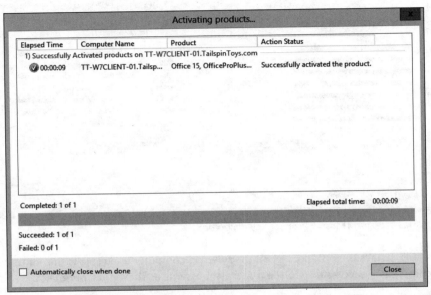

Elapsed Time	Computer Name	Product	Action Status
1) Successfully Activated products on TT-W7CLIENT-01.TailspinToys.com			
00:00:09	TT-W7CLIENT-01.Tailsp...	Office 15, OfficeProPlus...	Successfully activated the product.

Completed: 1 of 1   Elapsed total time: 00:00:09

Succeeded: 1 of 1
Failed: 0 of 1

☐ Automatically close when done

FIGURE 5-29 VAMT Activating Products window

In addition to the VAMT console, you can use Windows PowerShell to accomplish some VAMT management tasks. First, import the VAMT module by performing the following steps:

1. Start the 32-bit version of Windows PowerShell.

   The VAMT module is not supported when using the 64-bit version of Windows PowerShell. You can use the 32-bit version of Windows PowerShell while on a 64-bit installation of Windows.

2. Navigate to the VMAT installation directory. By default, it is located at %ProgramFiles(x86)%\Windows Kits\8.1\Assessment and Deployment Kit\VAMT3.

3. Run the Import-Module .\VAMT.psd1 command to import the module.

   After the import is complete, you have access to 12 cmdlets.

EXAM TIP

The VMAT module for Windows PowerShell is new to VMAT 3.1. Prior to VMAT 3.1, you could use the vmat.exe command-line utility to perform VMAT management tasks. However, vmat.exe is no longer available and does not come with VMAT 3.1. Watch out for answer choices that use vmat.exe, especially in scenarios that mention VAMT 3.1.

Key Management Service

The KMS is a server-based solution that provides activation for Microsoft products on a network. A client that has a product that requires activation will contact the KMS host on the network. The client does not have a product key because all product keys are specified on the KMS host. KMS uses remote procedure calls through TCP port number 1688.

EXAM TIP

The KMS threshold for Office 2013 is five computers; at least five computers must have requested activation before KMS begins activating clients. Therefore, the first four computers will not activate until the fifth has been deployed and requests activation.

By default, when a client is activated with KMS, the license is valid for 180 days. The client contacts the KMS host after 180 days to verify that the license is still valid. If the activation is unsuccessful in a 180-day period, Office enters the out-of-tolerance license state for 30 days. Users are prompted for activation during this 30-day time period. If Office is still not licensed after 30 days, users receive an unlicensed notification, and the title bar of the user interface becomes red.

To trigger activation, run the cscript ospp.vbs /act command. If successful, a successful message appears along with other license data, as shown in Figure 5-30.

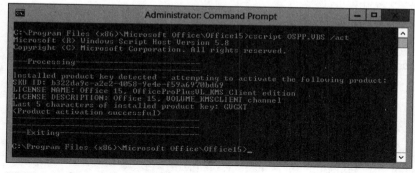

FIGURE 5-30 Command prompt activation

Multiple Activation Key (MAK)

To activate Office, you can use a MAK as a one-time activation process that communicates directly with Microsoft hosted activation services. Each MAK key has a predefined maximum number of activations, which are typically in the volume license agreement. The maximum activation limit does not always match the number of licensed installations.

Activations with MAKs can be performed in two ways:

- MAK independent activation
- MAK proxy activation by using VAMT

Independent activation requires each computer to contact the Microsoft hosted activation service. Activation can be performed over the Internet or by telephone. This type of activation is recommended for computers that are not always connected to a corporate network.

Proxy activation with VAMT centralizes individual requests from multiple computers to a single proxy, which contacts Microsoft directly. Proxy activation is configured with the VAMT and is recommended for large organizations with computers that have corporate network access. It is also useful in test environments where the computers might not have Internet access.

Active Directory–based activation

When using computers running Windows 8 or later, Office activation can also be performed by using Active Directory–based activation, which requires a computer running Windows 8, Windows 8.1, Windows Server 2012, or Windows Server 2012 R2 to support the activation of all deployments in the domain. The computer will have a generic volume license key or KMS key pair. When using Active Directory–based activation, the Office installation is activated for 180 days. The Software Protection Platform service (SPPSvc) occasionally attempts to activate Office, which will then reset the activation for another 180 days.

Updating a deployment

There are many types of updates for Office. They include:

- Service packs
- Security updates
- General updates
- Hotfixes

There are many methods to deploy the updates, including:

- Microsoft Updates
- Windows Server Updates Services (WSUS)
- System Center 2012 Configuration Manager (ConfigMgr)
- Microsoft Self-Extractor files
- Updates folder

Microsoft Updates is a common method of applying Office updates because they are downloaded directly from Microsoft during a normal update cycle. This method uses the settings that have been configured on the Windows client to download or install updates automatically.

Larger environments often use a WSUS server in addition to Microsoft Updates. In such environments, computers use the Microsoft Updates settings but contact and download the updates from a local WSUS server. This reduces the bandwidth to the Internet because only one computer is downloading updates. Each client then receives the updates from the local network.

Enterprises can also use ConfigMgr as a software distribution tool to control the deployment and update process for all client computers.

Microsoft Self-Extractor files are software updates in a downloadable file. This is useful if you want to control the update process manually, such as in a test environment. There are many command-line parameters to enable scripted deployment for larger environments.

The Updates folder of the installation source can also be used to slipstream updates to new deployments. This folder is only for new installations and does not affect any existing deployments. The files placed in the Updates folder will be used during the deployment process to update Office automatically during the installation.

Integrating Lite-Touch deployment

Office 2013 can be included in a Lite-Touch deployment by performing a deployment with the Microsoft Deployment Toolkit (MDT). The Deployment Workbench of MDT enables you to add applications to a repository, including Office 2013, for use with task sequences. To add an application to the deployment work, select the Applications tree items, as shown in Figure 5-31, and then click New Application.

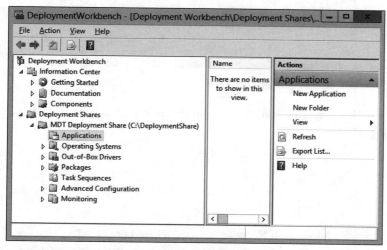

FIGURE 5-31 MDT Deployment Workbench

The New Application Wizard appears, as shown in Figure 5-32, in which one of three options can be selected. The choice you make depends on how you want to use the installation files to install the application during the deployment. The available options are:

- Application With Source Files.
- Application Without Source Files Or Elsewhere On The Network.
- Application Bundle, which only installs application dependencies.

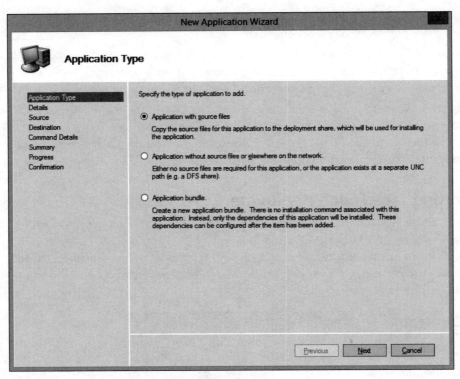

FIGURE 5-32 MDT New Application Wizard, Application Type page

The Details page of the New Application Wizard, shown in Figure 5-33, asks for details of the application, including:

- Publisher
- Application Name
- Version
- Language

The only required field is the Application Name field. However, additional details that are provided can be useful when there are application updates or when multiple languages are needed.

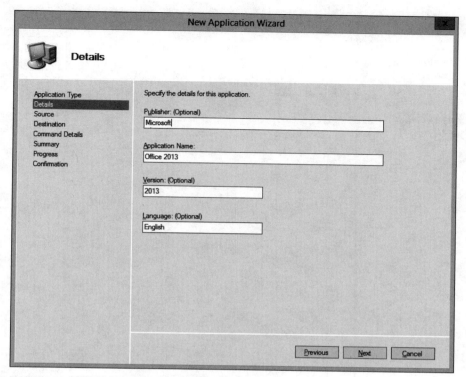

FIGURE 5-33 MDT New Application Wizard, Details page

The New Application Wizard then asks for the source installation files, as shown in Figure 5-34. Click Browse and then provide the folder location where the installation files are located. In this instance, Application With Source Files on the first screen of the wizard was selected; therefore, the installation files will be copied from the provided location to the deployment share. In this example, a location with the mounted Office 2013 ISO file is used.

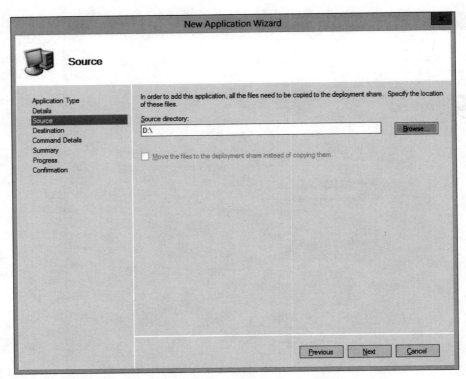

FIGURE 5-34 MDT New Application Wizard, Source page

The wizard then asks how you want to name the destination directory that will be created. By default, this is automatically populated with the name of the application, as shown in Figure 5-35.

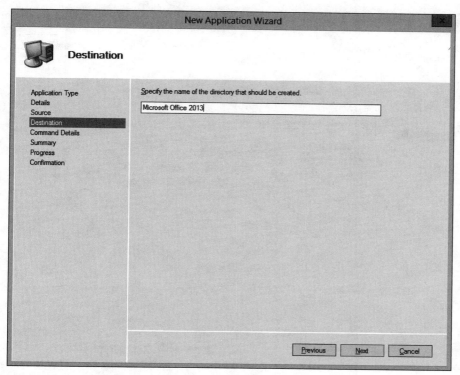

FIGURE 5-35 MDT New Application Wizard, Destination page

The wizard will then ask for a command to install the application quietly, or without user interaction, as shown in Figure 5-36. Because you are installing Office 2013, specify the setup utility and the /config parameter with the location of the Config.xml file. The Config.xml settings should include the necessary configuration for a quiet installation.

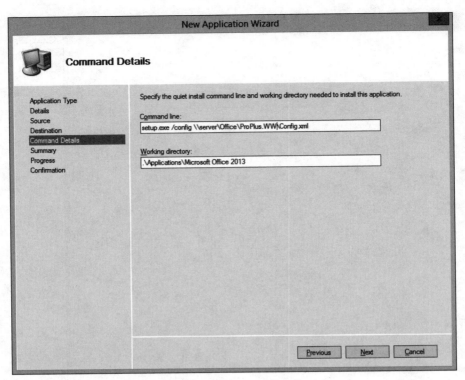

FIGURE 5-36 MDT New Application Wizard, Command Details page

The Confirmation page appears, as shown in Figure 5-37. On this page, you can review the information that has been specified during the wizard. Click Next to begin copying the installation files from the original directory to the deployment share. After the process has completed, a success confirmation appears. Click Finish to close the wizard and complete the process.

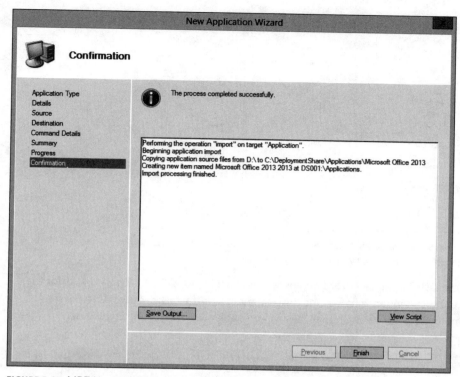

FIGURE 5-37 MDT New Application Wizard, Confirmation page

After you have added the application to the deployment share, it can be configured as part of a task sequence. The task sequence can then be included as part of an operating system deployment so that Office 2013 is installed automatically. To create a new task sequence, navigate to the Task Sequences menu, shown in Figure 5-38, and then click New Task Sequence from the Common Actions menu.

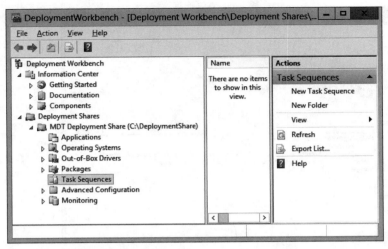

FIGURE 5-38 MDT Deployment Workbench, Task Sequences

The New Task Sequence Wizard begins, as shown in Figure 5-39. The wizard asks for the task sequence ID, sequence name, and any comments for the task sequence. Be descriptive when completing these fields so that they can be easily identified in the Deployment Workbench.

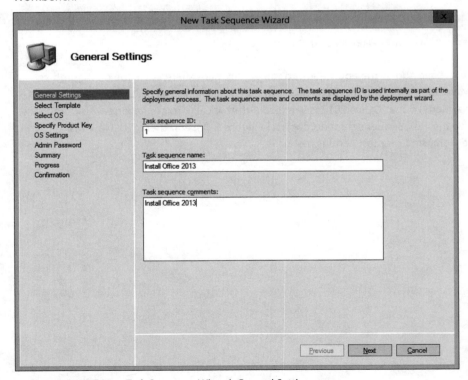

FIGURE 5-39 MDT New Task Sequence Wizard, General Settings page

The Task Sequence Wizard asks for the template to use for the task sequence, as shown in Figure 5-40. To install an application, select the Post OS Installation Task Sequence template.

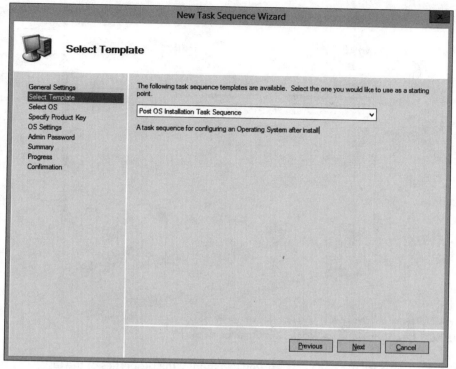

FIGURE 5-40 MDT New Task Sequence Wizard, Select Template page

After clicking Next, the remaining steps of the wizard are skipped, and you are taken directly to the Confirmation page, as shown in Figure 5-41. Click Next to confirm the settings and create the task sequence. The Confirmation page shows that the task sequence has been created successfully.

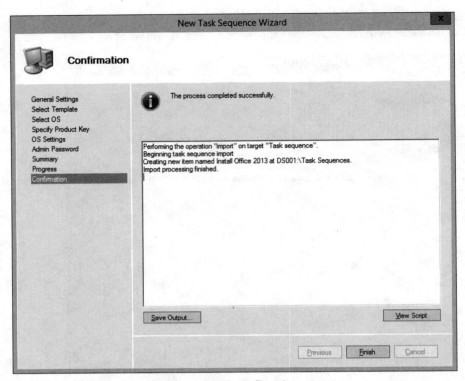

FIGURE 5-41 MDT New Task Sequence Wizard, Confirmation page

After the task sequence has been created, you can modify the properties of the task sequence and edit the steps that are taken during that sequence. Specify the application that was previously added to the application repository in the Deployment Workbench, as shown in Figure 5-42.

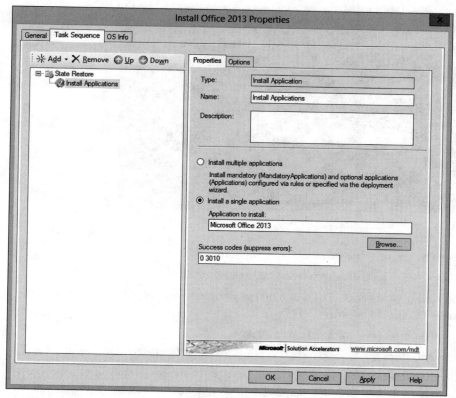

FIGURE 5-42 Task Sequence Properties dialog box

Re-arming Office 2013

After you install Office 2013, Office can remain unlicensed during a 25-day license grace period before activation notifications appear. To maximize the user experience, especially when deploying Office in an image, it is important to freeze the grace period so that future deployments are not automatically out of license immediately after deployment. If you don't freeze the grace period, activation notifications appear to users during their first use of an Office application. To rearm Office on a computer, open an administrative command prompt. Navigate to the %ProgramFiles(x86)%\Microsoft Office\Office15 directory. Run the ospprearm.exe command. If successful, a success message appears, as shown in Figure 5-43.

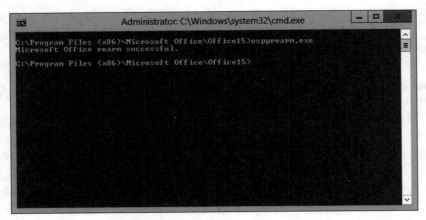

FIGURE 5-43 Re-arming Office 2013

You should be aware of the following facts about re-arming Office:

- You can re-arm an Office installation up to five times.
- When using a KMS host, you re-arm one additional time to bring to six the total number of allowed re-arms.
- Re-arming resets the grace period to 30 days.
- Re-arming stops the grace period timer until an Office application or ospp.vbs is run.
- Re-arming resets the computer ID (CMID) so that subsequent installations are counted as unique for KMS activations. Remember, KMS requires a minimum of five unique activation requests of Office before it begins activating Office.
- If you are using MAKs, you should activate Office remotely to ensure that users do not get activation notifications upon first running an Office application. You can activate Office remotely by using the VAMT or ospp.vbs.

Providing slipstream updates

Updates for Office can be downloaded from the Microsoft website as .exe files. To provide the update automatically during an installation, the .msp file must be extracted from the .exe file and included with the installation files. To extract the .msp file from the .exe file to E:\Updates, run the following command:

```
outlook2013-kb273132-fullfile-x86-glb.exe /extract:"E:\Updates"
```

After the update has been extracted, you are prompted to accept the license agreement. After accepting the license agreement, the MSP file is extracted to the location you provided, and a confirmation window appears, as shown in Figure 5-44.

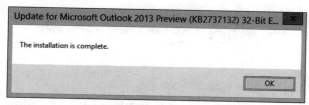

FIGURE 5-44 Update confirmation window

You can also verify that the extraction was successful by navigating to the directory you provided in the command. A license agreement file, MSP file, and XML file should exist for the update that was extracted, as shown in Figure 5-45.

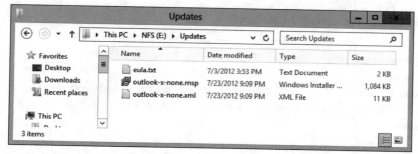

FIGURE 5-45 View of the extracted files in File Explorer

After the MSP files have been extracted from the EXE, they can be provided with the installation files. If the extraction was not to the Updates folder of the installation files, copy the files to the Updates folder. You must repeat this process for each update that must be included when performing a deployment or installation.

In larger deployments, multiple installation locations might be necessary—for example, a deployment for multiple offices. For bandwidth or other reasons, each office might require a local copy of the installation files. You can update the Config.xml file to include multiple network locations by using the SUpdateLocation parameter. The syntax for use in the Config.xml file is:

```
<SetupUpdates [CheckForSUpdates="Yes"  |"No"] [SUpdateLocation="path-list"]/>
```

To check for updates in a location on a server named tt-util-01 and a server named tt-util-02, you would use the following syntax:

```
<SetupUpdates CheckForSUpdates="Yes" SUpdateLocation="\\tt-util-01\updates;\\tt-util-02
\updates"/>
```

EXAM TIP

Update files typically reside in the Updates folder. However, if another location or directory must be used, it is possible to list alternate locations with the SUpdateLocation parameter in the Config.xml file.

Alternatively, you can specify additional locations by using the Office Customization Tool (OCT). These network locations would be included in the custom MSP file that is created when saving the OCT settings.

> **MORE INFO**   **DISTRIBUTING UPDATES FOR OFFICE 2013 PRODUCTS**
>
> For more information about distributing updates for Office 2013, see *http://technet .microsoft.com/en-us/library/cc178995%28v=office.15%29.aspx*.

Thought experiment
Deploying Office at Alpine Ski House

You work as a systems administrator for Alpine Ski House, an outdoor recreational company specializing in ski vacations with four locations. Eight hundred employees are spread across the four locations. Alpine Ski House currently uses Office 2010, and each client computer has a local installation of it. The company has decided to deploy Office 2013, and you plan to explore deployment methods and potential customizations.

1. Some of the ski instructors have a portable computer that is only occasionally connected to the network. You want to allow the ski instructors to install Office 2013 manually when it is convenient for them. What should you do?

2. The management team has requested only Office Word and Excel to be part of the Office 2013 installation for a couple of departments. How should you handle this?

3. The IT team struggled to keep up with updating Office 2010. Sometimes, updates weren't installed at regular intervals or were delayed. For Office 2013, the company has requested more timely updates. What should you do to automate timely updates of Office 2013?

Objective summary

- Office 2013 can be deployed by a variety of methods when using an MSI. There are many supported deployment methods, including
  - Local and network installations
  - Scripts
  - Software distribution products
  - Application virtualization
- Each of these deployment methods can be customized for the specific environment by using either the Office Customization Tool or the Config.xml file.

- After Office has been deployed, you can activate it by using the Key Management Service, a multiple activation key, or Active Directory–based activation.
- Office updates can be applied by using the traditional Microsoft Updates service, a WSUS server, ConfigMgr, or self-extractor files or by slipstreaming the updates as part of the deployment.
- You can slipstream updates into an Office 2013 installation by extracting the MSP file from the downloadable EXE file.

Objective review

1. Which of the following are supported methods of deploying an Office 2013 MSI? (Choose two. Each correct answer presents a complete solution.)

   A. Group Policy software installation

   B. Group Policy startup script

   C. AppLocker

   D. Windows Intune

2. Which Office customization method uses an MSP file?

   A. Office Customization Tool

   B. Config.xml

   C. Group Policy script

   D. Windows Intune

3. Which activation methods verify the Office license every 180 days? (Choose two. Each correct answer presents a complete solution.)

   A. Key Management Service

   B. Multiple Activation Keys

   C. Active Directory–based activation

   D. Windows Server Update Services

Objective 5.3: Deploy Office 2013 by using Click-to-Run

Click-to-Run technology is a streaming and virtualization method of deploying Office applications. You can use the streaming technology to enable users to use an Office product before all its applications have been downloaded to the local computer. The virtualization aspect of the technology isolates the run-time environment for Office so you can run two versions of Office, such as Office 2010 and Office 2013, side by side on the same computer. However, the versions must be on the same architecture, either 32-bit or 64-bit. Click-to-Run is an alternate method of deploying Office to the MSI method that was discussed earlier in this chapter. Click-to-Run is available for the following Office products:

- Office Professional 2013
- Office Home and Business 2013
- Office Home and Student 2013
- Office 365 ProPlus
- Visio Pro for Office 365
- Project Pro for Office 365
- SharePoint Designer 2013
- Lync 2013
- Lync 2013 Basic

To determine whether Office was installed by using Click-to-Run, check to verify that the VirtualOutlook key exists in the following registry location:

HKEY_LOCAL_MACHINE\Software\Microsoft\Office\15.0\Common\InstallRoot\Virtual\VirtualOutlook

If the key exists with a value that indicates the product language—for example: en-us— Office was installed by using Click-to-Run.

> **This objective covers the following topics:**
> - Configure licensing
> - Customize deployment
> - Configure updates
> - Monitor usage by using Office Telemetry Dashboard

Configuring licensing

Click-to-Run is available from both a traditional license purchase, such as retail or volume license, and from Office 365. The licensing model you choose doesn't affect how Click-to-Run operates. If using a traditional license, you can use Click-to-Run to distribute the installation files from the Office 2013 product. If using Office 365 with the appropriate licensing, you can still deploy Office 2013 by using Click-to-Run. The licensing type that you use depends on the business requirements.

Customizing deployment

When using Click-to-Run, you use a Configuration.xml file to configure installation and update parameters. The Office Deployment Tool (ODT) includes a sample Configuration.xml file that you can customize for your specific deployment. You can customize the configuration file to handle the following tasks:

- Add or remove products from the installation
- Add or remove languages from the installation
- Specify the display options
- Configure the logging location
- Configure software updates

The following is a sample Configuration.xml file

```
<Configuration>

  <Add SourcePath="\\tt-util-03\Office\" OfficeClientEdition="32" >

    <Product ID="O365ProPlusRetail">

      <Language ID="en-us" />

    </Product>

  </Add>  -->

  <Updates Enabled="TRUE" />

  <Display Level="None" AcceptEULA="TRUE" />

  <Logging Path="%temp%" />

  <Property Name="AUTOACTIVATE" Value="1" />

</Configuration>
```

Another benefit of using Click-to-Run is that language-neutral resources are packaged together and contain all the resources. Language-specific resources are packaged separately and strictly only for that language, for example, en-us for English (United States). Then, you have the option to install multiple languages, or the product can be installed in each language. If you are using Office 365 with Office ProPlus, you can use the Office 365 portal to manage language installations, or end users can select additional languages from the portal. A view of the ODT folder with the setup program and the configuration file is shown in Figure 5-46.

EXAM TIP

You can't customize the installation location for Office when using Click-to-Run. You must deploy it to the system drive only.

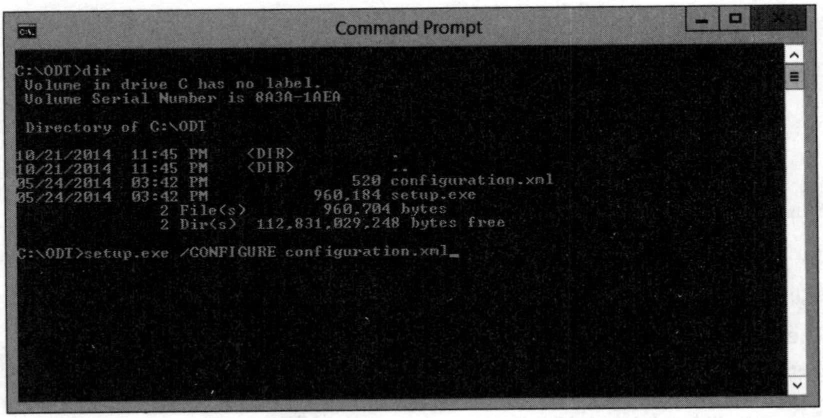

FIGURE 5-46 Office Click-to-Run setup

MORE INFO   CLICK-TO-RUN CONFIGURATION.XML FILE

For more information about the Click-to-Run configuration.xml file, see *http://technet .microsoft.com/en-us/library/jj219426%28v=office.15%29.aspx.*

Configuring updates

When using Click-to-Run, you can choose from three options for software updates:

- **Automatically update Office from the Internet**   For this option, Microsoft pushes out updates over the Internet as they are released. Office installations are automatically updated after the updates are finished downloading. If any Office applications are running when the update installation begins, those updates will be delayed until the application is closed and opened again.

- **Automatically update Office from an internal location**   This option is similar to the default option of automatically updating from the Internet. The key difference is that the update location is customized and usually points to an internal file server.

- **Disable automatic updates**   In some organizations, internal testing is required before updating applications. This is especially true in large enterprise environments or environments with a lot of complexity. In this case, you can download a monthly release of updates, test the updates, and then use your preferred deployment solution to push the updates out. Following are some of the most common reasons for disabling automatic updates:

    - Test compatibility of the updates with existing software. You might want to ensure that the updates work with Office add-ons or other infrastructure applications such as Microsoft Lync and Microsoft SharePoint.

- Adhere to a change control process. If you have specific change control windows, you might have to disable automatic updates to ensure that the updates are installed in the change control window.

- Provide a consistent support experience. You might want all users at a specific location to get the updates at the same time or for all users company-wide to get the updates at the same time. This enables your support organization to prepare for extra activity if necessary. You can also provide notification to users about the upcoming updates and any changes that they should be aware of.

For the option that automatically updates Office from the Internet, a daily scheduled task performs a check against the web service at http://officecdn.microsoft.com/. If an update is available, Office schedules a random time for the update to be downloaded and installed. The local computer checks the difference in data and downloads only the required files for the update, which reduces the required bandwidth. The Updates Enabled line of the Configuration.xml file dictates the update method. For this method, the line will read True, with no other configuration parameters, as follows.

```
<Updates Enabled="TRUE" />
```

If an internal location has been specified for updates, an administrator controls the update process. Each month, a new build version of Office is available to download by using the Office Deployment Tool. The administrator then specifies the network location that is accessible by the clients to store the files. Just as in the automatic update method, a daily scheduled task runs and checks the location of the network files. If updates are detected, they are applied in the background without requiring any interaction by the user. The Configuration.xml file entry would look like the following example:

```
<Updates Enabled="TRUE" UpdatePath="\\Server\OfficeShare\NewOfficeBuild" />
```

When you disable automatic updates, Office will not use an internal location or the Microsoft CDN servers to apply any updates. Instead, you control the update process by using your application deployment solution. However, you can set the Configuration.xml file to specify the exact version of Office that should be installed, and the client will ensure that the version is always the same as what is specified. For example, the configuration.xml entry would look like the following example:

```
<Updates Enabled="FALSE" />

<Add SourcePath="\\tt-util-04\Updates\" Version="15.0.xxxx.xxxx" OfficeClientEdition="32" >
```

EXAM TIP

Be aware of the difference in parameters for configuring automatic updates as well as the location of the software binaries. You can view the list of available parameters for the Configuration.xml file at *http://technet.microsoft.com/en-us/library /jj219426%28v=office.15%29.aspx.*

Monitoring usage by using Office Telemetry Dashboard

Office Telemetry is a new feature in Office 2013 that monitors the compatibility of documents, gathers environment-specific information such as hardware and software versions, and tracks issues that end users run into while using Office. Because Office Telemetry wasn't available in previous versions of Office, an agent must be deployed to collect information from a computer that is running Office 2003, Office 2007, or Office 2010.

The following use cases are some of the most common uses of Office Telemetry Dashboard:

- Maximize the chances of a successful migration from a previous version of Office to Office 2013. By using Office Telemetry Dashboard from the beginning of your migration, the support team can proactively monitor the telemetry data and take immediate action. This enables you to adjust your migration schedule for optimal times to reduce poor end-user experiences.

- Gather data in an Office 2013 pilot. If you're still in a pilot stage of an Office deployment, telemetry data can help paint a very clear picture of usage and issues. The team can spend time resolving issues prior to beginning a production rollout of Office 2013.

- Analyze your existing Office documents to see whether they perform adequately in Office 2013. For example, your accounting or tax department might work with very large and complex Excel spreadsheets. Will the user experience be acceptable when opening and working with those spreadsheets? Use Office Telemetry Dashboard to find out.

Office Telemetry Dashboard requires Excel 2013 and is installed automatically with Office Professional Plus 2013 and Office 365 ProPlus. It also requires the use of a SQL database. If an existing SQL server is in the environment, a new database can be created when you launch Office Telemetry Dashboard. Alternatively, you can use Microsoft SQL Server Express to create a new SQL instance and database. To get started, type **Telemetry Dashboard** from the Start screen and then run Office Telemetry Dashboard or Office Telemetry Dashboard For Office 2013. Excel will run and display a custom Office Telemetry Dashboard spreadsheet, as shown in Figure 5-47.

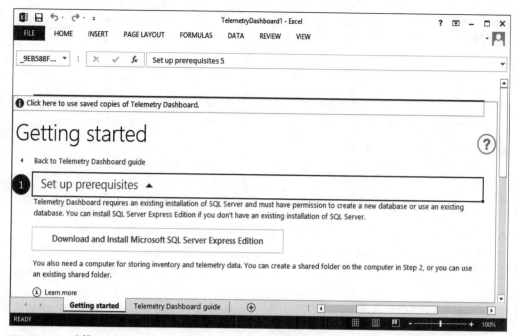

FIGURE 5-47 Office Telemetry Dashboard—Set Up Prerequisites in the Getting Started dialog box

Office Telemetry Processor is the agent that collects the data from Office and imports it into the database. The installation information is shown in Figure 5-48.

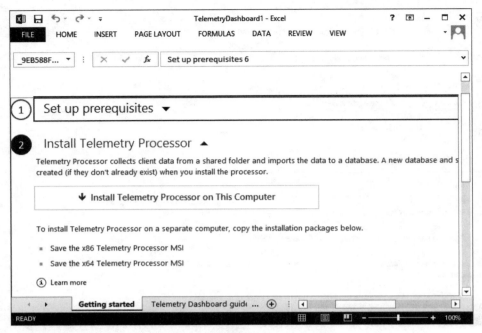

FIGURE 5-48 Office Telemetry Dashboard, Install Telemetry Processor

Office Telemetry Processor is a simple wizard installation. However, the SQL Server database must be online before reaching this point. The wizard prompts for the SQL Server and instance name and enables you to select or create a database in the instance, as shown in Figure 5-49.

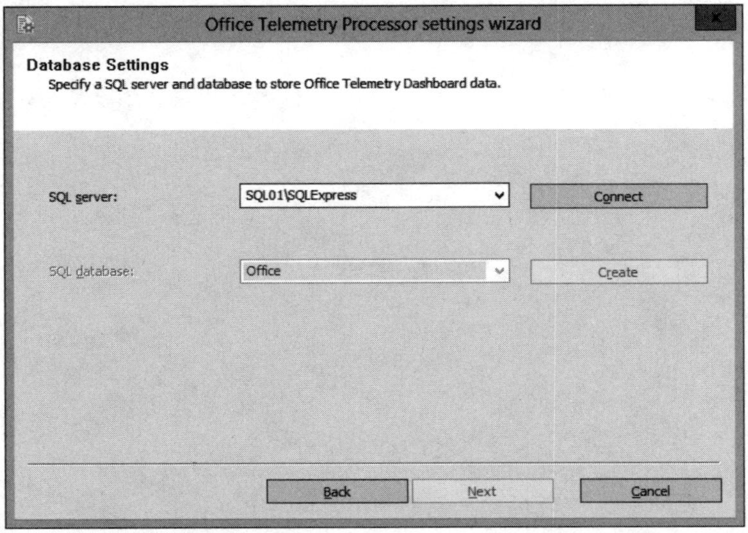

FIGURE 5-49 Office Telemetry Processor Settings Wizard

The next step in Office Telemetry Dashboard is to deploy Office Telemetry Agent to the necessary computers, as shown in Figure 5-50. As mentioned earlier, Office 2013 includes an agent that collects compatibility data. This is not true for Office 2003, Office 2007, or Office 2010, which require an additional agent. Save and deploy the agent to the computers that are running older versions of Office. The agent is packaged as an MSI file, so you can deploy it using Group Policy. You can also use Group Policy to configure Office Telemetry Agent by using the provided administrative templates.

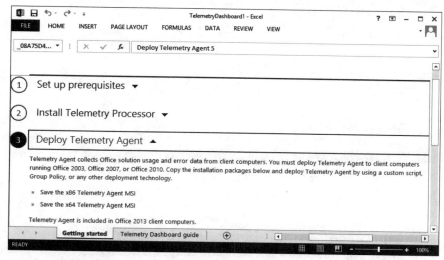

FIGURE 5-50 Office Telemetry Dashboard Deploy Telemetry Agent

After the agents have been deployed and configured, you can connect to the SQL database that was previously configured. The data that Office Telemetry Agent imported into the database appear. Various tabs are available to perform additional tasks, such as to

- Summarize the telemetry data from the Office clients.
- List the Office document files and their usage data.
- List Office solutions such as COM and other add-ins.
- List the servers that are running Office Telemetry Processor.
- List the versions of Office that have been deployed.
- Create custom PivotTable reports.

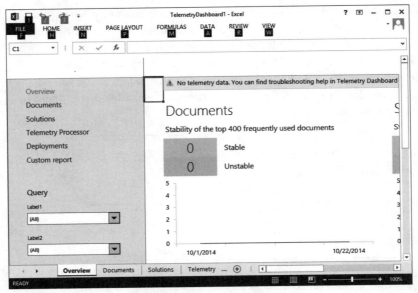

FIGURE 5-51 Office Telemetry Dashboard, Overview worksheet

Thought experiment

You are planning to migrate 300 computers from Office 2010 to Office 2013. During the migration, users must be able to run both versions of Office simultaneously. All compatibility issues must be centrally reported. You must also ensure that all Office updates are tested before being implemented on client computers.

1. How does selecting a license affect the available deployment methods?

2. What configuration parameters should be included in the Configuration.xml script?

3. What should be used to satisfy the reporting requirement?

Objective summary

- Click-to-Run is available for several versions of Office and Office applications.

- Office 2013 licensing is available in two forms: traditional and Office 365. Either licensing type can be used with Click-to-Run.

- The Configuration.xml file specifies the parameters for customizing a Click-to-Run installation.

- There are three methods of updating Office software after it has been deployed by using Click-to-Run.

- Office Telemetry Dashboard tracks Office application compatibility.

- Office Telemetry Dashboard requires a SQL Server database.
- Office Telemetry Dashboard can take an inventory of the Office deployment.

Objective review

Answer the following questions to test your knowledge of the information in this objective. You can find the answers to these questions and explanations of why each answer choice is correct or incorrect in the "Answers" section at the end of this chapter.

1. Which Office version does not support Click-to-Run?
   A. Office Professional Plus 2013
   B. Office 365 ProPlus
   C. Office Home and Student 2013
   D. Office Professional Plus 2010

2. How does virtualization technology enhance Office compatibility?
   A. Enables you to install the 64-bit version of Office 2013 locally on a computer running a 32-bit version of Windows.
   B. Allows multiple versions of Office to be installed.
   C. Enables end users to manage software updates.
   D. Prevents end users from denying software updates.

3. Which part of a Click-to-Run installation is not customizable?
   A. Installation location
   B. Activation
   C. Source file location
   D. Product language

4. How is Office Telemetry Agent configured after it has been deployed?
   A. Office Customization Tool
   B. Office Deployment Tool
   C. Group Policy
   D. Configuration.xml file

5. What must be configured before setting up Office Telemetry Processor?
   A. SQL Server instance
   B. Group Policy objects
   C. Telemetry Agents
   D. Office 2013

Answers

This section contains the solutions to the thought experiments and answers to the objective review questions in this chapter.

Objective 5.1

Thought experiment

1. To avoid affecting copy operations, you must ensure that the copy operations occur at the Contoso datacenter. A VDI would enable call center employees to connect to a virtualized support computer and perform copy operations from the Contoso datacenter, which would eliminate call center employees' home Internet connections from the copy operations.

2. Deploy the applications to a virtual machine. In the case of personal virtual desktops, the application installations would be limited to one installation per call center employee. If supported, you might also be able to install some of the applications on an RD Session Host server, which would substantially reduce licensing costs.

3. Use the Application Compatibility Toolkit (ACT) to assess and resolve application compatibility. Take an inventory, test compatibility, analyze the compatibility data, and, finally, resolve any compatibility issues.

Objective review

1. **Correct answer:** C
   A. **Incorrect:** 60 days is incorrect because the grace period is 120 days.
   B. **Incorrect:** 90 days is incorrect because the grace period is 120 days.
   C. **Correct**: The grace period is 120 days.
   D. **Incorrect**: 180 days is incorrect because the grace period is 120 days.

2. **Correct answer:** B
   A. **Incorrect:** Deploying the RDS Gateway server and the reverse proxy server in the perimeter network is incorrect because the RDS Gateway should be placed in the LAN and protected by the reverse proxy server. This also allows you to join the RDS Gateway to the internal domain and have AD DS authentication without opening up a large amount of ports between the perimeter network and the LAN.
   B. **Correct:** Deploying the RDS Gateway server in the LAN and the reverse proxy server in the perimeter network is correct because the RDS Gateway should be placed in the LAN and protected by the reverse proxy server. This also allows you to join the RDS Gateway to the internal domain and have AD DS authentication without opening up a large amount of ports between the perimeter network and the LAN.

C. **Incorrect**: Deploying the RDS Gateway server in the perimeter network and the reverse proxy server in the LAN environment is incorrect because the reverse proxy server will handle connections from the Internet; the perimeter network is the correct network segment for that duty.

D. **Incorrect**: Deploying the RDS Gateway server and the reverse proxy server in the LAN environment is incorrect because the reverse proxy server will handle connections from the Internet; the perimeter network is the correct network segment for that duty.

3. **Correct answer:** A

A. **Correct:** App-V is the correct answer because it offers offline access to virtualized applications.

B. **Incorrect:** System Center App Controller is not correct because it is a self-service virtual machine management platform and does not virtualize applications.

C. **Incorrect**: Client Hyper-V is incorrect because it virtualizes computers, not applications.

D. **Incorrect**: VDI is incorrect because it virtualizes client computers, not applications.

Objective 5.2

Thought experiment

1. For a manual installation, you should use a network-based installation. This enables the ski instructors to perform the Office 2013 installation at their convenience. Copy the Office product and language files to a network share and grant the user accounts Read permission on the network share. The ski instructors can then access the network share and run the Office setup normally.

2. You should run the setup.exe /admin command from where the Office 2013 installation files are located. That will start the OCT, which enables you to customize the installation so that only Word and Excel are part of the installation.

3. You should use WSUS or ConfigMgr. Both products can automate the distribution of Office updates, which allow for a routine deployment cycle.

Objective review

1. **Correct answers:** B and D

A. **Incorrect:** Using a Group Policy software installation is incorrect because only a startup script can be used to deploy Office by using Group Policy.

B. **Correct:** A Group Policy startup script in a GPO is the only supported Group Policy method for deploying Office.

C. **Incorrect**: AppLocker does not deploy software.

D. **Correct**: Windows Intune can deploy MSI software and Office through MSI.

2. **Correct answer:** A

    A. **Correct:** The OCT uses MSP files.

    B. **Incorrect:** Config.xml is incorrect because it uses config.xml.

    C. **Incorrect**: A Group Policy script does not use an MSP file.

    D. **Incorrect**: Windows Intune does not use an MSP file.

3. **Correct answers:** A and C

    A. **Correct:** KMS validates a license every 180 days.

    B. **Incorrect:** MAKs use a one-time validation during installation.

    C. **Correct**: Active Directory–based activation validates a license every 180 days.

    D. **Incorrect**: WSUS is not an activation method.

Objective 5.3

Thought experiment

1. Licensing is only a business aspect of Office 2013 and does not affect how Office 2013 can be deployed. Office 2013 can be deployed by using a traditional MSI or by using Click-to-Run, no matter which licensing model is chosen.

2. Given that the scenario requires updates to be tested before they are deployed, you must ensure that the UpdatePath parameter of the Updates Enabled section is specified to an internal network location. This ensures that the update files will be made available after they have been tested.

3. This scenario requires compatibility issues to be reported. After Office Telemetry Dashboard has been configured, you must ensure that Office Telemetry Agent has been deployed for all previous versions of Office.

Objective review

1. **Correct answer:** D

    A. **Incorrect**. You can deploy Office Professional Plus 2013 by using Click-to-Run.

    B. **Incorrect:** You can deploy Office 365 ProPlus by using Click-to-Run.

    C. **Incorrect**: You can deploy Office Home and Student 2013 by using Click-to-Run.

    D. **Correct**: Click-to-Run was first introduced for Office 2013; it does not support deployments of Office 2010.

2. **Correct answer:** B

   A. **Incorrect:** Virtualization technology for Office does not enable you to install the 64-bit version of Office 2013 on a computer running the 32-bit version of Windows.

   B. **Correct:** Virtualization technology enables you to run two versions of Office on the same computer. For example, you can run Office 2010 and Office 2013 on the same computer. Normally, this isn't a supported configuration, but the virtualization technology segments each Office installation into a virtual container, which makes it a supported configuration.

   C. **Incorrect:** Virtualization technology isn't applicable to software updates or to delegating administrative rights to end users.

   D. **Incorrect:** Virtualization technology isn't applicable to software updates or to preventing end users from denying software updates.

3. **Correct answer:** A

   A. **Correct:** The installation location is not customizable. The default location for installation is on the system drive in the Program Files\Microsoft Office 15 folder.

   B. **Incorrect:** Activation is configurable. One example is the AUTOACTIVATE attribute, which enables or disables automatic activation.

   C. **Incorrect:** The source file location can be customized. One example is for setting updates to a specific location.

   D. **Incorrect:** The product language can be customized based on your requirements.

4. **Correct answer:** C

   A. **Incorrect:** The OCT customizes the installation of Office. Telemetry is data gathered after the installation, so the OCT doesn't deal with telemetry.

   B. **Incorrect:** The ODT is used for the installation of Office and doesn't deal with telemetry data that is available after installation.

   C. **Correct:** There are two ways to configure Office Telemetry Agent. One way is by using Group Policy and the other is by modifying the registry.

   D. **Incorrect:** The Configuration.xml file is used to customize the installation and updates for Office and doesn't deal with telemetry data.

5. **Correct answer:** A

   A. **Correct:** SQL Server is required as part of the Office Telemetry Processor setup. You cannot complete setup without having SQL Server available and a database created. You can create the database during the setup.

   B. **Incorrect:** You do not need to configure Group Policy before setting up Office Telemetry Processor.

   C. **Incorrect**: Configuration of Office Telemetry Agent is not a prerequisite for Office Telemetry Processor.

   D. **Incorrect**: Configuration of Office 2013 is not a prerequisite of Office Telemetry Processor.

Index

Numbers and Symbols

X

Z

About the author

BRIAN SVIDERGOL specializes in Microsoft infrastructure and cloud-based solutions built around Windows, Active Directory, Microsoft Exchange, Microsoft System Center, virtualization, and the Microsoft Desktop Optimization Pack (MDOP). He holds a bunch of Microsoft and industry certifications, including the Microsoft Certified Solutions Expert (MCSE), Server Infrastructure. Brian coauthored the *Active Directory Cookbook*, 4th Edition. He served as an MCT Ambassador at TechEd North America 2013 and delivered two Exam Prep sessions, one on the 70-411 exam and one on the 70-412 exam. He also works as a subject matter expert on many Microsoft Official Curriculum courses and Microsoft certification exams. He has authored a variety of training content, blog posts, practice test questions, and college exams and has been a technical reviewer for more than 25 books.